Sounds of Chicago's Lakefront

A CELEBRATION OF THE GRANT PARK MUSIC FESTIVAL

Tony Macaluso, Julia S. Bachrach, and Neal Samors

introduction by Van Cliburn

foreword by Ron Magers

Chicago's Books Press

Publisher's Notes

Designed and produced by
Jell Creative, Inc., Chicago, Illinois.

Printed in Canada by Friesens Corporation.

Distributed by the Chicago's Books Press
282 Stanton Drive, Buffalo Grove, IL 60089

ISBN: 978-0-9797892-6-7

For more information on this book,
please email the author at
tony.macaluso@cityofchicago.org

Grant Park Music Festival
205 East Randolph Drive, Chicago, IL 60601
www.grantparkmusicfestival.com

Many of the photographs were cropped
to accommodate the book's trim size.

Front cover photo

A view from the lawn of the Jay Pritzker Pavilion,
Millennium Park, during a performance in 2008.

Back cover photos

Left: The original Grant Park band shell, 1937.

Right top: Grant Park Music Festival
    Principal Conductor Carlos Kalmar, 2008.

Right bottom: Audiences on the lawn of the
    Jay Pritzker Pavilion, Millennium Park, 2006.

Flap photos

Front: Jay Pritzker Pavilion

Back: Authors Tony Macaluso, Julia S. Bachrach,
    and Neal Samors, 2009.

Photos on the next three pages

iii: A closeup of the billowing overhang
    of Jay Pritzker Pavilion.

iv: The original Grant Park band shell, 1938.

vi: Chicago's lakefront seen from the
    Shedd Aquarium with the original
    band shell to the far left, circa 1940.

The Grant Park Music Festival is presented by:

City of Chicago
Richard M. Daley, Mayor

Chicago Department of Cultural Affairs
Lois Weisberg, Commissioner

Chicago Park District
Timothy J. Mitchell, General Superintendent & CEO

The Grant Park Orchestral Association

Dedication

This book is dedicated to the many musicians of the
Grant Park Orchestra and Chorus who have filled
Chicago's lakefront with the sounds of magnificent
music since 1935. Some of you are mentioned by name
in the following pages. All of you are here in spirit.

Contents

Acknowledgments

We would like to thank the Sheldon Good Charitable Foundation, Roosevelt University, Carl Birkelbach, and Raymond A. Frick, Jr. for their generous gifts in support of this publication.

This book, like the Grant Park Music Festival itself, would not have been possible without the extraordinary support of the Chicago Park District, Board President Gery J. Chico, and General Superintendent & CEO Timothy J. Mitchell; the Chicago Department of Cultural Affairs and Commissioner Lois Weisberg; and the board and the staff of the Grant Park Music Festival.

Head researcher Laurel Prag.

Interviews, transcriptions, and additional research Annie-Claude Chartrand, Britt'ni Fields, Agnieszka Kozlowska, and Gina Scalise.

Manuscript editing Aimee B. Anderson, www.readswrite.com.

In addition, we are grateful to many other people who contributed to the realization of this book Bernie Judge and James W. Palermo for project conception assistance; Leigh Levine and Christine Worthing for artistic advice; Izabella Woronko for fundraising support; Tim Samuelson, City of Chicago Cultural Historian, for research advice; Jessica Maxey-Faulkner and Gia Biagi of the Chicago Park District; Eric Bronsky for archival photography advice; Leon J. Hoffman, Ph.D., for historical advice; Peggy Cassidy, Rosemary Dolinski, Joellen Freeding, Elaine Prag, and Sharon Gilkerson for proofreading and research; Rob Medina of the Chicago History Museum, Virginia Davis and the staff of the *Chicago Sun-Times,* for archival assistance; Gary Matts and Terry Jares from the Chicago Federation of Musicians; Grant Park Principal Conductor Carlos Kalmar and Chorus Director Christopher Bell for their artistic leadership; and the Grant Park Music Festival Board of Directors: Fred Brandstrader, President, Bill Ritchie, Vice President, Marta Farion, Secretary, Cassandra Francis, Treasurer, Carl Birkelbach, Donald E. Casey, Jr., Lisel Cherry, Ron Emmerman, Joan Fencik Parsons, Julius Few, Raymond A. Frick, Jr., Eileen Friestad, James Gandre, Douglas Kinney, Olga Markoff, Julian Oettinger, Steve Robinson, Beth Clark Rodriguez, and Lois Weisberg.

Design and production Jell Creative: Veronica Bardauskis, Ty Cooper, Joe Grossmann, Jorie Hamm, Orrin McCormack, Wailam Pan, Kelsey Stegner, Mallori Stone, and Charlie Thomason.

For their support and patience, special thanks to Glenda and Giulio; Lloyd H., Marissa, and Paili Bachrach.

Published by Chicago's Books Press (chicagosbooks.com), an imprint of Chicago's Neighborhoods, Inc.

Preface

by Tony Macaluso

"Is it really free?" This question, and its many variations, is asked countless times each summer by tourists and Chicago residents alike as they seek out or discover the Grant Park Music Festival in Millennium Park. People are astonished that a first-rate orchestra and chorus fill Chicago's lakefront throughout the summer with the sounds of Beethoven, Mahler, and adventurous programming such as the orchestra paired with a silent film from India.

The Grant Park Music Festival has been providing free concerts since 1935, when the Festival was born out of a mix of visionary ideas, creativity, and tenacity in the face of historic hardship, namely the Great Depression. Chicago has long had a capacity for turning obstacles into opportunities. Much as the disaster of the Great Chicago Fire of 1871 led to the creation of the celebrated free and clear downtown lakefront, so the idea of presenting first-rate classical music for free in Chicago's front yard was supported in part because there was a tremendous willingness to experiment during the Depression. This eagerness to try new things has remained part of the Festival's makeup and has helped to keep it vibrant ever since.

Each summer since 1935 in Chicago's Grant Park, the Festival has presented roughly ten weeks' worth of free concerts to enormous audiences. From the beginning, the Festival showcased the highest-level guest artists, but equally important, it went on to develop its own professional orchestra (formed in 1944) and chorus (1962), making the Grant Park Music Festival far more than just a showcase for art from elsewhere, but rather a true ensemble of musicians from around the country.

This book features interviews with dozens of the musicians who have been part of the Festival, ranging from guest artists who made a single appearance to musicians who served as members of the orchestra and chorus for decades. For every musician whose voice is represented here, there are dozens who might have been interviewed had time and space permitted.

Another frequently asked question about the Festival is, "Who makes it happen?" For much of its history, the Festival was funded almost entirely by the Chicago Park District, with crucial early support also coming from the Chicago Federation of Musicians. Currently, it is presented through a balance of public and private support. On the public side, the Chicago Park District provides just over half of the Festival's operating costs, while the City of Chicago's Department of Cultural Affairs provides important logistical support. Meanwhile, nearly half of the Festival's funding comes from foundations, corporations, and above all, from thousands of individuals who make donations, attend the Divertimento Gala, or support the Festival through a membership program (while nearly ninety percent of the space in the pavilion is free, some seats are reserved for members). As a result of this support, the Festival presents more than thirty concerts each summer and draws an annual audience of over three hundred thousand people, an audience as diverse as the city itself.

This book was published in celebration of the Festival's seventy-fifth season. Looking back, it is fascinating to ponder whether those who helped create the Festival in 1935 would have dared to dream that their inventive response to the hardships of the Depression would still be a vibrant part of Chicago's cultural life well into the twenty-first century. This book is dedicated to the many tenacious musicians and administrators, as well as the loyal audiences who braved the countless thunderstorms, sirens, airplanes, gnats, sweltering heat waves, and other colorful urban and natural obstacles and who savored the magnificence of music along the lakefront over the past eight decades, helping to make the Festival an indomitable Chicago tradition.

The story that follows is, of course, one of passionate music making, but it is also the story of the creation of a public space where everyone can stop and listen, the result of the people of a great city working together as an ensemble.

Opposite: Pinchas Zukerman conducts the Grant Park Orchestra at the Jay Pritzker Pavilion, Millennium Park, 2008.

Foreword

by Ron Magers, ABC-7 Chicago

After coming to Chicago from Minneapolis in 1981, I first went to the Grant Park Music Festival in the mid-1980s, but only briefly. I work nights as a television news anchor so it has been hard for me to get over there on a regular basis. However, once the Festival moved into the new facility at Millennium Park, it was a little easier for me to get to the concerts. I started popping over there during what would be my dinner break in the early evening, and it was very, very pleasant. Then my wife and I decided that we would buy season tickets and have permanent seats. Since we became subscribers, we've been enthusiastic supporters and are regular attendees on most Wednesdays and Fridays, as well as an occasional Saturday.

Since I work in the Loop, when I walk over to the park on Wednesday and Friday concert nights, I'm part of a large group of people headed that way with chairs, blankets, and picnic materials. It really is a great feeling to be in the heart of an urban area amongst a bunch of folks headed for an outdoor evening in their neighborhood.

I am delighted that this Festival is still free, and now that it is located in this amazing facility, it is even more stunning. I tell friends who either don't live here in Chicago or who have never been to the Festival that they are clearly missing one of the real jewels of the city if they don't get to this facility and hear performances by the Grant Park Orchestra. The tradition of free municipal concerts has essentially disappeared everywhere except in Chicago and occasionally in small towns where I discover local groups performing concerts in their village band shells. There is certainly nothing in America on the level of the Grant Park Music Festival.

The fact that it's available to everyone in such a wonderful facility with an outstanding sound system is nothing less than amazing to me. If you sit on the grass at the very back of the

A panoramic view of Millennium Park, looking north, 2007.

facility, the sound will be very nearly as superb as if you were sitting in the first row. This experience is an acoustical wonder. The Festival also provides Chicagoans and visitors to the city an opportunity to enjoy our city in the outdoors during warm summer weeks. How could I possibly find a better way to spend my dinner break than at a concert that is rarely more than seventy minutes, in the open air, with amazing acoustics, in an outdoor facility designed by a world-class architect, featuring a world-class conductor, symphony and chorus, and with major guest stars?

When I was growing up, I played in a high school band and took music appreciation in college, but I have never been a fan of classical music. Now, because I regularly attend the Grant Park Music Festival, regardless of the program, I have been exposed to classical music in a way that has given me a new appreciation and enjoyment. I look at it as not simply an enjoyable evening, but also one in which I usually learn something. Because of my experience here I now realize that there is almost nothing that I don't enjoy. The result is that I no longer try to make a judgment on whether I should go based on the program description alone.

There actually have been some programs where I said to myself, "I really don't think that's for me!" But I have gone anyway and enjoyed it so much that I was happy I went and just let the music wash over me.

As for memorable performances, I am Portuguese on my mother's side, and I have never before heard Portuguese fado music performed except on records heard at my family home in California. So, the fact that the Festival provided an entire program of such music including the singer Mariza, with her amazing voice and a stunning orchestra, was wonderful for me. That one really stuck out, but there have been numerous other indelible memories. Imagine hearing Stephen Sondheim done by Broadway performers with Mr. Sondheim, himself, in the audience with us.

I am convinced that Millennium Park has given us, as a city, an incredible edge. It is now the first place on my list of "must-sees" for visiting friends. If you haven't come to Chicago in the summer and seen Millennium Park and heard the musical performances at the Pritzker Pavilion, then you haven't seen Chicago's best.

Introduction

by Van Cliburn

History has always evaluated the greatness of a city by its citizens' steadfast devotion and constant dedication to the fine arts. Great music and great art have always been barometers for judging the stability, cultivation, and refinement of a people. And those eternal verities always transcend the quixotic generational trends and popular fads. The great and beautiful city of Chicago has among its many treasures the world-renowned Chicago Symphony Orchestra, the famous Art Institute, the superb Lyric Opera, and the spectacular Grant Park Music Festival. James C. Petrillo, the legendary head of the Chicago Federation of Musicians and later the president of the American Federation of Musicians, had an incredible vision for his beloved Chicago. His deepest desire was for everyone within and beyond the city to know the wonder, power, beauty, and spiritual nourishment to be found in classical music.

When I was five years old my parents took me to Chicago where my father had business appointments. For five or six glorious days I vividly remember how thrilling and beautiful the city was. It was summertime, and when we arrived the weather was warm and friendly. It seemed almost overnight that suddenly there was a chilling wind coming from Lake Michigan, and my parents had to take me to a store to buy me some warm clothes. I would certainly need them in the evening for my inspiring visit to Grant Park to witness its musical beauty. During that same period of time when I was five, I announced to my parents that I was going to be a concert pianist.

In the summer of 1958, I found myself performing on the stage of the shell of Grant Park that I had admired so much when I was five years old. I have a flood of memories of the extraordinary audiences—kind and thoughtful people who wished me well. I could scarcely believe how many people were there. Of course, when I was invited again years later, I immediately accepted.

On the twelfth of June, 1994, I performed with my friend Leonard Slatkin and the Grant Park Festival Orchestra. En route to the performance, I remarked to friends that I hoped there would be a few people who still remembered me and wanted to hear me play. The audience had an intimate ambience—so concentrated and magnetically inspiring. The silence was palpable. I was overwhelmed. To my surprise and shock, the next day the newspaper reported there had been an audience estimated at three hundred and fifty thousand. I said to myself, if that be true, Chicago is surely one of the greatest audiences in the world.

The mystery of music has always fascinated me: Consider that out of twelve tones come infinite possibilities of myriad combinations of the three elements we call music—melody, harmony, and rhythm. Then mathematics is added to the equation. Mathematics is indispensable in order to bring coherent definition and comprehensible structure. After that, the most important ingredient is the essential collection of the human thoughts, feelings, and imagination of the composer, who carries the responsibility of the painstaking procedure of putting pen to paper in careful notation and expressive directions for the use of the sounds. Therefore, the notes are then, as it were, 'engraved in stone.'

Music then becomes invisible architecture. Hence, music is to time as visible art is to space.

Beethoven's Ninth Symphony is the same notation whether performed in Moscow, Beijing, Buenos Aires, or Chicago. The cardinal exhortation for all performers the world over is always to be faithful to the text and directions of the composer. The differences in those four hypothetical performances will be clarity of the musical enunciation, strength of sonic presentation, and human individuality of knowledgeable, disciplined interpretation. A timeless factor is in the rule of the profession:

Van Cliburn at the Great Hall of the Moscow Conservatory during the 1958 Tchaikovsky Competition.

Van Cliburn sitting at a Steinway piano on June 1, 1994, eleven days before his return to the Grant Park Music Festival.

Opposite: A dramatic view of the Grant Park Orchestra from the catwalk above the Jay Pritzker Pavilion stage.

all instrumentalists and singers are prohibited from using any electronic devices, thus giving the audience purity of sound. In the case of large venues, only overhead, broadcast-style magnification is employed. That further underscores the fact that great music is eternal and indestructible.

Everyone is indebted to Tony Macaluso, Julia Bachrach, and Neal Samors for giving us a wonderful opportunity to review the past seventy-five years of classical music performed in Grant Park, and now in Millennium Park, an international historic landmark. Also, the observations and thoughts of Ron Magers are consequential in understanding the enormity of this magnificent

venue. We cannot forget the tireless efforts of Anne-Claude Chartrand, Agnieszka Kozlowska, Leigh Levine, Laurel Prag, Gina Scalise, Christine Worthing, and Izabella Woronko for enabling such an important endeavor to function from day to day.

Great music is international and universal: it is a language that in many cases is greater than the spoken word. And I shall always be grateful to the memories of the wonderful audiences and the thrilling moments that I have had in Chicago. Congratulations to the Grant Park Music Festival on its seventy-fifth season. You and the great city of Chicago have confirmed your devotion to the arts and your indelible place in history.

A Grant Park Gallery: *The Programs and Posters*

Soon after the Chicago Park District established the Grant Park Concerts in 1935, it began promoting the free musical series through a variety of media including printed posters and programs. Two years earlier, the South Park Commission had begun using funding from President Franklin Delano Roosevelt's New Deal to produce flyers and educational pamphlets that were designed, written, and printed by its own employees. After the consolidation of the Chicago Park District in 1934, funding through the Works Progress Administration (WPA) and Federal Arts Program fostered the creation of similar materials.

An array of program covers from Grant Park concerts (top row from left: 1941, 1953, 1957, and 1958; bottom row from left: 1967, 1968, 1977, 1980, and 1981).

Each year, Park District graphic designers developed artwork for the Grant Park concerts. The materials were produced by a printing and engraving shop in the basement of the old Administration Building just north of Soldier Field. The posters were displayed in field houses, buses, and at elevated stations throughout the city. The programs were distributed at the concert series. Even after federal relief funding ended, the Park District continued to produce these specially designed materials. Today, a large collection of annual posters and concert programs provides a nostalgic reminder of Chicago's tradition of "concerts under the stars."

Posters from the Grant Park Music Festival (top left: circa 1940; bottom row from left: circa 1940, circa 1940, 1988, and 1999).

A Grant Park Gallery: *The Concerts Rendered*

These lush images give a sense of the romance of the Grant Park Music Festival's venues during the twentieth century. The original band shell (seen in postcards below) was located at the south end of Grant Park, across Lake Shore Drive from the Field Museum of Natural History. It stood from 1931 to 1978 and served as the home of the Grant Park Music Festival for forty-four seasons (the Festival began in 1935, several years after the band shell was built). The Petrillo Bandshell (seen in the watercolor, right) was built in 1978 and stood further north in Grant Park. It served as the Festival's home until Millennium Park opened in 2004.

The original Grant Park band shell seen in four vivid postcard images from the 1930s.

Opposite: The Petrillo Bandshell seen in a watercolor image from the 1970s. (Buckingham Fountain sprays skyward in the upper right corner.)

A Grant Park Gallery: *Architectural Poetry*

Architecture and music have always been profoundly inter-twined at the Grant Park Music Festival, whether it be Chicago's renowned skyline that has served as the backdrop for the concerts or the Festival's own band shells. Several of the Festival's homes (actual and imagined) are seen here.

Almost immediately after the Festival began in 1935, proposals for a new band shell design began to be proposed. There had been a long-standing hope that the Festival would receive a world-class home, a hope that was fulfilled when Frank Gehry's Jay Pritzker Pavilion in Millennium Park opened in 2004.

Clockwise from top left:
The original Grant Park band shell shortly after it was completed in 1931 stands starkly unadorned. (It would later be surrounded by flowers, shrubbery, and backstage buildings.)

A model of the Petrillo Bandshell, named after the Festival's legendary founder.

An unrealized amphitheater designed for the Festival, which was unveiled by the Chicago Park District in 1946 and which would have been located directly east of the Art Institute.

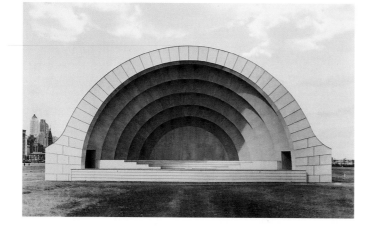

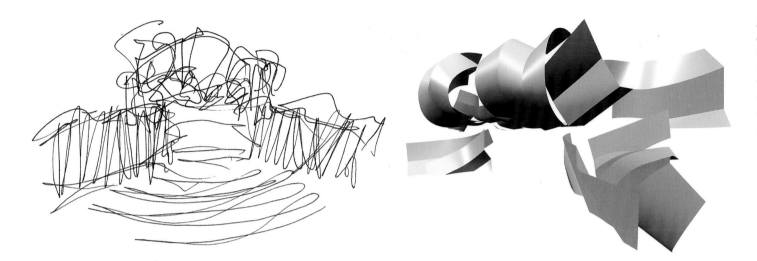

A series of renderings produced during the development of the Jay Pritzker Pavilion, which became the Festival's home in 2004 (clockwise from top left): an early conceptual sketch of the pavilion by Frank Gehry; a computer model; and a late-stage physical model.

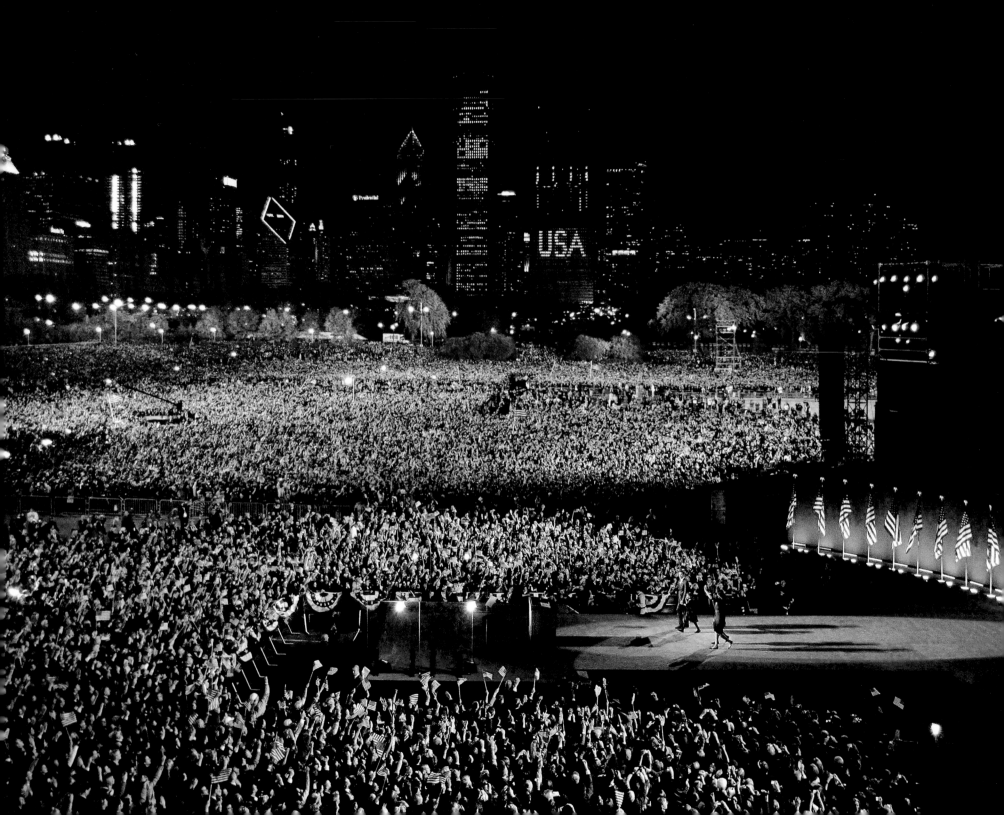

CHAPTER ONE

Front Yard for All

The History of Grant Park

On November 4, 2008, the whole world came to Chicago's front yard when hundreds of millions of television viewers watched Barack Obama's election night rally. Grant Park instantly became one of the earth's most famous public open spaces.

But in Chicago, the lakefront park has always been the premier gathering place. For over one hundred and fifty years, crowds have been drawn to this space by circuses, baseball games, protest rallies, military drills, aviation exhibitions, appearances by royalty, festivals, and parades, as well as open air concerts. The site has also long provided valuable and even sacred parkland along the city's lakefront.

The history of Grant Park is the story of a place that is essential to the identity of the city—a place that has attracted the masses and inspired the passionate involvement of generations of Chicagoans.

Barack Obama chose Chicago's front yard for his election night rally because of its symbolic significance. Photo 2008.

Foresighted Chicagoans

Even before Chicago's official incorporation as a city in 1837, foresighted citizens rallied to protect lakefront open space. In the mid-1830s, when early residents learned that Fort Dearborn, a military outpost near the juncture between Lake Michigan and the Chicago River, would soon be sold off for development, they held a meeting to discuss the need to save some of the property as parkland. By this time the streets had been platted, and there was only a narrow strip of land between Michigan Avenue and the lake. The group adopted a resolution to reserve a twenty-acre lakefront parcel "for a Public Square accessible at all times to the people."[1] In response, much of the area between Randolph and Madison streets, spanning both sides of Michigan Avenue, was set aside as "public ground."[2] (The area west of Michigan Avenue between Randolph and Washington streets was named Dearborn Park, and although designated as public ground, it later became the site of the Chicago Public Library, now the Chicago Cultural Center.)

Efforts were soon underway to save a larger lakefront area south of Madison Street. The federal government ceded vast acreage to the state with the intention of using revenues from land sales to help finance the Illinois and Michigan Canal. In 1836, the Canal commissioners—Gurdon Hubbard, William Archer, and William Thornton—designated the entire stretch east of Michigan Avenue from Madison Street to just south of Eleventh Street as "Public Ground—A Common to remain forever Open, Clear, and Free of any building, or other Obstructions Whatever."[3] The federal government reaffirmed this commitment three years later when the United States Secretary of War finalized the transfer of the Fort Dearborn land and marked the

area of the sale map between Randolph and Madison streets east of Michigan Avenue with the notation, "Public ground forever to remain vacant of buildings."[4]

ENJOYING AND PROTECTING LAKE PARK

By 1847 the City of Chicago had become the owner of the entire stretch between Randolph Street and Eleventh Street, officially naming it Lake Park. (The "breathing space" was also often called Lake Front and Lake Shore Park.) Over the next couple of decades, Lake Park provided a popular spot for strolling, picnicking, and open-air concerts despite its raw appearance and problems with shoreline erosion. Strong winds and wave action made Lake Park muddy and unpleasant; however, this did not deter visitors. In fact, an early published account described the park as "a place for recreation and the enjoyment of the scenery and fresh air."[5]

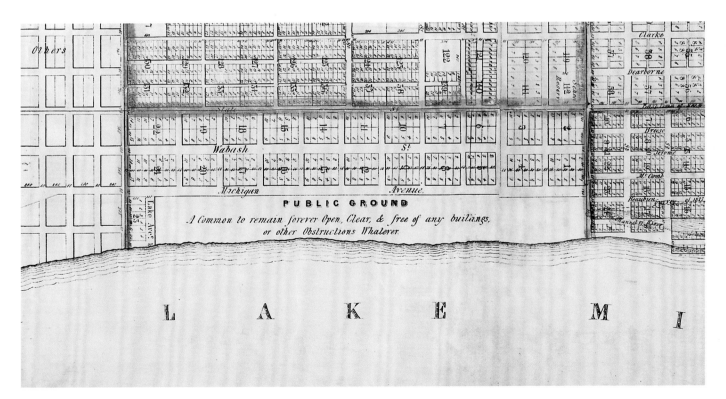

The Canal commissioners produced this map in 1836, setting forth their intention to protect lakefront property as open space.

Opposite: In the 1850s the Illinois Central Railroad Company built tracks on a trestle in the lake east of the existing park. Photo circa 1868.

Lakeshore erosion soon posed such a major threat that city officials considered abandoning the park and its surrounding area. A few months after a terrible summer storm in 1850, the *Chicago Daily Tribune* reported that the "public ground had been well nigh swept away, and unless something was done speedily the hungry waves would soon begin the work of destruction upon private property."[6] The city's flimsy revetments were not substantial enough to protect the shoreline and the mansions along Michigan Avenue. In 1852 a clever solution to this problem was conceived. The newly chartered Illinois Central Railroad Company (IC) agreed to construct a masonry breakwater that would protect the park and Michigan Avenue in exchange for permission to build a train trestle in the bed of Lake Michigan.

The IC Railroad Company bought some of the old Fort Dearborn property north of the park and added landfill between Randolph Street and the Chicago River. Soon after the construction of a passenger terminal and sheds, the entire area surrounding the mouth of the river was industrialized. Despite the smoke and soot, nearby ramshackle warehouses and wharves, and lack of trees or other landscape improvements, many Chicagoans considered Lake Park an important amenity. A citizen suggesting that trees be planted in the park wrote: "There does not exist the city that can boast of a more pleasant promenade than our Lake Park. In the summer nights, the moon shining brightly, and the cool, refreshing lake breeze gently blowing, it is delightful."[7]

PROMENADE MUSIC

Between the late 1850s and the 1871 Great Chicago Fire, many Chicagoans enjoyed open-air concerts during summer evenings in Lake Park. At this time, the city had several resident bands. Most were formed by musicians who had settled here from Germany, and fellow immigrants often supported them through private subscriptions.[8] German composer and musician Henry Ahner founded the Great Western Band, which began playing in Lake Park in 1857. After Ahner's death the following year, the band

continued under the leadership of another German immigrant, William Burkhardt. The Great Western played at the south end of the park, between Van Buren and Harrison streets. The concerts were held from late June through August, sometimes as often as one concert per week, on Thursday or Friday evenings. Band members wore a "very striking uniform," with a hat "trimmed with silver and red plumes, black coat with silver trimmings and silver shoulder guards, and dark pants with broad silver stripes."[9]

In addition to Lake Park, the Great Western performed regularly in nearby Dearborn Park and in marching processions through downtown streets. The band also occasionally played at the Wigwam, a large hall near the Chicago River at the corner of Wacker Drive and Lake Street that housed political conventions and meetings. In the late 1860s, the Great Western combined with another local band, the Light Guard Meeting. Led by A. J. Vaas, the Great Western Light Guard Band performed popular and symphonic music with as many as one hundred members.[10] In 1869, Vaas's full field band of twenty-two pieces played a summer series of concerts in Lake Park, funded through a subscription by nearby residents. The "promenade concerts" were held on Monday evenings from a gas-lit, covered bandstand.[11]

During the mid-nineteenth century, a number of local bands and orchestras gave outdoor concerts. Photo circa 1900.

Schemes for Enlarging and Selling Off Lake Park

In the late 1860s, prominent Chicagoans discussed enlarging Lake Park by filling in the existing harbor between the narrow strip of parkland and the train tracks. The group began raising private money in 1867 to commission an elaborate plan with elements symbolizing the region around the Great Lakes. Within the next few years, the city's Board of Public Works adopted a much simpler version of this scheme that did not incorporate symbolic elements.[12] The city's plan "called for a long pond at the center of the park which would be dotted by…a profusion of islets."[13] It also had lawns, terraces, walks, and fountains that were designed to take full advantage of the site's lakefront views.

As the city began slowly increasing Lake Park's acreage through landfill, several politicians supported a controversial plan to sell off part of the park. Chicago was developing into one of the nation's major railroad hubs, and three companies—the IC, Chicago Burlington and Quincy, and Michigan Central—wanted expanded tracking and a large terminal on the downtown lakefront. The proposed Lake Front Act (also called the Harbor Act) attempted to accommodate the needs of the growing railroads and to establish a private development agency for Lake Park's harbor. The bill conveyed the area north of Monroe Street to the railroads and granted the IC the rights to submerged lands south of Monroe Street. In 1869 the state approved the act over the objections of Governor John M. Palmer. Critics called the plan "the lakefront steal" because it would have robbed the city of property meant "for all time to come on our lake-front."[14] The railroad companies would pay only $800,000 for land that had been valued at millions. (The proposed proceeds were to benefit other parks throughout the city.) Many Chicagoans vehemently objected to the deal. The city comptroller refused to accept the initial payment, and the city council never finalized the sale. Although this protected the existing parkland, the provision granting the IC railroad lakefront riparian rights continued to be debated in the courts for many years.

After the City's Board of Public Works added new acreage by filling in the basin west of the train trestle, a new harbor was created on the east side of the tracks. Photo 1891.

The Great Chicago Fire and Aftermath

On October 8, 1871, the Great Chicago Fire raged for more than two days, spreading across nearly four square miles, and leaving one hundred thousand people homeless. Lake Park sat along the eastern edge of the burnt district. Among thousands of destroyed buildings were elegant mansions lining Michigan Avenue and the IC Railroad terminal building just north of Lake Park. Mr. Horace White, a resident of Michigan Avenue between Monroe and Adams streets, described the scene as he and his neighbors tried to escape before the fire had reached their area. He wrote, "We dragged seven trunks, four bundles, four valises, two baskets, and one hamper of provisions into the street and piled them on the wagon. The fire was still more than a quarter of a mile distant, and the wind, which was increasing in violence,

was driving it."[15] White explained that he and his family stood amidst a vast crowd while policemen tried to direct the chaotic mass to Lake Park, which was perceived as a much safer location. "From this imposing row of residences the millionaires were dragging their trunks and their bundles….There was real danger to life all along the street but nobody realized it, because the park was ample to hold all of the people."[16]

After the fire the city had to dispose of thousands of tons of charred rubble and debris. Considering that Lake Park was on the edge of the fire district and efforts to fill in the small harbor were already underway, the area between the existing shoreline and the train tracks was an obvious location. Soon, countless wagonloads "of ashes, stone-fragments, brick-bats, mortar-dust,

Left: The Great Fire devastated the downtown area, 1871.

Right: After the fire, Lake Park and other downtown locations quickly adapted into temporary business locations, 1871.

slag, metallic debris, melted and agglomerated nails, spikes, horse-shoes, bars, bundles and other forms of iron, china and glass-ware and ten thousand other relics" were dumped into the basin.[17] In addition to the accelerated landfill process, the fire had another significant impact on Lake Park. To help keep local companies from having to close down, the city allowed businessmen to build temporary commercial structures in the park. One- and two-story sheds and "pine lumber" shanties soon filled the lakefront open space.[18] The park became even more of an eyesore because garbage heaps were regularly dumped near the tracks so that railroad cars could haul them away.

After the temporary businesses were removed, Lake Park continued to play a role in boosting the post-fire economy, when a group of Chicago businessmen decided that it would be the perfect location for a world-class trade show. They "raised a sub-scription of $150,000 to pay for the initial costs of a fair with the continuing expenses to be borne by the entertainments which accompanied the commodities to be displayed."[19] Architect William W. Boyington designed a magnificent iron-and-glass Inter-State Industrial Exposition Building, soon built on the north side of the park. In the fall of 1873, a crowd of fifteen thou-sand gathered for the grand formal opening of the Exposition. They were entertained by a forty-piece band organized by A. J. Vass (who had also been the leader of the Great Western Light Guard Band) and Professor Flodoard Hoffman. Vaas & Hoffman's band played from an "airy perch up in the gallery."[20]

When the annual Inter-State Industrial Exposition was not in session, the enormous building served "a range of other activities such as dog, cat, cattle, horse, and chicken shows," political conventions, a bicycle tournament, and musical programs including operas and concerts.[21] One figure who attracted large audiences to the facility was Theodore Thomas. A beloved German-born violinist and orchestra leader, Thomas played

regularly in Chicago during this period and went on to settle here, founding the Chicago Orchestra in 1891 (later known as the Chicago Symphony Orchestra).

In the 1870s, the Exposition Building was "transformed at one end into a beer garden replete with overhead lights and potted plants," and Thomas's "concerts gave listeners not only brilliant and light music but symphonic movements not frequently presented in the summer."[22]

Housing more than 230,000 square feet of exhibit space, the Inter-State Industrial Exposition Building had a series of curved roofs, cupolas, and a central glass dome supported by enormous trusses. Photo circa 1885.

Baseball and Circuses

Lake Park became a hub of activities in addition to those held at the Inter-State Industrial Exposition Building. Just before the Great Fire, the city leased an area on the north side of the park to a professional baseball club. After the original stadium burned down, the baseball grounds were rebuilt, and by the late 1870s the Chicago White Stockings played there. (This National League team was the precursor to the Chicago Cubs.)[23] The games attracted thousands of spectators, and the White Stockings won several National League pennants in the early 1880s.[24]

In 1883, the city tried to evict the baseball club, during another attempt to sell parkland to the IC and Baltimore and Ohio railroad companies. The railroads attempted to acquire the entire harbor area, add landfill, and provide a depot and expanded tracking. Along with adjacent property owners, the baseball club filed lawsuits to prevent the scheme. The litigation continued for several more years; however, the property owners filed another complaint against the baseball club because they believed the sporting facility was a nuisance that violated the area's dedication as "open ground to be kept forever vacant of buildings of every description."[25] As a result, the courts forced the ball club out of the park at the end of its 1884 season.

Even after the baseball grounds were razed, the site remained cluttered with shacks and other buildings, including two federal armories. An unsightly maintenance yard was used "for storing paving blocks, tar wagons, stones, old lumber, and all sorts of rubbish."[26] For decades, the city had also leased out

Left: The Chicago White Stockings, 1889 (renamed the Chicago Cubs in 1902).

Right: A poster promoting one of the many circuses that performed in Grant Park, circa 1896.

Opposite: Aaron Montgomery Ward had two adjacent structures on Michigan Avenue for his business—the tower building with the pyramidal top, and the warehouse to the north. Photo circa 1915.

space in Lake Park to the Barnum, Sell's Brothers, Forepaugh, and other circuses. Enormous three-ring tents in the park featured elephants harnessed to chariots, trained monkeys, and sideshows such as the "Woman with the Iron Jaw."[27]

Adjacent property owners became increasingly unhappy. Mail-order magnate Aaron Montgomery Ward (1844–1913), whose Michigan Avenue office overlooked the park, filed an injunction in 1890 to stop the city from dumping garbage, maintaining sheds or other buildings, and holding circuses there. This proved to be the first in a long series of legal battles he waged to preserve the lakefront park. The court restrained the city from dumping or constructing sheds but allowed the circus leases to continue. City officials soon planned larger and more boisterous events for the site such as "spectacular" pyrotechnic displays, a show called the "Fall of Pompeii," and Buffalo Bill's Wild West show.[28] Despite the ruling, the sheds remained, and the city even began building a new barn for garbage horses and wagons.

The legal disputes relating to the railroad company's claim to riparian rights resulted in an 1892 United States Supreme Court ruling clarifying that the "lakefront water rights…belonged to the city 'in trust for public use.'"[29] This squelched the plans for the railroad terminal; however, other buildings remained in place including a power plant, the city's sheds, and the partially built barn. Ward filed another lawsuit, and in 1893 the judge ruled in his favor, restraining the city from leasing any part of Lake Park for circuses and ordering the removal of the buildings.[30] Although the circuses had their final performances there that June, debates about buildings in the park and riparian rights would continue for many years.

World's Columbian Exposition

In 1890, when Chicago won the bid to host the World's Columbian Exposition, several downtown businesses lobbied for Lake Park as its location. Renowned landscape architect Frederick Law Olmsted, Sr. (1832–1902) was asked to help identify the fair site. Two decades earlier, Chicago's South Park Commission had hired Olmsted to lay out an immense park composed of the Eastern Division (Jackson Park), the Western Division (Washington Park), and the broad tree-lined Midway Plaisance connecting the two areas. Olmsted recommended Jackson Park as the site for the World's Fair. Like Lake Park, it offered dramatic views of Lake Michigan and access by steamship and other boats. But Jackson Park was much larger, and it could offer a vast expanse of unimproved lakefront property. Working with Chicago's famous architect and planner, Daniel H. Burnham (1846–1912), Olmsted soon created plans to transform the raw south-side site into a gleaming "White City" with magnificent waterways and Beaux Arts–style buildings.

Although Lake Park was no longer under consideration, local directors of the exposition agreed to build the World's Congresses Hall there, with the understanding that the structure would later house the Art Institute of Chicago. The proposal called for razing the Inter-State Exposition Building and replacing it with a permanent building designed by the firm of Shepley, Rutan and Coolidge. Completed in time for the World's Fair opening in May of 1893, the World's Congresses Hall hosted meetings devoted to promoting an understanding between people of various cultures and religions throughout the world. The congresses covered broad topics related to art, science, religion, business, sociology, and social reform, including meetings on destitute children, the advancement of women in society, and the concept of Sunday as a day off from work.

After a six-month period that ended in late October, more than twenty-seven million people had visited the World's

Columbian Exposition. The South Park commissioners worked swiftly to return the site back to parkland. In Lake Park, the World's Congresses Hall was converted into a museum even more quickly. By early December of 1893, the building had been remodeled and officially reopened as the Art Institute of Chicago. The following year, two lions sculpted by Edward Kemeys were installed, flanking the entryway of the museum. Plaster versions had been similarly displayed guarding the exposition's Fine Arts Palace, and Mrs. Henry Field paid to have them recast in bronze for the new Art Institute building.

The Art Institute of Chicago opened soon after the World's Columbian Exposition closed. Photo circa 1915.

Opposite: Court of Honor of the World's Columbian Exposition in Jackson Park, 1893.

Renewed Interest in Chicago's Front Yard

After the World's Columbian Exposition closed, many prominent Chicagoans, including Daniel H. Burnham, began envisioning an improved Lake Park with extensive acreage added through landfill, landscape improvements, and new amenities which they believed would enhance Chicago's "front yard." Burnham proposed several new permanent structures in Lake Park to house the Field Museum, Crerar Library, the Illinois National Guard, a new city hall, and other municipal buildings. Department-store magnate Marshall Field had recently given $1 million to purchase anthropological artifacts that had been exhibited at the exposition. The Field Columbian Museum soon occupied the old Fine Arts Palace in Jackson Park. Within a year, there was strong consensus that the institution should erect a permanent building downtown, in Lake Park. Field agreed to give millions more for the new museum.

In 1895 Burnham created a preliminary plan in which, on a small scale, Lake Park would emulate the "White City." Envisioning the monumental neo-classical Field Museum as the centerpiece, Burnham symmetrically surrounded it with the other proposed buildings. Other prominent designers and organizations began suggesting alternative schemes that included some of new buildings but also respected the views of

Even with few landscape improvements, large crowds frequented Chicago's front yard. Photo circa 1890.

Lake Michigan. Among them, an early mentor of Burnham, Peter B. Wight, created a plan on behalf of the Municipal Improvement League, in which buildings flanked outer edges, leaving open water basins in the center to emphasize the lakefront views.[31]

The following year, the city began transferring ownership of Lake Park to the South Park commissioners, who soon renamed it in honor of Ulysses S. Grant. Although Ward had won a permanent injunction against any buildings or other intrusions in the park, the city appealed. Burnham continued with plans for a formal landscape featuring three major cultural buildings: the Field Museum flanked by an enlarged Art Institute and a

new Crerar Library. The South Park commissioners strongly supported this scheme.

By now, Ward had commonly become known as the "watch dog of the lake-front," but his legal battles to protect the character of the downtown park were far from over.[32] Although he had previously agreed to the construction of the Art Institute and a temporary post office in Lake Park, when foundations were laid for a six-lap bicycle track in 1897, he complained that it violated an injunction that he had won the year before. Despite the enthusiastic support of cycling clubs, the courts ordered the track's removal.

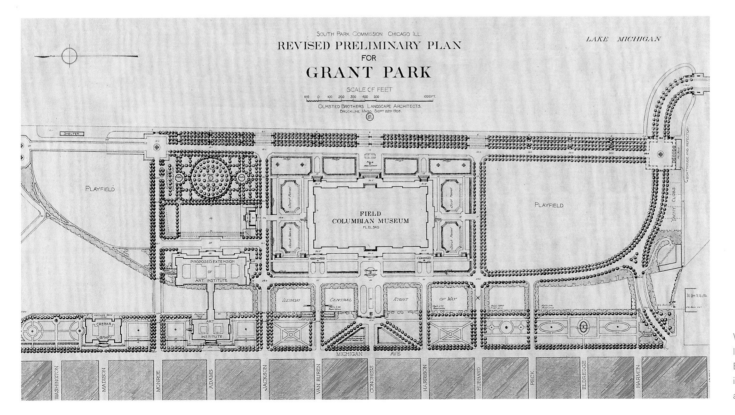

Working closely with Burnham, landscape architects the Olmsted Brothers produced a series of plans in 1908 that placed the Field Museum as the focal point of the design.

A Larger Park for the New Century

In 1903, three bills passed by the state seemed to clear the way for Burnham's proposed improvements to the park. These bills gave the commissioners the right to enlarge Grant Park; permitted cities and park districts to purchase, erect, maintain, and levy taxes for museums in public parks; and brought new clarity to the long-term dispute with the IC over riparian rights.[33] The commissioners hired the Olmsted Brothers (sons and successor firm to Frederick Law Olmsted, Sr.) to help Burnham fully develop his plans for the expanded two-hundred-acre park. Each of their series of plans placed the Field Museum as Grant Park's centerpiece. Wight wrote to the Olmsted Brothers on Municipal Art League stationery arguing against the building's proposed location, but the design team would not be swayed.[34]

As Burnham began considering the finer points of the plan, he proposed four monumental statues—Columbus, Lincoln, Washington, and Field. In a letter to Henry Foreman, president of the South Park Commission, he asserted: the "four monuments... will cover the history we desire to refer to: That of the Discoverer of America; that of the Founder of America; that of the Liberator of America; and finally, as typical of Peace and Prosperity, that of the Merchant and Manufacturer whose beneficence naturally follows and completes the work for which the first three laid the foundation."[35] Burnham went on to suggest that private funds could easily be raised for the Marshall Field monument.

While anticipating that the implementation of the ambitious plans would soon move forward, the South Park commissioners continued with landfill operations. The raw, newly created ground was leveled so that people could begin using it for baseball and football games.

Meanwhile, Ward vowed to continue his fight to protect the lakefront open space. Marshall Field died in 1906, leaving an $8 million bequest to build the long-proposed museum on any publicly owned site within six years. At the same time, ground was broken for the Crerar Library east of the IC tracks between Madison and Monroe streets. The South Park commissioners were confident that Ward would lose his battle in the state supreme court. In 1908, they displayed a model of the Olmsted Brothers' final plan for Grant Park in an Art Institute gallery.

WARD'S VICTORY SPURS LANDFILL TO THE SOUTH

In 1905 Edward H. Bennett (1874–1954) a talented young architect, joined Burnham's firm and began working closely with him on sketches for a magnificent stretch of parkland between Grant and Jackson parks. Four years later, Burnham and Bennett produced the ambitious *Plan of Chicago.* Parks and green spaces provided the nucleus for the entire plan, and Grant Park was an important focal point. South Park Commission President Henry G. Foreman described the plan's overall scheme for parkland as a "half wheel," with "Grant Park as the hub," diagonal streets as the spokes, the older system of parks and boulevards as the "support of the spokes," and an outer belt of lakefront parkland and forest preserves.[36] For the lakefront parkland proposed south of Grant Park, Burnham and Bennett suggested using new landfill to create a series of manmade islands, lagoons, harbors, beaches, meadows, and playfields.

Many Chicagoans blamed Ward for Grant Park's raw and unfinished appearance over a long period of time. In a rare interview, Ward voiced frustration about the lack of public support for his efforts to protect the open space. He said, "Had I known in 1890 how long it would take me to preserve a park for the people against their will, I doubt if I would have undertaken it." Ward also explained, "I fought for the people of Chicago, not the millionaires.... Here is park frontage on the lake, comparing favorably with the Bay of Naples, which city officials would crowd with buildings, transforming the breathing spot for the poor into a showground of the educated rich."[37]

Despite public opinion, Ward won his final lawsuit in the Illinois state supreme court in December of 1910. To create an alternative site for the Field Museum, the South Park commissioners began new negotiations with the IC Railroad Company. This resulted in an agreement by which the IC finally surrendered its rights to the submerged lands south of Twelfth Street in exchange for expanding its right-of-way between Twelfth Street and Jackson Park.

The commissioners could then create new landfill at the south end of Grant Park for the museum site. The arrangement also provided an opportunity to begin forming the new stretch of lakefront parkland that would eventually link with Jackson Park. Burnham produced revised plans for the neo-classical museum building in 1911, the year before his death. (It took another decade before the Field Museum of Natural History would finally open to the public.)

After Ward's last lawsuit, the South Park commissioners filled the lakefront on the south side of Grant Park to create an alternative site for the Field Museum. Photo circa 1920.

Parades, Special Events, and Tournaments

As fill operations progressed, most of Grant Park's landscape remained raw and unimproved. Despite these conditions, the park hosted tournaments, parades, and other special events. In July of 1910, well over a million people attended a twelve-day military tournament and exhibition, which included parades, drills, and historical pageants. Later that fall, tremendous crowds gathered in the park to witness airplane maneuvers above Chicago's lakefront for the first time in history. Crowds cheered as Walter L. Brookins flew a Wright biplane thousands of feet above the skyline.[38]

Harold McCormick, a prominent Chicago businessman, helped to organize one of the nation's first international aviation meets, held in and above Grant Park for ten days in August of 1911. Although two pilots died, several others set world aviation records, and the event was considered a success. The following year, the park hosted another meet in which aviators won cash prizes in contests of speed, skill, and duration. Spectators continued to watch with great enthusiasm, and several smaller aviation events occurred in Grant Park over the next several years.

As the president of the American Olympic Games Committee, McCormick organized an enormous athletic carnival in the park in 1913, with many of the same events as offered at the Olympics, such as track and field, shooting, fencing, and equestrianism.

View of aviator C. P. Rodgers flying over boats in Lake Michigan during the International Aviation Meet, 1911.

Over the next few years, other organizations sponsored sporting events there. For instance the Illinois Athletic Club presented track and field, the Grand American sponsored a trapshooting tournament, and in 1916 the *Chicago Tribune* held an ice-skating event in the park.

When the focus shifted during World War I, Grant Park continued to serve as an important gathering place. More than a hundred thousand Chicagoans joined a 1917 "Win the War" rally with a parade along Michigan Avenue, speeches, military drills, and performances by army aviators in and above the park. The following year, throngs gathered in the park daily for a larger two-week Government War Exposition with many performances by the Army Navy Band, trench battle and tank demonstrations, outdoor war motion pictures, parades, and specially designated days such as Red Cross Day.

While many of these large events were staged in the landfill area east of the IC tracks, there were also band performances on the southeast side of the park near Michigan and Congress avenues. The South Park commissioners erected a temporary bandstand in 1915, and William Weil's Chicago Band performed summer concerts there, sometimes as often as biweekly.[39] The wooden bandstand remained for five or six years.

Left: Naval recruiters on elephants in Grant Park, 1917.

Right: Marathon runners taking their positions for a race during an athletic carnival, 1913.

Refining the Classical Vision

By 1915 the commissioners were eager to finally begin large-scale improvements to the entire park, so they hired Edward H. Bennett to create revised plans. Bennett was uniquely qualified to reinterpret Burnham's design ideas for Grant Park. Not only had Bennett been classically trained at the École des Beaux Arts, but he had produced many earlier park designs for D. H. Burnham & Company. The coauthor of the *1909 Plan,* Bennett had recently been appointed consulting architect to the Chicago Plan Commission.

Bennett paid homage to Burnham's earlier vision, while also protecting lakefront views. Designing in the French Renaissance style, he relied on formal symmetry and outdoor room-like spaces defined by tree allées, and he incorporated lawn panels and gardens, formal walkways, terraces, fountains, and elegant details to be made of ornamental concrete. The South Park commissioners placed a model of the proposed work on display. Construction began at the northwest side of the park, featuring classical balustrades, rostral columns, and a peristyle surrounding a shallow circular fountain at the far north end.

As the commissioners focused on completing Grant Park, they also worked to develop the new linear park that Burnham

and Bennett had proposed between Grant and Jackson parks. A 1919 agreement between the City of Chicago, the South Park commissioners, and the IC helped further both projects. Not only did this result in the electrification of hundreds of miles of tracks, but it also provided for the depression of tracking to a level of nine to fourteen feet below grade, with viaducts and bridges connecting the divided landscape.

In 1920 all of the necessary property rights and government approvals were finalized to allow the landfill operations to begin south of the Field Museum, and voters approved a $20 million bond issue to create the new linear park. The plan called for a long stretch of parkland with five islands extending into the lake. Only the Northerly Island (now a peninsula) was ever realized. Landfill on the mainland progressed slowly southward, eventually resulting in more than five hundred acres. Although the ambitious vision set forth by the *Plan of Chicago* was never fully realized, the South Park commissioners named Burnham Park a few years later to honor the great urban planner.

One of the first priorities for the new landfill area was to build a large multi-use stadium there. Athletic competitions and large festivals had taken place in a temporary stadium for

Rendering entitled "General View of Grant Park for the South Park Commissioners," Bennett, Parsons, Frost and Thomas, circa 1922.

years, and there was great need for a larger and more permanent structure. The South Park commissioners sponsored an architectural competition. Architects Holabird & Roche's proposal for a U-shaped, classically inspired stadium was selected as the winning entry for what would soon become known as Soldier Field.

Although Edward H. Bennett's stadium plans did not win the competition, his firm continued to design Grant Park. Bennett, Parsons, Frost, and Thomas produced a complete vision for the park in a 1922 presentation drawing. A large ornamental fountain would serve as the centerpiece—a monumental focal point that could convey the French Renaissance style without obstructing views of Lake Michigan. In 1924, philanthropist and art patron Kate Sturges Buckingham agreed to donate the fountain in tribute to her brother, Clarence. Bennett submitted sketches, and Miss Buckingham agreed to cover the estimated costs of approximately $350,000 to build, maintain, and operate the "electrically operated" fountain.[40] By the time the Clarence Buckingham Memorial Fountain was dedicated three years later, Miss Buckingham's financial commitment added up to $1 million for the fountain's construction and perpetual care.

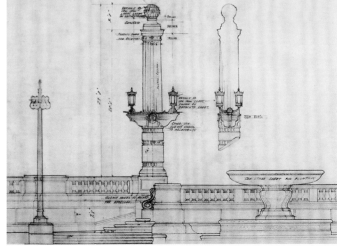

Above: Construction of rostral columns and balustrade, circa 1916.

Left: Construction of the Buckingham Fountain, circa 1926.

Right: Sketch by Edward H. Bennett of rostral column and fountain, circa 1915.

The Front Yard Takes Shape

After Grant Park had remained barren and unimproved for decades, in the mid-1920s it finally began to develop into an exquisite front yard with many cultural attractions. More than a decade earlier, after discussing the popularity of the aquarium at the World's Columbian Exposition, the commissioners had decided that Grant Park should have a world-class aquarium.

They met with the trustees of the Field Museum to consider having the two cultural facilities jointly operated, but the idea did not progress.[41] In the early 1920s, the Lincoln Park Zoo opened a small aquarium. The South Park commissioners wanted to build a much larger aquarium near the Field Museum and Soldier Field. John G. Shedd (1850–1956), retired president of Marshall Field & Co.,

Aerial view of south end of Grant Park looking towards Burnham Park landfill area, 1931.

Opposite, above: Newly finished Clarence Buckingham Memorial Fountain, circa 1928.

Opposite, below: Edward H. Bennett's implemented plans for Grant Park included the Congress Plaza with a grand stairway leading into the park, circa 1940.

donated $3 million to this ambitious project. In 1927 ground was broken for the Beaux Arts–style building designed by architects Graham, Anderson, Probst and White.

By the time the John G. Shedd Aquarium opened a few years later, Grant Park's Clarence Buckingham Memorial Fountain had already become Chicago's most beloved monument. Designed by Edward H. Bennett along with French sculptor Marcel Loyau and engineer Jacques H. Lambert, the fountain was touted as "the largest structure of its kind in the world." The Latona Basin in Versailles, France, provided the inspiration for the four-tiered basins of elaborately carved stone. However, the Buckingham Fountain is unique because it symbolizes Lake Michigan. This is conveyed through enormous water displays as well as four pairs of bronze sea horses, which represent each of the states bordering the Great Lakes.[42] These Art Deco–style sculptural elements received critical praise and garnered Loyau the Prix National award at the 1927 Paris Salon.

The Clarence Buckingham Memorial Fountain was especially impressive as one of the world's first decorative fountains to "use modern mechanical systems to create a dynamic light and water display on a massive scale."[43] Some of the displays rely on more than fourteen thousand gallons of water per minute. The original colored lighting was carefully orchestrated with the water displays. According to an early brochure, during the planning stages, Miss Buckingham worked closely with technicians to test and blend the lighting colors to create the effect of soft moonlight.

The park commissioners erected a temporary bandstand near the fountain for its formal dedication on August 26, 1927. An hour before the ceremonies, John Philip Sousa's band began entertaining the audience of fifty thousand. At 9:04 p.m., Edward H. Bennett turned on the power.[44] Sousa "stood waving his baton" as the band "played the march king's own 'Stars and

Stripes Forever.'"[45] The fountain began to glow in misty blue lights, and within moments the audience witnessed the first half-hour-long water display in the monument's history.

Another monumental sculptural installation was the Abraham Lincoln, also known as the Seated Lincoln. Installed in 1926, this solemn-looking sculpture of the martyred president had been produced nearly twenty years earlier by Augustus Saint-Gaudens, one of the nation's most revered artists. Architect Stanford White produced its enormous one-hundred-and-fifty-foot-wide marble setting (known as an exedra). Bennett deemed the area on which the monument sits the Court of Presidents. The commissioners had intended to mirror the Lincoln and its exedra with a similarly impressive monument of George Washington. This never occurred, however, and the Court of Presidents was left only half finished.

Despite the unfinished quality of the Court of Presidents, much of Grant Park's landscape was finally under construction. Bennett had designed a series of bridges that crossed the IC tracks and right-of-way, with classical balustrades and pylons made of ornamental concrete. The monumental Congress Drive provided a formal axis and view to the Buckingham Fountain. West of the Court of Presidents, twin bridges along Congress Drive connected to an elliptical roadway and an elegant formal plaza with grand stairway leading to Michigan Avenue. As the Congress Plaza was being constructed in 1928, South Park Commission President Edward J. Kelly (who went on to become mayor of Chicago five years later) described it as "the most beautiful park approach in the world."[46]

The Art Institute's B. F. Ferguson Fund commissioned a pair of bronze Native American equestrian figures to flank Congress Plaza. Although acclaimed Croatian sculptor Ivan Mestrovic poised the idealized warriors as if to shoot an arrow and throw a spear, he omitted the weapons, leaving them to the imaginations of the viewers.

FETES AND FESTIVITIES

Between the end of World War I and the late 1920s, Grant Park reestablished itself as one of the city's most popular places for outdoor celebrations and special events. Children's play pageants had singing, dancing, athletic drills, and contests. Some pageants

Left: Group laying wreath at the newly installed Lincoln Monument, circa 1926.

Right: Graf Zeppelin flying over Buckingham Fountain in Grant Park, 1929.

focused on a theme, such as fire prevention, while others were Mardi Gras celebrations with bicycle and doll parades and children in costumes.

During this period, the circus returned to Grant Park. Beginning in the summer of 1919, the commissioners permitted the newly merged Ringling Bros. and Barnum & Bailey circus to give shows in the park for a week and a half, despite Ward's earlier efforts. With seven hundred fifty performers and over one thousand animals, the circus pitched a tent-city along with the big top. For decades, the circus continued this annual tradition, eventually moving to the large parking lots next to Soldier Field.

Beginning with an enormous rodeo in 1925, Soldier Field quickly became a major venue for festivals, celebrations, concerts, and sporting events. Among the earliest events that attracted huge crowds were the 1926 Eucharistic Congress, the Dempsey-Tunney boxing match the following year, and dozens of Army Navy and collegiate football games. In August of 1927, enormous crowds flocked to Soldier Field for a reception honoring the world-famous aviator, Charles Lindbergh.

Large gatherings were also held in other parts of Grant Park. In 1929 Chicagoans gathered near the Buckingham Fountain to watch Hugo Eckner's Graf Zeppelin soar over the city's skyline in an eighteen-minute-long flight.[47] The same year, the park hosted events celebrating the Light's Golden Jubilee, honoring the fiftieth anniversary of Edison's incandescent bulb. One of many celebrations around the country, Chicago's involved a spectacular display of lights around the Buckingham Fountain and congratulatory messages to Edison in skywriting above Grant Park.

The combined Ringling Bros. and Barnum & Bailey circus pitched tents in Grant Park for the "Greatest Show on Earth" for many years. Photo 1930.

World's Fair Preparations

During the festive and prosperous mid-1920s, Mayor William E. Dever organized a committee to plan a major celebration to honor the one hundredth anniversary of Chicago in 1933. Looking back to the success of the World's Columbian Exposition, the group suggested using this opportunity to host a second world's fair. In 1927 Dever's successor, Mayor William Hale Thomas rejected the idea, but the advocates persevered. After they received support from U.S. Vice President Charles S. Dawes, the mayor reconsidered. The vice president's brother, Rufus Dawes, headed the fair's board of trustees.

Despite the October 1929 stock market crash, the trustees continued with plans for the fair. There had been an early decision to finance the event entirely through private sources. More than one hundred thousand people had purchased subscriptions before the economic crisis, and afterwards, businesses were still willing to pay for exhibit space to participate in this international event.

As plans progressed, the new landfill spanning Northerly Island and Burnham Park's mainland between Twelfth and Thirty-ninth streets was considered an ideal location for the fairgrounds. Close to hotels and other downtown amenities, there

would be good transportation, access to adjacent museums, and Soldier Field would serve as a venue for pageants and festivals.

With "the dramatization of the progress of civilization during the hundred years of Chicago's existence" as the theme, fair planners named the World's Fair "A Century of Progress."[48] With the focus on science and technology, it was especially fitting that Max Adler, retired vice president of Sears, Roebuck and Co., provided a major donation to build a permanent planetarium on Northerly Island. Designed by architect Ernest Grunsfeld, Jr., the domed granite building opened in 1930.

The following spring, as fair buildings were under construction, the Chicago Concert Band Association made an offer that prompted the construction of a new band shell at the south end of Grant Park. Made up of prominent Chicagoans, the association offered to organize "a concert band of the highest rank, composed of seventy carefully selected musicians" to give free summer concerts if the commissioners would agree to build a band shell with electric lighting and dressing rooms.[49] General Superintendent George Donahue asked the park commissioners to approve a $12,500 construction budget, asserting that with this investment, each of the fifty free summer concerts would cost only about $300, "no more has ordinarily been paid for a mediocre band."[50]

South Park Commission architect E. V. Buchsbaum designed the band shell, which was made of wood and fiber. Although the *Chicago Tribune* described the Art Deco structure as "a huge fan," many people believed it resembled the Hollywood Bowl, the well-known band shell that had recently been built in California.[51] Considering the hardship of the times, the commissioners anticipated that the free concerts would be extremely popular and planned to accommodate an audience of twenty thousand. At the ground-breaking ceremonies Mayor Cermak proclaimed that "good music has a wider appeal and is entertaining to a far greater number than perhaps any other form of art or science."[52]

Despite some rain on the evening of August 24, 1931, more than ten thousand people filled the lawn in front of the new band shell for the opening of the free concerts. The Chicago

Concert Band played some "earnest music" by Wagner during the first part of the program with lighter selections such as a Brahms waltz and a Sousa march towards the end.[53]

After the first season, the band shell continued to be well used. In July of 1932, Franklin Delano Roosevelt appeared there during his campaign for the presidency. Supporters flocked to the lawn to greet Roosevelt before a motor parade took him to the Chicago Stadium, where he delivered his acceptance speech as the Democratic nominee for president. Throughout the rest of the summer, Chicagoans enjoyed a second season of free concerts from the band shell. The opening performance by the Cavallo Symphonic band included "Onward Chicago," a march composed in honor of the upcoming Century of Progress exposition.[54]

Construction of the band shell, 1931.

Opposite: Aerial view of Burnham Park in 1931 during construction of the Century of Progress exposition.

Second World's Fair Brightens Spirits

Crowds on Northerly Island enjoying A Century of Progress in its second season, 1934.

Opposite, left: The Ford Symphony Gardens was one of several band shells at the fair. Photo circa 1934.

Opposite, right: The sky ride had observation decks that stood six hundred feet tall and rocket cars that extended along cables at a height of 219 feet. Photo circa 1934.

A team of the nation's leading architects planned the fairgrounds and designed the major buildings. This architectural commission included Raymond Hood and Harvey Wiley Corbett of New York, Paul Phillipe Cret of Philadelphia, as well as Chicagoans John A. Holabird, Edward H. Bennett, and Daniel H. Burnham's sons, Daniel, Jr., and Hubert. Their initial plans for A Century of Progress followed the classical Beaux Arts style of the 1893 World's Fair. Prompted by the forward-looking theme and oddly shaped site, however, they decided to take a bold new approach, emphasizing asymmetry, bright colors, and modernistic buildings.

In late 1930 two additions to the architectural commission, theatrical designer Joseph Urban and landscape architect Ferrucio Vitale, helped to make A Century of Progress quite unlike any fairgrounds that had ever been seen in America before. Urban selected a palette of twenty-three bright colors that included Persian orange, tomato bisque, and turquoise. Modern lighting techniques such as neon and choreographic search lights intensified the sense of color. Large garden beds with annuals in vivid hues relating to the colors of nearby fair buildings heightened the effect.

More than a dozen foreign countries participated, lending to the fair an international ambience. Myriad exhibits introduced the public to the latest achievements in science and technology, such as a voice-controlled robot, baby incubators, and an automobile production line. Visitors were also entertained by pageants, theater and concerts, the Enchanted Island for children, sideshows, the famous fan dancer, Sally Rand, and numerous rides including the iconic Sky Ride.

When the fair closed on November 12, 1933, its planners believed that A Century of Progress had been a great success. Well over twenty million admission tickets had been purchased, representing the highest attendance for any international fair by that time. Because admission only generated enough income to retire half of the bonds, A Century of Progress was extended into a second season from May 26 to October 31, 1934. By the time it closed at the end of the second season, more than thirty-six million visitors had attended, and the exposition had earned enough to repay the entire debt, while also generating additional funds that were donated to Chicago museums and other non-profit initiatives.

Consolidated Chicago Park District

By the early 1930s the South Park Commission was one of twenty-two independent park districts operating simultaneously throughout Chicago. The Great Depression had rendered most of the districts financially insolvent and drastically hindered the operations of all of them. To streamline services and gain access to relief funding through President Roosevelt's New Deal, voters approved the Park Consolidation Act of 1934, unifying the twenty-two agencies into the Chicago Park District.

Between 1935 and 1941, the Park District received approximately $100 million in federal funding through the Project Works Administration (PWA) and the Works Progress Administration (WPA). This allowed for various improvements in Grant Park, such as building the Outer Drive Bridge, planting thousands of shrubs, trees, and flowers, and installing an automatic sprinkling system. Since the overriding goal was to put Chicagoans back to work, the initiative not only supported construction but also cultural programs and special events. For example, children worked with artists to make kites and flew them in Grant Park kite tournaments. Adults made bows and arrows, which could be used in archery tournaments.

Two artistic special events were the Carnival of the Lakes, in which dozens of handmade water floats were sailed in a procession along the lakefront, and the Buckingham Fountain Spectacle. Presented with cooperation from Kate Buckingham, the spectacle was choreographed and staged by artists, musicians, and dancers who worked with hundreds of children from parks throughout the city. For three consecutive evenings in July of 1936, crowds gathered near the fountain. Dancers in waterproof costumes emulating mermaids, nymphs, frogs, and other whimsical creatures wove in and out of the illuminated mists while Walter Steindel's radio orchestra played opera music. One observer reported that "fairyland itself had been transported for the occasion into Grant Park, in the heart of the city."[55]

Chicago Park District employees planting trees in Grant Park, 1936.

Launching the Concert Series

The newly consolidated Chicago Park District had several thousand employees responsible for managing and operating the city's existing one hundred and thirty parks and approximately forty miles of planted boulevards. Mayor Edward J. Kelly appointed the agency's five-member Board of Commissioners including James C. Petrillo, president of the Chicago Federation of Musicians. Petrillo had previously served on the board of the West Park Commission, which was known for its high-quality music program. After suggesting that the Park District should sponsor free symphonic concerts in Grant Park, Petrillo and board president Robert Dunham came to an agreement. Petrillo would raise the money for the first season, and if the concerts attracted huge crowds, the Park District would provide a budget to continue the program.

In preparation for the first concert on July 1, 1935, Chicago Park District laborers spruced up the landscape and hung

Chinese lanterns along the edges of the white, fan-shaped band shell. They cleaned up the plaza area around the band shell and put out rows of seats. Despite late afternoon rain showers, thousands gathered to hear the debut concert. It had been suggested that programs should combine the work of European and American composers. Eric DeLamarter conducted the Chicago Symphony Orchestra in a program that included Wagner's *Tannhauser* and John Powell's *Natchez on the Hill*.[56]

The 1935 season continued with free concerts nightly from July 1 through Labor Day. An estimated two million people attended the first season's sixty-four concerts, and thousands of others listened at home on their radios. The endeavor was so successful that the following year the Chicago Park District assumed complete financial responsibility and continued to jointly sponsor the annual outdoor concert series with the musician's union.

Left: Tennis lessons for women in Grant Park, 1935.

Right: The Chicago Park District used funds from the WPA to improve Grant Park's roads and landscape and to support programs. Photo circa 1936.

WWII and Aftermath

Grant Park's role as the city's front yard was especially symbolic after America entered World War II. The armed forces used Hutchinson and Butler fields for physical training and drills, and a victory garden was planted next to the Art Institute. In July of 1942, when a twenty-three-year-old Chicagoan, Martin Wilson Nolan, became the city's ten-thousandth Naval recruit, a huge celebration was staged at the band shell. After a performance by the Chicago Opera orchestra, five hundred sailors from Navy Pier stood at attention for the color guard and "tossed their white caps high in the air," as Nolan arrived on stage for the induction ceremony.[57]

The park hosted a 1944 Army Show with mock battlefields near Soldier Field and special war exhibits at the Congress Plaza. Among events held at the band shell were ceremonies honoring the second anniversary of the founding of the WAVES, concerts by the United States Army Band, and other performances of patriotic music, which were broadcast by a radio program called *Chicago Theater on the Air.* During the intermission of live Grant Park concerts, radio news flashes helped keep the band shell audiences in touch with the latest information about the war.

In 1944 the Chicago Park District made some minor improvements to the band shell such as a public address system, and a new, resident Grant Park Symphony Orchestra was organized. After the war, the concerts became even more popular. By 1949 the series attendance totalled more than one million, including an audience of seventy-five thousand for a Rogers and Hammerstein program in July. This fifteenth season of "Concerts under the Stars" featured thirty-one symphonic programs. A *Sun-Times* editorial raved, "The Park District concerts have been drawing big crowds... As described in the song, 'the best things in life are free.' The stars belong to everyone and so does the music."[58] Uses of recreational facilities also increased during this post-war period, and softball, baseball, soccer, and tennis were especially popular in the park during the summer months.

United Nations for
Victory Parade, 1942.

Continuity and Change

Prosperity had returned to America. After the election of Mayor Richard J. Daley in 1955, Chicago began to modernize, while also retaining older values. During this automobile age, new highways, roadway improvements, and parking structures were considered a high priority. While building a modern expressway system that caused large-scale upheaval in many Chicago neighborhoods, Mayor Daley made significant improvements to downtown. He encouraged the construction of new and taller buildings, and the Loop became even more vibrant than before.

The influx of automobiles spurred major construction projects in Grant Park. In 1953 the park's first underground garage opened beneath the northern lawn and promenade area along Michigan Avenue. The project involved razing the historic peristyle and relocating elm trees to Northerly Island. As construction of the Congress Expressway (later named the Eisenhower) progressed, the Chicago Park District demolished the elegant stairway in the center of Congress Plaza to build a roadway extension connecting the expressway with Lake Shore

Drive. Ceremonies celebrated the first car to enter Grant Park via the expressway on August 10, 1956. Five years later the south underground garage opened to the public. In the early 1960s only a few small projects were undertaken to enhance the passive enjoyment of the park. These included a garden by landscape architect Dan Kiley planted just south of the Art Institute and new rose gardens flanking the Buckingham Fountain.

Traditional values were well reflected in Grant Park's programs and ceremonies at this time. Venetian Night, first celebrated in 1958, featured a parade of decorated and illuminated boats much like the earlier Carnival of the Lakes. Other celebrations honored nature. Beginning in 1955, the Park District's annual Arbor Day festivities in Grant Park included giving out fifteen hundred tree seedlings. For more than a decade, a Blossomtime Festival was celebrated in May, when Grant Park's profusion of flowering trees and shrubs were in bloom. The weeklong event included the coronation of a Blossomtime Queen, who had the honor of turning on the Buckingham Fountain for the season.

In 1959 the park became an authentic royal venue, when Queen Elizabeth II visited Chicago during a trip to the United States and Canada to dedicate the opening of the Saint Lawrence Seaway. On Chicago's "Queen's Day," the *Brittania* yacht docked in Lake Michigan, and "fireboats sent streams of water cascading into the air, as the royal party approached the specially built jetty in a sleek barge from the Brittania."[59] Queen Elizabeth and Prince Philip then proceeded along a red carpet to the Buckingham Fountain while a band played "God Save the Queen" followed by the American national anthem. (This is how Queen's Landing received its name.)

Grant Park's role as a gathering place took on new meaning in the 1960s as a growing number of people became involved in the civil-rights and anti-war movements. Among several nationally significant events in the park and Soldier Field was Dr. Martin Luther King's Freedom Rally in July of 1966. Later that fall nearly one thousand demonstrators marched through the Loop and rallied in Congress Plaza in hopes of persuading Senator Everett Dirksen to support President John F. Kennedy's civil-rights bill in 1966.[60]

Grant Park's most memorable protest rally occurred during the Democratic National Convention in 1968. As the party prepared to endorse a candidate who supported America's involvement in the Vietnam War, protestors began demonstrating in several locations in Chicago. Mayor Daley called in thousands of national guardsmen and policemen, and the treatment of the protestors became increasingly violent. Some of the most volatile incidents occurred around the band shell and near the General Logan Monument, which protestors had symbolically blindfolded. After the riots were broadcast on national television, many people began to think of Chicago and Grant Park as frightening places. In truth, however, many peaceful demonstrations soon followed, including a rally against the police response during the convention. Other large anti-war demonstrations continued in Grant Park through the early 1970s.

FIRST CAR TO ENTER GRANT PARK
OVER CONGRESS STREET HIGHWAY
AUGUST 10, 1956

Above: Mayor Richard J. Daley crowning Blossomtime Queen Mary Jean Ahern with queens from other cities, princesses, and Park District officials, 1957.

Below: Chicago Park District commissioners with first car to enter Grant Park from Congress Street highway, 1956.

Opposite: Queen Elizabeth and Prince Philip during the procession to Buckingham Fountain with Mayor Richard J. Daley, 1959.

Additional Changes Accommodate Uses

By the 1970s Grant Park's landscape was showing severe signs of wear. Attempts to accommodate ever-increasing numbers of people and automobiles were wreaking havoc on the front yard. In response to rising incidents of crime and vandalism, the Park District removed shrubs and increased lighting to provide better surveillance. In 1974 Paul Gapp, the award-winning architecture critic for the *Chicago Tribune* described the broken fountains, eroded ornamental concrete, and "weed-choked grass and patches of bare and rutted earth," in the park, arguing that landscape improvements should be a "front-yard priority."[61]

Among Grant Park's most deteriorated features was the forty-year-old band shell. In recent years, several "stagehands, performers, and even a grand piano had fallen through the stage floor."[62] Although many new band shell plans had emerged over the years, none had yet moved forward. In 1972, the park district began considering a controversial proposal to build a massive $31 million concrete-and-fiberglass band shell over a new underground garage in place of the existing surface parking lot at Monroe Street. After community groups charged that this structure would violate the A. Montgomery Ward restrictions, Chicago Park District officials decided to build a less expensive demountable band shell at Butler Field. Named in honor of James C. Petrillo, the new band shell opened in time for the summer concert season in June of 1978. Although the structure was designed to be dismantled, that fall Park District officials decided to save money by leaving it up, and the band shell was never dismantled.

At the same time, there were continuing demands for additional recreational facilities in Grant Park. The Park District responded with a major development at Monroe Street, including underground parking, locker rooms and bathrooms, tennis courts, an outdoor skating rink, playground, chess and checker tables, and picnic areas. In August of 1979, Mayor Jane Byrne dedicated the new Daley Bicentennial Plaza in honor of Mayor Richard J. Daley (1902–1976).

The Petrillo Bandshell not only provided a new venue for the Grant Park summer concerts, but also for huge special events that attracted audiences swelling to over a million people. In October of 1979, a terraced altar platform was erected next to the band shell from which Pope John Paul II officiated the largest public mass ever held in Chicago. A few years later, Joseph L. Bernardin delivered a homily from the same area soon after his appointment as Chicago's archbishop. The Petrillo Bandshell also became the locus for new festivals sponsored by the Mayor's Office of Special Events, such as Taste of Chicago, the annual July 3rd fireworks display with a coordinated Grant Park Orchestra concert, and the Chicago Jazz, Blues, and Gospel Fests. These traditions carried through the 1990s. Among other noteworthy events at the shell were appearances by the Dalai Lama and rallies celebrating the Chicago Bulls championships.

Couple enjoying the music at the new Petrillo Bandshell, circa 1980.

Opposite: Aerial view of crowds during Pope John Paul II's appearance in Grant Park, 1979.

A New Era

The election of Mayor Richard M. Daley in 1989 marked a new era for Chicago's parks, especially the downtrodden front yard. Years of decay and the impact of millions of annual visitors had taken a major toll on Grant Park's landscape and amenities. The Chicago Park District began an intensive study of the park, which generated design guidelines in 1992, and a series of physical improvements soon followed. Throughout the park, historic monuments, sculptures, bridges, and decayed ornamental concrete elements were conserved, repaired, and replaced. The diminished tree canopy was greatly enhanced by planting hybridized elms and other compatible species. New contextually designed facilities provided long-needed restrooms and concessions near the Buckingham Fountain. In 1995, a northbound stretch of Lake Shore Drive was relocated west of Soldier Field and the Field Museum. This $100 million project transformed two miles of asphalt into new green space. Plazas, gardens, and improved pedestrian linkages between the museums have replaced the paved roadway.

As impressive as the Museum Campus project has been, the most dramatic transformation has occurred along the far north end of Grant Park. For years, Chicagoans had put up with an eyesore in this area—a vast area of derelict rail yards and surface parking east of the lawn along Michigan Avenue. After the City of Chicago finally acquired much of this site in 1997, Mayor Daley announced plans to extend the park's underground garage system and build innovative parkland on top of it. Garage revenue as well as many millions from private donors have made possible the creation of Millennium Park, a world-class center for art, music, architecture, and landscape design.

Completed in 2004, Millennium Park is an exciting space that offers a variety of free cultural activities, outdoor exhibits, festivals, family programs, tours and nature walks, and other special events. A team of the nation's most acclaimed architects,

The Crown Fountain in Millennium Park has a collection of one thousand faces of Chicagoans that are randomly projected on two fifty-foot-tall glass towers. Photo 2004.

Opposite: The five-acre Lurie Garden in Millennium Park was inspired by Chicago's "City in a Garden" motto. Photo 2006.

landscape designers, horticulturalists, and artists contributed to the development of the twenty-five-acre site. Crowds have been flocking to the two major interactive works of public art—the Crown Fountain by Jaume Plensa and Anish Kapoor's *Cloud Gate,* which is known by Chicagoans as "the Bean." The Lurie Garden weaves together an exuberant palette of native perennials, a tall evergreen hedge, and a boardwalk edged by a linear water feature. Other permanent facilities that enhance visitors' experiences are McDonald's Cycle Center, McCormick Tribune Plaza and Ice Rink, Boeing Galleries, Wrigley Square, Chase Promenade, Exelon Pavilions, and the BP Bridge.

One of the most crucial goals for Millennium Park was to offer better facilities for theatrical, dance, and musical programs in Grant Park. The Harris Theater for Music and Dance and the Jay Pritzker Pavilion are fulfilling this challenging ambition. Cleverly tucked into the park's landscape, the Harris Theater provides numerous Chicago arts organizations with an indoor venue for performances ranging from classical ballet to contemporary dance as well as opera to folk music. After a history of more than one hundred fifty years of outdoor music in Grant Park, the Pritzker Pavilion provides Chicago's front yard with its first state-of-the-art concert venue. Architect Frank Gehry, winner of the National Medal of Art, created a lively one-hundred-twenty-foot-tall, stainless steel pavilion with an overhead trellis that supports a remarkable sound system providing a superior outdoor listening experience to the entire audience. The pavilion is now the home of the Grant Park Music Festival, and it is also used for many other free concerts and special events.

Along with Millennium Park, other recent improvements are invigorating Grant Park, such as the Music Garden and Summer Dance Program near the restored Spirit of Music monument and the new *Agora* installation by internationally acclaimed sculptor Magdalena Abakanowicz. The Parkways Foundation is working

with the Park District to raise millions for the Buckingham Fountain restoration, and other exciting improvements will follow as the result of a major gift from the Tiffany & Co. Foundation to restore the rose garden south of the fountain.

After three-quarters of a century of marvelous outdoor concerts, the Grant Park Music Festival contributes to this vitality. Along with all of the recent cultural amenities and programming, this renewed popularity proves that Daniel H. Burnham and Edward H. Bennett were exactly correct when they predicted that "civic beauty satisfies a craving of human nature so deep and so compelling that people will travel far to find and enjoy it," in Chicago's front yard.[63]

CHAPTER TWO

The 1930s

From the Depression, a Music Festival for the People Is Born

Chicago's lakefront had been the site of concerts of various sorts for nearly eighty years when the Grant Park concerts, later known as the Grant Park Music Festival, began in 1935. The Great Western Light Guard Band, for instance, played regularly, starting in the 1860s in a gas-lit music pavilion on the lakefront. The creation of a long-standing lakefront concert series that attracted tens—and even hundreds—of thousands of people per night, however, was a product of the unique circumstances of the 1930s.

A crowd gathers to hear violinist Albert Spalding in 1938. Spalding was the Chicago-born nephew and namesake of the Hall-of-Fame baseball pitcher and sporting-goods impresario.

Songs for a Cruel World

The combination of the Depression and the availability of several new forms of technology rattled the process of presenting and experiencing live music. In addition to economic woes, innovations such as records, radio, and sound films were making live music more dispensable and were leading to a shrinking number of jobs for musicians. The consequences were stark. In the late 1920s, before the arrival of sound films, about two thousand musicians were employed in Chicago movie theaters; by the mid-1930s there were only 125. In turn, the general public was hard pressed to afford tickets to live music. Circumstances were ripe for creative projects, but implementing such projects required a forceful push from individuals. James C. Petrillo, the legendary head of the Chicago Federation of Musicians, was more than glad to provide the initiative.

Before exploring the drama of the Festival's creation and early years, however, it is worth recalling the atmosphere of

Grant Park in the early years of the Depression. While the park was always a site of citywide celebrations, in the 1930s it was also filled on summer nights with desperate crowds and hobo squatter camps.

FROM THE ARCHIVES

The hardships of the homeless were vividly described in this *Chicago Daily Tribune* article from 1930:

"Last Sunday afternoon, while sitting at the pedestal at the Logan monument, at Michigan Boulevard and 8th Street, I was addressed by a middle aged American man of decent appearance with the remark, 'It's a cruel world.' He told me, that for the last three weeks he had passed the nights sleeping in Grant Park. The last couple of nights had been very cool, he said; and the rain during the night had soaked and drenched his clothes. He had not had anything to eat the whole day, he added, except a

Unemployed squatters on
Chicago's west side, 1932.

sandwich which another man of the army of unemployed, who had two of them, had shared with him. He was on the road for the last four months, he said, trying to find employment. On asking him how many men he thought were passing the night similarly, sleeping in Grant Park and under the viaduct of the adjacent road, he estimated the number to be between eight and nine hundred.

"'Do the police interfere with you sleeping here,' I asked. 'Not until about 5 o'clock in the morning,' he answered. 'Then the motor cops come around and start clubbing us at our feet, cursing, and swearing at us while driving us away.' There is, I believe, a society for the prevention of cruelty to animals. Would it not at least, be equally proper to organize one for the prevention of cruelty to the unemployed America's workingmen?"[1]

Above: Chicagoans line up for jobs in 1933.

Left: Members of the Illinois Women's Alliance campaign for relief and fairer taxation, circa 1935.

Right: The southeast corner of Grant Park in 1936 with the newly constructed band shell.

President Harry Truman joins Grant Park Music Festival founder James C. Petrillo (right) in a memorable piano-and-trumpet rendition of "Hail, Hail, the Gang's All Here," at an American Federation of Musicians gathering in 1954.

James C. Petrillo: The Organizer

The prime mover behind the creation of the Grant Park concerts, James C. Petrillo, was born in Chicago in 1892, the year before the World's Columbian Exposition. Petrillo was precocious, having organized a four-piece dance band in which he played trumpet at the age of fourteen. Despite being underage, he was given a special dispensation by the American Musicians Union that enabled him to join the union. Shortly thereafter, Petrillo began working in an organizing role for the American Musicians Union, and at the age of twenty-two, in 1914, he was elected president of the Chicago chapter of the AMU, although he was defeated for re-election in 1917.

Due to the advent of sound film and the production of records, leading an organization such as the Chicago chapter of the Federation of Musicians during the 1930s became immensely more challenging. The fight against recorded music and other new technologies that were threatening musicians' livelihoods would remain a major focus for Petrillo for the rest of his career. In the 1940s he would become a nationally renowned figure, both beloved and vilified, and featured on the cover of *Time* magazine, in large part due to his leading a nationwide recording ban over the way royalties were handled.

FROM THE ARCHIVES

By 1918 Petrillo had begun to make his mark as an organizer. According to author Robert Leiter:

"He was assigned the task of organizing the musicians in the Chinese restaurants. The task was difficult since Chicago was torn by labor wars and racketeering. But Petrillo already was accustomed to rough tactics. His methods were not tactful but they were very effective and in a short time he unionized most of those restaurants. As a result he was elected vice president in 1919." [2]

CHAMPION FOR PERFORMERS' RIGHTS

Petrillo quickly earned a reputation as a highly skilled advocate for Chicago's musicians, winning salary increases for performers in venues ranging from restaurants to the opera, and unionizing musicians performing in Chicago hotels in 1931. By the time of the birth of the Grant Park concerts in 1935, he was renowned throughout the country for his success in winning rights for musicians, notorious for tough tactics and folksy ways. By the early 1940s he would be elected the national president of the American Federation of Musicians.

James C. Petrillo and President Lyndon Johnson, circa 1965.

Petrillo Fights for Free Concerts in Grant Park

One of Petrillo's solutions for these hard times was to organize a free outdoor concert series in downtown Chicago that could both employ hundreds of languishing musicians and provide entertainment and culture for Chicagoans coping with the Depression. Petrillo determined that the key to realizing this vision was to gain the support of Chicago's formidable network of park districts.

Prior to 1934, when the Chicago park commissions were brought together by the Park Consolidation Act in order to gain federal funding under the New Deal, there were twenty-two separate park systems in Chicago. Petrillo succeeded in getting appointed to the West Park Board in 1933. He immediately began lobbying for a series of free music performances in the parks.

As Petrillo noted in a 1975 interview, the idea wasn't warmly embraced. "The first time I mentioned park concerts, they laughed in my face. The park employes hadn't been paid for 21 months. Where are you going to get money for park concerts when the policemen aren't being paid?"[3]

The situation changed significantly in 1934 when all twenty-two of the city's park boards merged and the mayor of Chicago, Ed Kelly, gained the right to make appointments to this new citywide Park Board. Petrillo immediately went to work trying to get appointed, with the goal of realizing his vision of free outdoor concerts. Gaining a seat on the new, unified, and much more powerful Chicago Park District Board was no simple task, yet Petrillo was undeterred.

Years later, in an interview with the *Chicago Tribune,* Petrillo described how he advocated for the festival:

"I had a meeting of all the employers in Chicago who hired musicians, everybody. I told them what I was after and I told them: 'You're not doing me a favor, but I'd like you to go to the mayor and tell him what you think about me. If you want to, it's all right; if you don't want to, it's all right, too. If you think I'm a son of a bitch, okay, tell him. No strings.' So some of them went to see Kelly, and I figure they did a good job. Later, I met the mayor at a Cubs game and asked him if he had reconsidered. 'No,' he says. 'I'm loaded. You can't imagine how many people want to get on that board.' It was mostly political, you see, and I had no backer, no political backer."[4]

Petrillo eventually succeeded in being appointed to the board with the help of a skillfully assembled coalition of allies—ranging from the Italian Consul General to many of the owners of the venues where the members of the unionized musicians performed—lobbying on his behalf. He immediately raised the subject of free concerts with the first president of the newly consolidated Chicago Park District, Robert Dunham, who, according to Petrillo, somewhat warily agreed to have the Park District sponsor the programs if Petrillo could guarantee large crowds. He immediately set to work, using the reach of the union to bring in big names.

"We did anything we could. We brought in Heifetz and Kostelanetz and his wife (What was her name?), Lily Pons, and Lawrence Tibbett. One night they said we went as high as 250,000. It was for a violinist who didn't play very well but was on a show with Jack Benny—Dave Rubinoff."[5]

Throughout the spring of 1935, it was uncertain whether the concerts would actually proceed as Petrillo and the Park District

James C. Petrillo continued to play trumpet during his many years as a labor leader. Photo circa 1960.

negotiated the budgets and sought to pull together an artistic lineup. Only in June did the official announcement come, as the *Chicago Daily Tribune* noted:

"It was good news when the papers the other day printed the information that the commissioners of the Chicago Park District had decreed nine weeks of free symphony and band concerts in Grant Park this summer. It indicated more than anything since the beginning of the depression that Chicago still has claims to being a musical center and desirous of providing summer time entertainment of a high order. Apparently the crystallizing force in this movement was James C. Petrillo, and apparently he operated in a threefold capacity, as park commissioner, as president of the Chicago Federation of Musicians, and as public spirited citizen. Otherwise the action might not have been taken, at least not to the generous extent that is being offered Chicago citizens."[6]

The Power of the Union

The Chicago Federation of Musicians was formed in 1896, and according to its official history: "Its origins date back to 1864 to the Chicago Musicians' Protective Union founded by German American band musicians. It was a member of Chicago General Trades Assembly and had a strong voice in working conditions for local musicians particularly in theaters and museums."[7]

LOOKING BACK

Ed Ward, the former president of the Chicago Federation of Musicians, talks about the vital role the unions played in helping musicians: "Before the union, musicians were really on their own. Going back to the Romantic era, they were usually kept in the court by the king, like servants. When musicians started to work in orchestras around the turn of the century, everybody was at the mercy of management and conductors, who could be fair or could be despots. Musicians could be fired at the whim of a conductor who may have simply had a bad day. Then the unions started getting involved in the negotiations. Previously, if the player had a problem, he could go and say, 'You can't fire me, it isn't right!' and they could say, 'Yeah we can, good-bye, there is the door.'

"When the unions came in, it put a middleman between management and labor. In modern times, I like to think of it as a way of insuring the best conditions for both sides. Over the years, it basically established very simple concessions by management; no, we cannot rehearse over three hours. Before that, a conductor could keep the musicians on stage far beyond what would be reasonable in the workplace.

"When musicians would go on strike, people would ask, 'How can you justify asking for $66,000 per year? How can you justify that when a good salary for someone is $25,000?' I said, 'Well, you have to understand that in order to get this job each player had to beat out two or three hundred other people wanting that job.'

"People expect, when they go to Grant Park or Lyric Opera or the symphony, to hear the best that there is. Whether the musician was getting a divorce, if she was getting the flu that day, or had problems with his children, they are expected to give one hundred percent everyday. If you go down Clark Street, we have a baseball field where we pay people millions of dollars a year to get a hit one out of every four times at bat. That is why they are worth that and more than that. When people leave the opera, they don't go out humming the scenery."

The former headquarters of the Chicago Federation of Musicians at 175 West Washington Street, circa 1950. James C. Petrillo's office, located on the second floor, had bulletproof windows and an elaborate security network. This was not necessarily an extreme precaution, given the tenacity of Petrillo's struggles on behalf of his members.

Building the Band Shell

The band shell that served as the home of the Grant Park concerts and later the Grant Park Music Festival, from its inception until the Festival moved to the Petrillo Bandshell in 1978, never had a name. It was built on a shoestring budget in just three weeks in 1931 for a shorter series of concerts. The program had the enthusiastic support of Mayor Anton Cermak (who two years later would be killed in Miami during an attempted assassination of the newly elected president, Franklin D. Roosevelt). Cermak, who had been elected mayor just a few months earlier, shook up Chicago politics by riding a wave of anti-Prohibition sentiment to victory.

FROM THE ARCHIVES

In the summer of 1931, Mayor Cermak spoke at a groundbreaking ceremony for the band shell:

"Good music has a wider appeal and is entertaining to a far greater number than perhaps any other form of art or science.... This summer as we look forward hopefully and confidently to better times, I feel these concerts will be among the many things which will inspire us and give even more determination quickly to achieve the welfare of all people, which is and should be the normal condition of men in America."[8]

The band shell's first concert took place in August of that summer, and the *Chicago Daily Tribune* chronicled the debut, complete with its weather challenges.

"It took more than a spurt of rain at 8 o'clock to discourage the musicians of the Chicago Concert band from giving their first concert in Grant Park last night. For that matter, it discouraged only a few of the audience. The rest camped under umbrellas and newspapers, and when the spurt was over vacant seats and standing room were speedily filled until some 10,000 or 12,000 persons were there."[9]

A MIXED-USE SPACE

During the subsequent three summers, the band shell was used for sporadic concerts featuring a variety of orchestras, big bands, and guest artists, but not until 1935 would a unified concert series be organized as a result of Petrillo's efforts.

Above and below: The Grant Park band shell was assembled in the summer of 1931. Four years later, it became home to the newly formed Grant Park concerts. It would serve stoically for forty-eight summers.

Opposite: Chicago Mayor Anton Cermak, shovel in hand, participates in the groundbreaking of the Grant Park band shell in the summer of 1931.

Launching the Grant Park Concerts

The first season of the Grant Park Music Festival began July 1, 1935, and sixty-four concerts followed between then and Labor Day. Among the regular performers that season were the Chicago Symphony Orchestra, the Woman's Symphony Orchestra, and the Civic Opera Orchestra, each performing five or six times. In addition, a host of big bands, led by Bohumir Kryl, Armin Hand, Max Bendix, George Dasch, Glenn Bainum, and Victor Grabel, entertained. Within a few weeks, an estimated thirty to thirty-five thousand people were attending the nightly free concerts, with millions more listening via nationwide radio broadcasts.

The Grant Park Music Festival's first season, the summer of 1935, was an eventful and turbulent time. In the final months,

Franklin Roosevelt oversaw the creation of Social Security, Nazi Germany grew increasingly intolerant with the implementation of the Nuremburg Laws, and the Chicago Cubs were on their way to a World Series appearance (they would lose to Detroit). By the summer's end the Festival had drawn an estimated audience of 1.9 million, and there was much talk of making the new concert series permanent.

The opening performance of the Festival, a peculiar mix of Wagner, Johann Strauss, and relatively obscure American composers, featured the Chicago Symphony Orchestra (the Grant Park Orchestra would not be formed until 1944). While rain kept the crowd to a modest size, Mayor Ed Kelly singled out Petrillo for

Summer nights in Grant Park quickly became major social occasions that drew people from all across the city, as this photo from Lily Pons's epic 1937 concert shows.

credit for bringing the concerts to life. The *Chicago Daily Tribune* noted that "the band shell has been ornamented with shrubs and Chinese lanterns until it is a pleasure to the eye."[10]

FROM THE ARCHIVES

By the end of the first week, the *Chicago Daily Tribune* was reflecting on some of the surprises of the new lakefront concert series:

"It begins to look as though several cherished and ancient theories were due to go into the discard before the present summer series of concerts from the band shell in Grant Park is over. One of them is that a symphony orchestra is the chosen delight of only the cultivated few. Another is that mere music

does not appeal to the public. A glance at last night's audience would to some degree have dispelled both."[11]

The concerts grew so popular that, in 1937, the *Chicago Daily Tribune* even compared Petrillo to Santa Claus:

"Yesterday was Christmas in Chicago, and the city's citizens swarmed to Grant Park to enjoy at absolutely no cost a show which any theater in the land would mortgage its future to obtain. Cast in the rôle of Santa Claus was James C. Petrillo, commissioner of the park district, and president of Chicago Federation of Musicians."[12]

Daily Life at the Concerts in the 1930s

Within a few weeks of the inauguration of the Grant Park Concerts in the summer of 1935, the throngs of people gathering along the lakefront for classical music night after night averaged in the tens of thousands. The largest attendance in the Festival's history is believed to have been Lily Pons's concert in 1939, which drew well over three hundred thousand people. These nightly gatherings developed their own character, mixing high art and populist, Midwestern charm.

Hype and Mangled Names

The press was not shy or slow to lodge complaints about hyperbole over guest artists and stumbles by the announcers, as this 1938 article notes:

"All summer long we have had to submit to a master of ceremonies who told what each piece of music was, or who the soloist was to be. Every guest artist has been 'built up' in the most exaggerated manner. Local singers who have never set foot on the stage of an opera house have been described as famous opera stars. Sub-standard performers have been made to sound like Ponses and Martinellis...

"Then, too, the announcer should recognize the educational responsibility of his position. Mispronounced proper names and garbled foreign titles should not be tolerated. Great gobs of boring descriptive matter about composers drawn from incompetently compiled musical textbooks do not add to the gayety of the concerts and merely serve to foster the unfortunate impression that good music cannot get along without the crutch of dry literary interpretation."[13]

Bigger Than a Heavyweight Bout?

By the third concert season, Chicago arts journalists, perhaps in keeping with the city's reputation for windy boastfulness, were

These girls take their Wagner seriously. The one on the right is not musically inclined, although she does think "Cross Patch" and "It's a Sin to Tell a Lie" are awfully cute tunes. The girls asked her along because they hated leaving her all alone in the apartment. Right in the midst of "Tristan" she's telling any one who wants to hear about how cute her brother's little girl is, only six mind you, and does a marvelous imitation of Popeye the Sailor.

Music critic being very caustic about the concert. His girl friend is too busy scratching mosquito bites to pay attention.

not afraid to start comparing the new lakefront music festival with the biggest audiences in any field:

"It has long been gospel in the United States that big sports events draw the tremendous crowds. The sports people will have to look to their laurels after the appearance of Rubinoff and his violin at the Grant Park concert. Estimates of the attendance ran as high as 225,000....The sports promoters may object that people pay to see their spectacles, and that if Joe Louis and Max Schmeling were to fight for nothing on the Chicago lake front they might attract a million people. Conceded, but this does not detract from the service rendered by the Music Festival and the Grant Park concerts in uncovering the latent interest of Chicagoans and their neighbors in music."[14]

A Living Wage

Meanwhile, behind the scenes the Grant Park concerts were, to most accounts, succeeding in their other aim, which was to provide a living wage for hundreds of musicians. According to *Intermezzo,* the official newspaper of the Chicago Federation of Musicians, in 1938 musicians were being paid ten dollars for a two-hour concert at a time when the minimum wage in the United States was twenty-five cents an hour. *Intermezzo* also made it very clear who was in charge of selecting conductors, guest artists, and other musicians, a task that was not treated lightly at a time when competition for work everywhere was fierce:

"The leaders for concerts in Grant Park and outlying parks have been picked by the President [i.e., James C. Petrillo]. These leaders will have full authority to select their own personnel. Do not ask the officers of the Local to put you on these jobs, because it will be impossible for them to do so as we are holding the leaders strictly responsible for the efficiency of these bands and orchestras. If they are not up to par, Mr. Leader will be dispensed with. He must protect his own job and, by doing so, will give the best possible concerts that can be given."[15]

"Get your ice cold lemon pop here!"

Intermission. Showing music lovers strolling about greeting friends and telling each other how awful the conductor is. From the left, a voice teacher, a girl music student (she's had ten radio auditions the past year), her mother, and a concert accompanist.

As a special treat, this evening's concert will be enlivened by Miss Betty Scrapple, premiere danseuse of the mechanistic ballet, in her interpretation of "Marche Militaire." Some say her conception is a portrayal of the horrors of war and some say it just means military preparedness.

The *Chicago Daily Tribune* printed these cartoon images of audiences typical of the Grant Park concerts in the summer of 1937.

They Scream for Ice Cream, Fighter Planes, and Other Disruptions

Food was always a big part of the picnic-like ambiance, and vendors were drawn to the crowds with an enthusiasm that sometimes unnerved patrons more used to traditional classical concert-hall norms, as demonstrated by this letter to the *Chicago Daily Tribune* in 1935:

"All of the time prior to the concert there are venders of all sorts of eats yelling their wares. Two of these venders last evening yelled so loudly that they deafened us to such an extent that personally I had a headache before the concert commenced. One man in particular, selling ice cream, just stood there and screamed with all his might. I asked him to tone down, but he replied that he had to sell. I told him that we were not deaf or else we would not be at the concert." [16]

Shouts of ice cream vendors were nothing compared to the barrage of fighter planes that rattled concertgoers at a 1937

performance that coincided with an airplane show along the lakefront. The next day's newspaper account ran:

"Mars again threw the Muses for a loss last night when a few volleys of artillery fire and a flock of raiding airplanes from the nearby Carnival of the Lakes came very near breaking up a Grant Park concert by the Chicago Symphony orchestra. However, the plucky little Muses came back fighting and the evening ended in a draw." [17]

Petrillo and other concert organizers, however, quickly learned to take the offensive to shut down potential disruptions before they could spoil the slow movement of a violin concerto, as with this preemptive strike in 1937 on the railroads that intersected Grant Park, as described in the *Chicago Daily Tribune*:

"It is reported that James C. Petrillo, president of the Chicago Federation of Musicians, has dickered with the Illinois Central

Concertgoers sprawl across Grant Park on a lazy summer afternoon in 1939.

railroad to such good purpose that the carrier is resolved to allow its bananas to spoil in the cars rather than move a single freight train during the Heifetz program next Sunday night."[18]

Babies, Limburger, and Strange Politics

Perhaps the most striking portrait of the surprising diversity of Grant Park concert audiences in the era was captured in this poem, titled "Who Goes to Grant Park Concerts?" by Isabelle Young, published in the Chicago Federation of Musicians newsletter, *Intermezzo*, in the summer of 1940. Since the concerts have always been free and accessible, the fascinating mix of people drawn to the Festival, as described in the poem, has been a constant, although the choice of food and unsettling political benchmates is a thing of the past:

Who Goes to Grant Park Concerts?

"The young, the yare, the fond, the fair,"
The jolly old lady with fattish flare,
The meek, the mild, the tough, the wild,
The bothersome couple with crying child,
The ones who came early and brought their lunch,
And Limburger sandwiches loudly munch!
The co-ed, the spinster, the banker, the cop,
And gramma with the bun on top!
The rich, the poor, the sad, the gay,
The weak, the proud, in rich array—
The Brit, the Russ, the German, the French,
The Spaniard, the Swiss, all squeezed on a bench…
And Jew and Nazi sit side by side!
Listening to the trombone slide!
For this is America, praised be God—
Still clear the sky—still green the sod![19]

A Tribute Following Gershwin's Death

In the summer of 1937, shortly following the death of George Gershwin at the tragically young age of thirty-eight, the Grant Park concerts honored the beloved American composer with an emotional concert heard across the country and described by the *Chicago Daily Tribune:*

"While lowering skies held back a threatening storm the crowd at the Grant Park band shell last evening heard Richard Czerwonky lead the Chicago Philharmonic orchestra in a half-hour tribute to the late George Gershwin. Over a nation-wide radio network of 109 stations the orchestra played the funeral music which closes Tschaikowsky's 'Pathetic' symphony, Gershwin's own 'Rhapsody in Blue,' and Siegfried's death music from Wagner's 'The Twilight of the Gods.'"[20]

The *Tribune* reprinted Petrillo's tribute to Gershwin delivered before the concert:

"America, strange new land to peoples of many tongues, forging ahead in the rapid pace that has made it a leader among nations, has lost a spokesman whose universal language is understood by all. His violins sing of conflict and sorrow, his horns blare the busy traffic of great cities, and drums accompany the riveting of huge skyscrapers. They sing of America and to America.

"We all have lost a friend who spoke our language. We, as musicians, have lost in George Gershwin a master craftsman."[21]

George Gershwin's music has been a mainstay at the Grant Park Music Festival for seven decades, from the memorial concert performed following his death in 1937 through the gala Divertimento concert of his work performed in 2008. Photo circa 1935.

Radio Days: Grant Park on the Airwaves

The first commercial radio broadcasts were only fifteen years old at the time the Festival began, but classical music on the airwaves had already become a big business. Classical programs such as *The Voice of Firestone* and *The Bell Telephone Hour* had enormous audiences, and in 1937 Arturo Toscanini began broadcasting NBC Symphony Orchestra programs.

During the 1930s, Grant Park concerts were broadcast by dozens of radio stations across the country, bringing live classical music to people in unlikely places.

LOOKING BACK

One vivid example is described by Wally Kujala, who went on to become a member of the Grant Park Orchestra and the Chicago Symphony as a renowned flutist.

"We lived in Huntington, West Virginia, and I was already taking flute lessons. My parents were rather poor. My father was a musician; he played the bassoon during the days of the Work Progress Administration, which was started by President Roosevelt, the WPA. I used to listen to the radio a lot. Grant Park Orchestra was on every week. That is when I really started to pay attention to what was going on in Chicago. In those days there were a lot of symphony broadcasts on all the networks, unlike what you would see today. Typically, Sunday afternoons the New York Philharmonic was on, Saturday afternoon Met Opera, Friday afternoons Philadelphia Orchestra, Saturday night NBC Orchestra. This was all part of my diet growing up musically, and Grant Park was one of them."

Arturo Toscanini led the renowned NBC Symphony Orchestra radio broadcast in the 1930s.

Great Artists of the 1930s

During the 1930s the Grant Park Concerts spared no expense in bringing many of the biggest names in classical music to Chicago's lakefront. In addition to such well-known guest artists as Lily Pons, Jascha Heifetz, Bobby Breen, Rudy Vallee, and Helen Morgan (profiled on the following pages), the 1930s saw the first appearances of conductor Andre Kostelanetz (1936–1937, 1939); violinists David Rubinoff (1936 and 1937), Mischa Elman (1936), Efrem Zimbalist (1938), and Albert Spalding (1938); pianist Moriz Rosenthal (1938); sopranos Marion Claire (1937 and 1938), Edith Mason (1938–1942), and Vivian Della Chiesa (1936–1941); tenors Tito Schipa (1937), John Carter (1938 and 1939), and Lawrence Tibbett (1939); and baritone John Charles Thomas (1936 and 1938).

Soprano Lily Pons during her 1937 Grant Park performance when, according to the *Chicago Daily Tribune,* more than three hundred fifty thousand people poured into Grant Park to hear her sing. Andre Kostelanetz, her husband at the time, conducted.

Lily Pons

Soprano, 1937 and 1939

One of the great sopranos of her era, Lily Pons was born in southern France and first gained attention singing for wounded soldiers in hospitals during World War I. She made her opera debut at the age of thirty and her debut at the Metropolitan Opera—where she would be a principal soprano for almost three decades—in 1930, singing Donizetti's *Lucia di Lammermoor*. When George Gershwin died in the summer of 1937, the year of Pons's debut in Grant Park, he was in the midst of working on a piece written specifically for her. Her two appearances with the Grant Park Music Festival were among the most popular in the Festival's history, drawing crowds in the hundreds of thousands.

FROM THE ARCHIVES

The *Chicago Daily Tribune* ran the following descriptions of Lily Pons's Grant Park appearances:

"Chicagoans streamed to Grant Park by the tens of thousands last night to make for Lily Pons the largest audience of her career. Here was music and a single voice, a calm night, and a sky of stars. To the east stretched the lake. Between it and the skyline, like a shining white cornucopia pouring forth sound, was the bandshell—and Lily Pons—with the blue white light of the Lindbergh beacon cutting the deep blue sky above.

"It was, however, a crowd that must have come for music, rather than for curiosity, for an intense silence fell upon it whenever Miss Pons, whom most of them saw only as a tiny figure in misty white with something orange thrown about her, began to sing. He who talked, or even whispered, while her voice trilled forth, amplified by the public address system, was scorned into silence. For the first ten minutes of the concert the thousands standing behind the first standing rows were unable to see the band shell. But woman's vanity came to their aid when a young girl fished a pocket mirror from her bag and held it up as a periscope. Others quickly imitated. Soon mirrors flashed from almost every hand." [22]

<hr>

The *Chicago American* described Lily Pons's return performance:

"Musical attendance records the world over were shattered last night when a surging mass of 330,000 Chicagoans riotously greeted the performance of Lily Pons and her conductor-husband, Andre Kostelanetz. Between appearances the beautiful Miss Pons told a reporter in almost frightened tone:

"'Thees is ze most threeling moment of my life. For the first time I nearly have stage fright when I see thees huge crowd. Nevair have I been so thrill—even in my first appearance at the Metropolitan Opera. And to theenk, all these people come to hear one who as a little girl milked cows and sang to them, in the country in France! Please tell all Chicagoans I love them. They have overwhelm me!'" [23]

Jascha Heifetz

Violinist, 1937

Recognized as one of the great violinists of the twentieth century, Heifetz was born in Lithuania around the turn of the century (the exact year of his birth is disputed) and became a music sensation as a child, performing an outdoor concert in Saint Petersburg in 1911 to an audience of over twenty-five thousand people. He made his United States debut at Carnegie Hall in 1917. His performance was one of the highlights of the third season of Grant Park concerts. Audiences flocked to hear the great violin virtuoso.

FROM THE ARCHIVES

The mass appeal of Jasha Heifetz's performance in Grant Park was vividly described by the *Chicago Daily Tribune:*

"The ancient but still potent lure of music, plus the fame of one of the art's greatest living practitioners, drew to the vast audience area at the south end of Grant Park yesterday one of the largest crowds of this whole crowded summer....All through the late afternoon hordes of people kept streaming over the viaducts and ramps that lead to the band shell. They took seats as long as there were any left—or set up headquarters on the broad lawns between the two drives. There were family picnics, some equipped with huge bludgeons of salami two and three feet long....Then came the big moment of the evening. The announcer finished a brief eulogy, and the great violinist walked out on the platform to the accompaniment of applause which failed to be deafening only because it had the sky and the horizon, rather than roofs and a wall, to confine it and echo it back."[24]

Jascha Heifetz gave what was, by many accounts, one of the most riveting performances in the history of the Grant Park Music Festival in the summer of 1937.

Children from all across Chicago came out in droves for the much-beloved radio and film child-star, Bobby Breen, in his two 1930s Grant Park appearances.

Bobby Breen

Actor and Singer, 1937 and 1938

Immensely popular radio and film child-star, Bobby Breen drew thousands of giddy fans, especially other children, during his appearances in Grant Park in the 1930s. Curiously, Breen made a pop-culture comeback more than thirty years later, when his image appeared amidst the crowd on the cover of the Beatles' *Sgt. Pepper's Lonely Hearts Club Band.*

FROM THE ARCHIVES

Child-star Bobby Breen's 1937 Grant Park appearance was described by the *Chicago Daily Tribune:*

"The lightest weight soloist of the whole Grant Park concert series came, as luck would have it, on the windiest night of the season. But he stood his ground against the gale, and the swirling dust storms which it provoked, and proved to the thousands who had braved the weather to hear him that he ranks already, at the age of nine years, as a sterling trouper. He is Bobby Breen, the screen's latest juvenile sensation, and he sang at the lake front band shell last night with the Chicago Philharmonic orchestra under Richard Czerwonky's direction. A tiny, bright faced lad with a huge shock of fair hair, he faced the throng as unconcernedly as he faces the cameras of Hollywood and gave a couple of more or less impromptu speeches in addition to his four scheduled songs.... Bobby positively oozes personality and sells his songs in the best Broadway tradition. The audience was delighted with the boy and with his work and would gladly have kept him there all night." [25]

Rudy Vallee

Singer, Actor, and Bandleader, 1937

In many ways the predecessor of Frank Sinatra and Bing Crosby, Rudy Vallee was an unparalleled pop star in the 1920s and 1930s, drawing frenzied mobs of fans wherever he performed. This Vermont-born son of French Canadian immigrants essentially defined the new artistic niche later termed the "crooner." When Vallee took a vacation from his national radio show in 1938, the year after his performance in Grant Park, he helped to break a key social barrier by insisting that Louis Armstrong be hired as his replacement—the first time an African American had served as the front man for a nationally syndicated radio program. Below is an impression from Vallee's Grant Park debut.

Adored crooner Rudy Vallee was one of the highlights of the Festival's first season. Photo circa 1935.

FROM THE ARCHIVES

The frenzied enthusiasm provoked by Rudy Vallee's appearance with the Festival is captured in this 1937 newspaper account:

"Seventy thousand people whooped it up for Rudy Vallee last night when America's No. 1 crooner and orchestra leader walked smilingly onto the stage of the Grant Park band shell. And what is more, the majority of those people ignored the light rain that fell almost constantly, and stayed right on through the entire time—the best part of an hour—that Rudy and his corps held the spotlight. This marked the entry of the Chicago Federation of Musicians and the Chicago Park district into big time vaudeville. They paraded a bill that any showhouse would sell its soul to secure, and offered it simply as a climaxing attraction on the program of the forty-seventh of the free lake front concerts."[26]

Helen Morgan

Singer, 1937

A Chicago-raised torch singer who made her reputation singing in the city's speakeasies in the 1920s, Helen Morgan became a sensation after her performance in the premiere of the musical *Showboat* in 1927 (and the film version two years later). Morgan brought her intimate club style to the formidable environment of Grant Park.

FROM THE ARCHIVES

The *Chicago Daily Tribune* pondered the challenges of creating an intimate atmosphere in Grant Park in this contemporary account of Helen Morgan's guest appearance:

"Up to a few hours ago night club singers who sit on the tops of pianos and croon their tales of faith and love and disappointment were entirely strange to Grant Park. There is something about these lakefront acres—a certain lack of intimacy, perhaps—which has always seemed to discourage any outpourings of this sort. But Helen Morgan came to the band shell last night and was as little daunted by the incongruity of her surroundings as by the heavy cold against which she was struggling. The confidences which she whispered to a microphone from her place atop the piano were carried to the far reaches of Grant Park by a sturdy public address system and were a source of considerable delight to the thousands of people who had gathered to hear her sing." [27]

Native Chicagoan Helen Morgan's appearance with the Festival in 1937 foreshadowed the later focus on local talent.

Planning for the Future

The initial season of Grant Park concerts in 1935 was in many ways a test engineered by Petrillo. As the popularity of the concerts became clear, the Chicago Park District quickly agreed to provide a large portion of the funding for the concerts the following year (and it has continued to do so up to the present).

FROM THE ARCHIVES

Almost immediately following the creation of the Grant Park concerts in the 1930s, discussions and debates about the need to build a new and better band shell began. In 1936 the following suggestion appeared in the *Chicago Daily Tribune:*

"Because of the popularity of the nightly free concerts in Grant Park which were started last summer city and park officials are discussing construction of a natural amphitheater somewhere in the park which could accommodate larger crowds and afford a more fitting setting than the band shell now in use."[28]

DEVELOPMENT ON HOLD

A new band shell and other upgrades would have to wait, however, until the creation of the Petrillo Bandshell in 1978 and then the Jay Pritzker Pavilion in Millennium Park in 2004. With the onset of World War II at the beginning of the following decade,

This massive crowd from a 1938 concert was typical of the music-hungry audiences that made their way to Grant Park in the late 1930s.

the Festival's function and its goals quickly began to change in unexpected ways.

By the end of the 1930s, the Festival had provided Chicagoans with five summers of free outdoor concerts. Starting in 1940, the Festival added an entire month of programs, including a series of concerts by high school bands and orchestras. This marked a new role for the Festival in helping showcase young musicians (later in the coming decade, the summer music program would host a number of high-profile, young-musician contests). These new initiatives prompted the *Chicago Tribune* to write, "Apparently this Petrillo is not quite the big bad wolf his detractors have

proclaimed him. This added series should prove a most interesting one and should draw record crowds to hear it. As for myself, I'll be on hand the first night—with bells on!"[29]

Despite the large crowds for the Grant Park concerts, each season tended to provoke fresh debate about how much funding would be available to support the concerts. In the coming decade many of these questions would be resolved, particularly with the founding of the Grant Park Orchestra in 1944. What began as a temporary experiment to address the needs of a hard pressed public and underemployed musicians in the Great Depression would begin to evolve into a lasting Chicago legacy.

CHAPTER THREE

The 1940s

The Consolation of Concertgoing during the War and Beyond

As Chicago moved from the Great Depression into economic recovery under President Roosevelt's New Deal and then into the Second World War, the Grant Park Music Festival steadily became more and more a part of the fabric of summer life in the city. One of the first big steps in the Festival's expansion was the creation of a new, resident Grant Park Orchestra in the summer of 1944. In turn, the following year the great Russian-born conductor Nikolai Malko became the Festival's first resident conductor and helped build the orchestra and expand the scope of the Festival's programming.

Nikolai Malko, the Grant Park Music Festival's first principal conductor (left), rehearses with an ensemble in 1945. Malko, born in Saint Petersburg, Russia, gave the world premieres of Shostakovich's first two symphonies and played a key role in deepening the Festival's artistic range.

Musical Democracy

Meanwhile, during the 1940s, the Festival invited a tremendous range of guest artists including tenor Mario Lanza, clarinetist Benny Goodman, soprano Kirsten Flagstad, and actor-singer Paul Robeson. In addition, the Festival became a fixture on the national radio scene as WGN radio's acclaimed and nationally syndicated *Theater of the Air* program began to be broadcast live from Grant Park in 1944. The program featured actors and narrators mixed with musicians (as well as a commentary by Colonel McCormick, publisher of the *Chicago Tribune)* presenting shows such as *A Midsummer Night's Dream, Peer Gynt, Peter Pan,* and *An Ode to Chicago.* In short, the Grant Park Concerts in the 1940s were full of dynamic public celebration in the midst of the war and post-war years.

FROM THE ARCHIVES
A *Chicago Daily Tribune* article from 1946 provides a vivid snapshot of just how fervently embraced the Festival was.

"The concerts in Grant Park are growing more and more popular as they are also growing more and more important artistically, and it is one of Chicago's well earned boasts that music is a vital part of Chicago's summer life, and as free to its inhabitants as the incomparable lake breezes which, lazy as they are at times, really can do a magnificent job of revivifying and consoling when they set their minds to it. There is nothing more truly democratically inspiriting than to feel oneself one of some 55,000 souls being spiritually lifted to the stars on the soaring planes of music which issue from the tiny band shell on the lakefront of Chicago's vast industrialism…

"It is becoming more and more chic to 'go to Grant Park.' One guest, recently deeply impressed by the concert, asked his hostess, 'Who pays for all this?' and she told him quite frankly, 'You do.' Chicago taxpayers really get their money's worth out of the share of their assessments which are spent on the free concerts in Grant Park."[1]

The Grant Park band shell framed by the striking silhouette of the Michigan Avenue skyline, 1947.

An Orchestra of Their Own

After nine seasons of presenting concerts performed by various local and touring orchestras and bands, the Festival took an important leap in the summer of 1944 when the Grant Park Orchestra was formed under the direction of concert manager Walter L. Larsen and manager of the Chicago Symphony Orchestra George Kuyper. Renowned conductor Rudolph Ganz conducted the initial concerts with the new orchestra.

FROM THE ARCHIVES

The significance of the creation of an independent orchestra was captured by Chicago arts journalist Claudia Cassidy:

"A lot of things have happened to the band shell since I saw it last, and all of them are good. It has been built out toward the audience so that everyone on the stage looks more comfortable and the music has a better chance to focus, and its restful blue paint and orange music stands turn all sorts of pleasant color tricks under a barrage of persuasive lights. You can even get a cushion to sit on this season, and, all things considered, it wouldn't surprise me in the least if the Chicago Park District also ordered the perfect opening night with its enormous moon rising out of the lake like a slice of pink watermelon.

"But these are mundane things to delight the hedonist. Your more implacable music lover found them secondary in importance to the good common sense of having one Grant Park orchestra chosen from the best men available. Even last night, when it was too new to be an ensemble, it had the unmistakable makings of an orchestra worth hearing. All it needs is what it will get, a chance to rehearse and develop." [2]

Above: Legendary Swiss-born conductor Rudolph Ganz leads the Grant Park Orchestra in 1944.

Below: The Grant Park band shell gets a touch-up prior to the start of the summer, circa 1940.

The Great Recording Strike: Petrillo Becomes a Household Name

"——and it comes out here."

PETRILLO SAYS ITS O.K. TO OPERATE!

Wait 'Til You Hear Him Now!

A series of newspaper cartoons, circa 1940, conveys the extent to which Grant Park concerts series founder James Petrillo had become a nationally renowned figure, especially as a result of his nationwide recording strike, which was aimed at giving musicians a more equitable share of the royalties.

At the beginning of the 1940s, the founder of the Grant Park Concerts, James C. Petrillo, leapt into the national spotlight. In the summer of 1940, he was elected president of the American Federation of Musicians (AFM) at the age of forty-six while also remaining head of the local Chicago chapter.

Two years after taking over the AFM, Petrillo led a widely discussed and debated nationwide recording ban aimed at forcing record companies to pay royalties to musicians. Petrillo had long regarded recordings as a major threat to musicians' livelihoods and had led local strikes against recording in Chicago in 1937. With the United States having just entered World War II at the end of the previous year, the ban was a risky political move, and many newspapers in the country were opposed to Petrillo. One of the most notable manifestations of the debate was the appearance of editorial cartoons depicting Petrillo as a sort of Caesar (his actual middle name) ruling over the availability of recorded music. Above are a few of the hundreds of cartoons that appeared during the more than two years of the strike. Petrillo took great pride in the notoriety and avidly collected the cartoons that caricatured him.

Record companies sought to fight the ban by relying more on vocalists and reissuing old recordings, but starting in the autumn of 1943, one by one nearly all of the major record companies began to acquiesce to Petrillo's demands. The same tenacity that had helped him initiate a massive experiment in free, municipally funded outdoor music in Chicago could be said to have helped Petrillo gain a victory against many of the world's largest recording companies in the face of considerable popular opposition.

The Music Festival and World War II

Grant Park, as Chicago's front yard, has been the site where Chicago has often celebrated and pulled together during difficult times. Feelings of patriotism ran high during the long ordeal of World War II. These feelings were expressed during numerous special events and concerts in the park.

FROM THE ARCHIVES

Several newspaper accounts of wartime park activities follow:

"Chicagoans who are kept in town by gas rationing, the difficulties of railroad travel, their war work or that strong fear of being more difficult to reach in case a son or daughter gets a sudden leave, or word should come from or about them, are finding more pleasant things than they had dreamed of in their city in summer. One of those very pleasant things is the series of open air concerts in Grant Park."[3]

"Against the background of a pageant of melody and color in the Grant Park band shell last night the 10,000th recruit, enlisted in the Chicago area was inducted into the navy. It was a ceremony at once symbolic and impressive. Before the gleaming white band shell and the Chicago Opera orchestra stretched a vast sea of faces, the faces of thousands and thousands of music lovers who had gathered for the twofold purpose of honoring the navy and listening to good music."[4]

"As a fitting climax to Fourth of July festivities, United States army musical organizations gave the first of a series of Tuesday night concerts in the Grant Park band shell last night before an overflow audience estimated at 30,000.... In an Independence day address before last night's audience, President Franklyn

During the Second World War, military themes were often woven into the Grant Park concerts, as with this July 1943 performance.

B. Snyder of Northwestern university declared that 'the prize for which we are fighting today is in essence just what it was in 1776—the priceless boon of freedom. We are fighting with England, Russia, and China,' he said, but not for them, 'tho we shall help them in every way that is consistent with our national welfare. Neither,' he added, are we fighting for 'any vague concept called worldwide democracy, noble as that concept is.' The fight, he said, 'is to preserve this America of ours.'"[5]

Daily Life at the Concerts in the 1940s

Young and Old

In the 1940s, the Festival attracted a wide range of people including these from opposite ends of the spectrum:

"A woman who goes to more summer concerts than any music critic, and who does not get paid for it, was honored at Grant Park last night when the Woman's Symphony orchestra, under Nicolai Malko's direction, played 'Happy Birthday,' and the people in the front rows stood and clapped. Yesterday was her 77th birthday.

"She is Mrs. S. Jacobs, who lives at the Hayes hotel, and who, since 1935 has been Grant Park's best customer. She has attended about 400 concerts, a record surpassed only by Herb Carlin, who manages them. In addition Mrs. Jacobs goes down to the band shell after the season is over, amuses herself amid the autumn mists by thinking over the concerts she has heard. This is more than Mr. Carlin does. Mrs. Jacobs is a vigorous, bright eyed lady who considers Grant Park, Orchestra hall, and the Art Institute her three heavens on earth."[6]

"Among the 45,000 attending the Grant Park concert Sunday night was a young man in his early 20s with a baby carriage beside him. Every once in a while he leaned over and placed a bottle in the baby's mouth. Out of consideration to the other music lovers, he and his charge were parked behind the band shell."[7]

Nestled in a basket, baby gets a first taste of classical music, 1946.

Strauss and the Shriners' Parade

The array of unexpected disruptions that have visited the Festival over the decades is vast, ranging from airplanes to police sirens to swarms of insects, but few compare to the 1949 clash of competing celebrations described by the *Chicago Tribune:*

"[Erich] Leinsdorf had the pleasure of conducting a Grant Park Symphony concert during a Shriners' convention. The Shriners had a permit to parade past the concert area, and as you know the nobles never move down a street without music of their own. Mr. Leinsdorf, sensing a battle, had lopped off some Bach and Beethoven from the program, managing to get the 'Midsummer Night's Dream' music played before the parade came by with its drums, buggies and shimmy whistles. Then he counterattacked—with the Strauss family's 'Thunder and Lightning,' 'Perpetual Motion' and 'Clear Track.' That was quite a musical occasion while it lasted, and I'd leave home any mad evening to hear it again."[8]

The Grant Park Orchestra, a few years after it was organized as an autonomous, professional orchestra in 1944.

The band shell seen in the larger context of Grant Park and Michigan Avenue in this shot from the 1940s taken from the Field Museum of Natural History.

Malko Takes the Baton

Nikolai Malko was widely regarded as one of the great conductors of the mid-twentieth century; he led the Grant Park Orchestra for ten seasons. Following his tenure with Grant Park, he left the United States to conduct the Sydney Symphony Orchestra, where he remained until his death in 1961.

In 1945, one year after forming an orchestra, the Festival added the role of chief conductor and selected the Russian-born Nikolai Malko to fill the role. The position was structured much like the Festival's current position of principal conductor. Malko was able to help the Festival in selecting programs and guest artists with a more comprehensive approach. He conducted the first four weeks of the season, guest conductors led most of the middle weeks, and he returned for the final weeks.

Malko, who would lead the artistic activities of the Grant Park Concerts until 1954, had a storied background. Born in 1883, he studied composition with the great Russian composers Rimsky-Korsakov and Glazunov at the Saint Petersburg Conservatory. After the revolution he served as conductor of the Leningrad Philharmonic and conducted the world premieres of Shostakovich's first two symphonies. He defected from the Soviet Union during a tour to Prague in 1928 and moved to the United States in 1940. The following year he began his relationship with the Grant Park concerts, serving as a guest conductor for several years before becoming chief conductor.

FROM THE ARCHIVES

Critics and musicians were often divided over Malko's artistic choices, but he clearly brought a level of ambition and creativity to the Festival's programming and a dose of musical heft to the summer concerts, as this contemporary review shows:

"With the weather—always a lake front variable—on its very best behavior, the Grant Park Symphony orchestra under Nicolai Malko's direction gave one of its sprightliest concerts last night. So good, in fact, were all the performances that it definitely marked the Orchestra's symphonic coming of age...

"The leaden weights that sometimes seem to perch upon the tip of Mr. Malko's baton were replaced by gossamer elves that radiated serenity and light, and that kept the music bouncing along up to the very last metronome mark of lively tempo. With its inhibitions thus unbound the orchestra leaped to the fray like the thorobred it can easily become, given half a chance, and quite likely surprised even itself by its clean, nimble performance."[9]

The Groundbreaking Chicago Woman's Symphony

The new Grant Park Orchestra, as with many orchestras of the time, consisted almost entirely of male musicians. However, through the 1940s the Festival also regularly featured Chicago's highly regarded Woman's Symphony, which typically presented a half dozen concerts each season, starting with the first Grant Park concert season in 1935.

The Chicago Woman's Symphony, which provided frequent performances at Grant Park in the early decades, was founded in 1925 during a period when female musicians were under-represented in other classical music organizations.

FROM THE ARCHIVES

In 1939, *Time* magazine ran the following article about the challenges and triumphs of Chicago's Woman's Symphony:

"Today there are at least twelve women's symphony orchestras in the U. S. Oldest: the Los Angeles Women's Symphony which has been flouncing its fiddle-bows for more than 40 years. Finest: the Chicago Woman's Symphony, which last week got to the start of its 15th season.

"Ten years ago the Chicago Woman's Symphony got itself a permanent woman conductor, a husky, blonde Swedish-American from Lindsborg, Kans., named Ebba Sundstrom, and went to work in earnest. But while its concerts swept by with an air of drawing-room dignity, its private meetings and rehearsals seethed with back-bitings, hair pullings. Socialite sponsors quarreled with each other; the women musicians quarreled with Conductress Sundstrom. Several times it looked as if the show could not go on...

"Since then the Chicago Woman's Symphony has had one guest conductor after another, with results that critics found scarcely an improvement on the Sundstrom era. But last week it sported a brand-new conductor, hoped this one was for keeps.

This time the conductor was a man: pint-sized, cadaverous Izler Solomon. Mr. Solomon started by firing six women, cowed five more into resigning, added 15 new players. Chicago wits nick-named the orchestra 'Solomon and his Wives,'...

"In the audience, among the mink-coated sponsors, there were still some stormy echoes...Acting-President Mrs. James George Shakman (whose Pabst Brewery money helps feed the orchestra's kitty) basked in a box. Beamed she: 'We are all work-ing in perfect harmony....The girls are such fine musicians, they should be supported. Why, think of all the money that is spent in night clubs!'"[10]

The Chicago Woman's Symphony, which performed frequently at the festival, rehearses in cramped quarters, circa 1945.

Great Artists of the 1940s

Michigan Avenue, near Washington Street, 1937. The peristyle in the distance stood from 1917 to 1953. A nearly full-sized replica was constructed in the same location for the opening of Millennium Park.

The 1940s at the Festival were years of exciting guest artists who frequently challenged the dissolving boundaries between classical and other music forms. Whether it was Benny Goodman's clarinet, Paul Robeson's booming and politically charged voice, or Mario Lanza's hybrid opera-Hollywood persona, there was a growing excitement over the possibilities for merging classical music with other genres in innovative ways. The festival quickly showed a great willingness to blend the old and new, a tradition that continues to the present.

Among other special guest artists of the decade were sopranos Kirstin Flagstad (1940), Marion Claire (1940–1942), Eileen Farrell (1948), Grace Moore (1940 and 1942), and Vivian Della Chiesa (1940, 1941, and 1946); tenors Giovanni Martinelli (1940 and 1941), Richard Tucker (1946), and Jan Peerce (1947); baritone Robert Merrill (1945–1947); and violinist Mischa Mischakoff (1947). The decade also saw esteemed conductors Frederick Stock (1940–1942), Leo Kopp (1940–1943 and 1946–1949), Arthur Fiedler (1947 and 1948), and Antal Dorati (1946–1949).

Native-born Chicagoan Benny Goodman with the Woman's Symphony in Grant Park in 1941. He drew a frenzied crowd of young fans during his sole appearance with the Festival.

Benny Goodman

Clarinetist, 1941

Born in Chicago's Maxwell Street neighborhood in 1909, Benny Goodman was the son of a stockyard laborer. He received early music lessons at the Hull House, which was founded by Jane Addams. By the age of sixteen, he was beginning to play clarinet with various Chicago big bands. By the time Goodman came to Grant Park in 1941, he had a fierce following of young fans.

FROM THE ARCHIVES

The *Chicago Tribune* celebrated Goodman's performance with the headline, "Classic Music or Swing," conveying the unease over his genre-defying style. Here are excerpts from the review:

"Enthusiasm mounted steadily, and when the men of Goodman's band started taking the places vacated by the woman's orchestra the thousands of high school youngsters packed in front of the band shell became all but hysterical. There was a strangled quality of unbearable excitement in their shouts and ejaculations, and when the great Goodman himself appeared they gave their last reserves of breath in a great welcoming yell. Not quite their last, at that, for when their idol—who was acting in the triple capacity of leader, clarinet player, and master of ceremonies—announced that the band would play 'Intermezzo' as its second number, a shout of such ecstasy went up that you would have sworn that the whole crowd had just been inducted into paradise. And apparently it was paradise. You never saw so many intent, shining faces in *this* sad old world." [11]

Mario Lanza

Tenor, 1947 and 1948

Lanza, whose given name was Alfred Arnold Cocozza, gained national recognition before he was even twenty when conductor Serge Koussevitzky singled him out for praise and helped him to win a scholarship to the Berkshire Music Center at the Tanglewood Festival. Lanza, who went on to a prolific Hollywood career (which perhaps diverted his attention from what seemed a promising opera career) before he died at the early age of thirty-eight, was often compared to the great tenor of the previous generation, Enrico Caruso, whom he played in a 1938 film.

Tenor Mario Lanza's two appearances with Grant Park in the late 1940s were among the highlights of the decade. In 1948 he came to Chicago as part of an eighty-six-city tour of the United States and Canada.

FROM THE ARCHIVES

When Lanza first came to Grant Park in the late 1940s, he was just beginning a massive eighty-six-concert tour of the United States following an interruption of his performing career to serve in World War II. Chicago journalist Claudia Cassidy was effusive in reviewing his first performance in Grant Park:

"Young Mr. Lanza was something approaching a sensation. You are a sensation in opera when customers whistle thru their fingers and roar 'Bravo!' A coltish youngster with wide shoulders and the general just-out-of-uniform air of 'Call Me Mister,' Mr. Lanza sings for the indisputable reason that he was born to sing. He has a superbly natural tenor which he uses by instinct, and tho a multitude of fine points evade him, he possesses the things almost impossible to learn. He knows the accent that makes a lyric line reach its audience, and he knows why opera is music drama.... [His performance of 'Celeste Aida'] was beautifully done, and the crowd roared while Mr. Lanza happily mopped his brow. He seemed more surprised, and just as delighted, as anyone else."[12]

Paul Robeson

Bass-Baritone and Actor, 1940

It would be hard to overestimate the immensity of Paul Robeson's achievements: the African American singer, actor, athlete, writer, courageous political activist (to name just a few of his many roles) used his astonishingly powerful bass-baritone voice to mesmerize audiences, condemn social injustice and fascism, and help set the tone for the civil-rights movement.

FROM THE ARCHIVES

From the 1950s on, Robeson would be increasingly besieged in McCarthy-era America for his leftist politics (his FBI file is one of the largest compiled for an American artist). In his appearance in Grant Park in 1940, he was widely embraced by an enormous audience, as critic Edward Barry notes:

"Paul Robeson, the great Negro bass-baritone, made his first Chicago appearance in nearly five years last night. He sang from the stage of the Grant Park band shell to an audience that packed the tens of thousands of available seats and overflowed onto the spacious lawns all about. Mr. Robeson's co-attraction was the orchestra of Rico Marcelli, altho for virtually all of his accompaniments he used the pianist Lawrence Brown. Mr. Robeson first won the enthusiastic friendship of his audience by the charm of his personality. He is a great giant of a man, with an infectious smile; bright, humorous eyes, and that dignity of bearing that springs from an honest sense of worth. The moment that he walked upon the stage the crowd that faced him from every

Paul Robeson, in a non-Grant Park Music Festival performance of *Othello*. The press gave rave reviews to his 1940 appearance in Grant Park.

corner of the big breezy auditorium put on a big demonstration in his honor...

"The singer produced his tones as effortlessly as if he had a pair of bellows within his chest. And the rhythmic strength of his singing gave the song a pounding, inexorable quality which accorded well with its character. The climax of the evening came when popular demand—in the shape of numerous shouted requests from the audience—compelled Mr. Robeson to do 'Ol' Man River.' He sang it with an awesome virility. There were cheers and screams at its end."[13]

Lorin Maazel

Conductor, 1941

For every well-established guest artist who performed with the Festival, there have been numerous young, up-and-coming artists, many of whom later went on to renowned careers. One of the youngest of the young was Lorin Maazel, who at the age of eleven took up the baton to conduct in Grant Park. Years later he would go on to serve as music director of the Cleveland Orchestra and the New York Philharmonic (leading the latter on its unprecedented tour of North Korea in 2008).

FROM THE ARCHIVES

Maazel's appearance with the orchestra was charmingly described in the *Chicago Tribune:*

"Eleven year old Lorin Maazel directed the Walter H. Steindel orchestra in two numbers last night. The huge audience gathered before the lake front band shell received the prodigy with gales of laughter, salvos of applause, and, finally, with cheers and whistles of astonishment. The laughter, which came at his entrance, was due to nothing but the sheer incongruity of the spectacle. Here was a tiny, wilful-looking child of the type that you would normally expect to see smearing his face with pie or running like a wild Indian down the alley. Yet he had come to Grant Park to conduct a symphony orchestra of 74 men. Nearly all of these men are old enough to be his father and some of them old enough to be his grandfather.

"The applause came in thunders after his performance of Beethoven's 'Egmont' overture. Lorin did everything expected of a conductor. He waved his baton vigorously, extended his expressive left hand warningly to keep down the volume, and gave each section of the orchestra its cues with unerring accuracy.

"He conducted Tschaikowsky's 'Marche Slav' with great zest and achieved a big climax toward the end. Then he bowed to the applause and cheers and whistles, and was off—presumably to the astronomical studies with which he is said to fill his leisure time."[14]

Lorin Maazel was only eleven when he led a concert in Grant Park in 1941. He is pictured here with another orchestra during the same period.

A New Home for the Post-War Years?

As the 1940s came to a close, the Festival, along with downtown Chicago as a whole, faced a great transition. Born during the Great Depression, when audiences were hungry for free entertainment in the heart of the city, the concert series flourished during the war as it provided both escape and catharsis. The post-war climate of increasing prosperity would bring new challenges. As more and more Americans bought homes and cars and as television permeated the culture, in order to remain relevant, the Festival would have to adapt.

Chicagoans were frequently dreaming of creative improvements for the Festival, and in the mid-1940s there was a strong push to build an adventurous new band shell.

FROM THE ARCHIVES

Chicago Daily Tribune critic Claudia Cassidy described a 1946 proposal for a project that never came to life:

"When it rains at Grant Park, where can you go? The tiny shed off the band shell doesn't hold many and tho I once sat out a rainstorm in the violin section, I am afraid Mr. Petrillo's union would demand dues if I tried again....

"Having splashed my way through a share of such concerts, I responded with alacrity when the Chicago Park District suggested that I come out to its handsome administration building to look at the scale model of the music court it hopes to erect on the lake front for the summer concerts of 1947, providing it can hurdle possible opposition and an approximate cost of $1,500,000....

"It sounds like a delightful place to go of a summer evening for concerts, ballet, operetta, possibly motion picture premières with visiting stars...any such lake front project will have one priceless asset. The lake will be stretched out to meet the sky in a cyclorama nothing man made can hope to match, but all mankind can enjoy."[15]

Following World War II, proposals for a new band shell were created.

Above: Park district officials show model of proposed band shell to a group of women. They intended to build the new shell directly east of the Art Institute. More than thirty years later, the Petrillo Bandshell was eventually constructed there.

Below: The band shell was to have had a pair of butterfly-like retractable canopies, here seen closed and covering the front portion of the seating area.

Photos 1946.

CHAPTER FOUR

The 1950s

In the Era of Sputnik: A Skinny Texas Pianist and Other Musical Triumphs

The 1950s raised difficult questions for the Grant Park Music Festival: in the new post-war world of increased prosperity, cars, and television, what was the role of free concerts along Chicago's lakefront? Was the Festival tenable in the age of the Cold War and rock 'n' roll?

In the years following World War II, many Depression-era arts programs did quietly slip away. The Grant Park Music Festival, however, was the rare WPA-era program that adapted and survived. While crowds of one hundred thousand or more no longer turned out quite so regularly as they had during the hard times of previous decades, in the 1950s the Festival continued to draw audiences in the tens of thousands. Looking back from the early twenty-first century, a phenomenal number of Chicagoans tell stories of having developed a hunger for classical music thanks in large part to the Festival's free offerings.

Van Cliburn is greeted at Midway Airport by a contingent of cowgirls prior to his 1958 performance with the Grant Park Music Festival. He had won the Tchaikovsky piano competition in Moscow in April of that year and instantly became a national hero.

From Small Town to Big City

Perhaps no event in the early years of the Cold War embodied the way classical music could catch the imagination of so many people as pianist Van Cliburn's unexpected vault to fame by winning the Tchaikovsky piano competition in Moscow in April of 1958. Through a bit of fortunate happenstance, the Grant Park Music Festival had previously booked the young Texan, while he was still an up-and-coming artist, to perform later that summer.

By the time he arrived in Chicago that July, he had captured the imagination of millions of people: a kid from small-town America who went to Moscow and won one of the most prestigious music competitions in the world, barely half a year after the launching of Sputnik had jolted the competition between the United States and the Soviet Union. Van Cliburn's visit to Chicago prompted a frenzy of celebration, including a ticker tape parade down Michigan Avenue.

The crowds gather at the Van Cliburn concert on July 16, 1958.

Daily Life at the Concerts in the 1950s

Strange Sounds from Soldier Field

Each decade pitted the Grant Park concerts against new acoustic nemeses. In the early 1950s, as critic Claudia Cassidy describes, hot rod races were among the new rivals:

"Last night on what must be the world's noisiest lakefront the free…concerts now sponsored by the Chicago Park District began their 19th season…It was rather like being immersed in layers of noise the blatantly amplified music tried to penetrate. From the rear the hot rod races roared the circuit of Soldiers' field, using the band shell to bounce the noise back from. From above, cruising planes took the short cut over our heads. From the sides, traffic zoomed and squawked and backfired, with piccolo overlay of the policeman's whistle. The night was full of a lot of things, all noisier than music." [1]

Peril in the Park

Was downtown Chicago, and Grant Park in particular, becoming less safe in the post-war years? Anecdotes began to appear in the early 1950s that underscored that idea, which would grow in future decades.

For example, in 1952 Walter L. Larsen, director of the Grant Park Concerts, told the *Chicago Daily Tribune* that, "because of the bums and sex deviates in the park and the concealment that heavy shrubbery offers them," he was often fearful when he left the park at night after the concerts. "There are people in the bushes and others making love," Larsen said. "I wouldn't cross the 11th st. footbridge for anything late at night. The bushes grow right up to the walk there. After hours, when crowds have dispersed, the park is a dangerous place to go." [2]

Soldier Field, located directly south of the original band shell across the street from Lake Shore Drive, was often the source of strange and unpredictable distractions for concertgoers. Here, Soldier Field is used for hot-rodding in the 1950s.

Opposite: By the 1950s lawn audiences had begun to have a more casual look, as seen in this image from late in the decade.

A New Mayor Shares
His Ideas on the Concerts

Richard J. Daley became mayor of Chicago in 1955 and for much
of the next twenty-one years made it a point of speaking to
crowds at Grant Park concerts, usually before the opening-night
concert. The *Chicago Daily Tribune* summarized Mayor Daley's
opening night comments as follows:

"The greetings came from Mayor Richard J. Daley, who
briskly congratulated musicians and management after being
introduced as 'the best mayor Chicago ever had' by Park District
Commissioner John F. McGuane. The commissioner also
remarked that there can be neighborhood concerts in addition to
those in Grant Park if everyone will work to make them possible.
He did not say how, nor did anyone mention that increasingly
wistful mirage of a suitable home for the Grant Park concerts,
for 22 badgered summers the orphans of every storm." [3]

Mayor Richard J. Daley addresses the
audience at Grant Park on opening
night in 1956. To the left is Edward
Gordon, then the Festival's assistant
director (he would take over in 1958);
at center is conductor Nikolai Malko.

Venice on Lake Michigan

In his third summer in office, in 1958, Mayor Richard J. Daley
also inaugurated the Chicago summer festival of Venetian
Night—a peculiar mix of festooned boats and fireworks.
That grew into an annual tradition that would continue to
the present day. The *Chicago Daily Tribune* described the first
Venetian Night:

"This event, being promoted by [Col. Jack] Reilly, director
of public events for Mayor Daley, is to be known as Chicago's
first annual Venetian Night festival. Col. Reilly will tell you it is
to be one of the most colorful events in the city's history.

"Three hundred boats, well lighted and decorated, will swing
into Burnham harbor, head southwest and then pass along the
lake shore to a reviewing stand at Congress street for all to see.

"Reilly and Henry W. Angsten, head of a committee of yacht
club officials, are proud to note that 'during the parade there
will be an overhead canopy of fireworks.' As others noted,
there will be a considerable number of noisy outboard motors.
Furthermore, those aboard may have difficulty restraining
themselves from sounding their horns and sirens.

"The difficulty is that also about sundown, and just a few
hundred feet from this same lake shore, a concert is to begin
in Grant Park. The Grant Park symphony orchestra, with
Irwin Hoffman as guest conductor, will be presenting such
numbers as Mendelssohn's rather quiet Piano Concerto No. 1
and Tschaikowsky's Fourth Symphony, not so quiet but still not
fitting competition for fireworks, sirens, and outboard motors.
Miss Lillian Kallir, pianist, faces the difficult prospect of reach-
ing her audience...

"Col. Reilly, who once prevented a small lamb from entering
Daley's office, did not seem to be upset over the impending
conflict. 'These fireworks are going to be high,' observed Reilly,
'and they will not make a lot of noise. They will be pretty.'" [4]

A musician's-eye view of the audience, with the dramatic backdrop of the Field Museum of Natural History, is seen in this mid-1950s image.

A Power Failure and a Moonlight Sonata

Over the decades some of the most memorable moments of Chicago's downtown, outdoor-concert tradition have been the result of unexpected synchronicities, accidents that might have gone awry but instead led to instances of beauty. The convergence of live classical music and bustling, unpredictable city was always full of surprises, as with this 1955 mishap described in a contemporary newspaper account:

"Electric power failed at the Grant Park band shell last night, for the second time in less than three weeks. The concert area was plunged into darkness shortly after intermission, during the first movement of Beethoven's 'Emperor' Concerto. The loudspeaker system went out along with the lights.

"The pity of it was that the piano soloist, Jacob Lateiner, seemed on his way to a compelling performance of the 'Emperor.' He, the Grant Park Symphony orchestra, and the guest conductor, Joseph Rosenstock, called off the rest of the scheduled music after waiting a while for a miracle of man made illumination.

"Nature, however, was there with a proud assist, in the shape of a full moon. By the light of that moon Mr. Lateiner played some other Beethoven music and Schubert for piano alone."[5]

An Extravagant Band Shell Proposal

A composite rendering of a proposed new venue for the Festival that would have been built directly east of the Art Institute. Throughout the summer of 1953, there was great public enthusiasm for the project; however, in the autumn of that year the project collapsed, largely due to a political decision to deny a bond issue that would have funded it.

In 1953 the Festival came close to having a new home built, a variation of the fifteen-thousand-seat band shell with a moveable, fan-shaped roof that was first proposed in 1946. That autumn, preparation was made to put a referendum on the November 3 election-day ballot allowing Chicago voters to decide whether to approve the $3 million project. Only a few weeks before the big vote, the entire project collapsed when the bond issue that would have helped finance the project was denied.

Chicago Park District President James H. Gately said of the project, "Chicago has the opportunity to acquire the nation's most beautiful music amphitheater.... It would be a great thing for our city to have such a facility near the heart of Chicago." [6]

FROM THE ARCHIVES

The 1953 band shell plan was not realized, but ideas for new venues, as always, remained part of a passionate, citywide discussion. Ideas were expansive and varied, as this 1955 suggestion to move the Festival to a completely different part of the city illustrates:

"The park superintendent would like to move the bandshell a few blocks north to a less noisy location. He thinks the move would help to increase...attendance, which has fallen off in recent years.

"May I suggest that the bandshell be moved to the west side, say in Garfield park, where it would be more convenient for a larger number of people? The suburbanites do not like to have to cross the Loop to hear a band concert." [7]

The New Skyline of the 1950s

Despite the fact that a new band shell was not built in the 1950s, by the middle of the decade the Festival's home began to be transformed in other ways. With the opening of the Prudential Building in 1955, the skyline of Chicago began to evolve after the long pause in skyscraper building that had settled in during the Depression and World War II. The previous skyscraper built in the city was the Art Deco Field Building, which was finished in 1934.

This new wave of skyscraper building would transform the ambiance of Grant Park, turning the Festival's home into an even more urban public space. In the following decades the John Hancock Building, the Standard Oil (now Aon) Building, Sears Tower (now Willis), Trump Tower, and many others would join the diverse architectural backdrop of the park.

FROM THE ARCHIVES

In September of 1955, the *Chicago Daily Tribune* ran a special magazine story titled, "A New Look at Chicago's Boom!" which captured the array of changes that had begun to sweep the city, including the opening of the Congress Expressway in 1955 and the development of an extensive subterranean garage system beneath Grant Park. Some excerpts follow:

"Something has happened and continues to happen in Chicago that deserves to be called a renaissance. It is a wide-spread, prolonged outbreak of creative energy and skill devoted to the remaking of this metropolis.... Altho fairly recent as a city-wide phenomenon, visible and audible to every citizen, this renaissance of the 1950s is no surprise to the native-born. It stems from the inspiring leadership of Daniel H. Burnham, master architect, whose plan for Chicago's future was issued in 1909, and of Charles H. Wacker, capitalist, philanthropist, and dedicated citizen, whose communication of the Burnham gospel became required reading in Chicago public schools. Their memory lives wherever American city planning is discussed....

"Building, demolition, and rebuilding form a phase of Chicago's renaissance more conspicuous to the citizenry at large than its improvements in transportation. They alter the sky line with massive evidence that the city is in colossal stride toward a new era. The Prudential building on Randolph street over the Illinois Central railroad tracks—a focal point in the lakefront silhouette—is a new but already familiar landmark. It is a soaring oblong buttressed by lesser oblongs at lower levels, clever in arrangement of forms yet not ultra-modern in style.... To thumbprint its tourist appeal: It cost $40,000,000 and is the highest skyscraper built in the United States since 1940....Verily, the planners of Chicago are on the march like the legions of Julius Caesar."[8]

Chicago's changing skyline hovers beyond the Grant Park band shell. In this 1954 photo the Prudential Building, which would be completed the following year, is in its early stages of construction just north of where Millennium Park would open fifty years later.

Great Artists of the 1950s

In the 1950s the focal point of the Grant Park concerts began to shift from an emphasis on stellar, household-name guest artists to solid performances of programs by the increasingly professional Grant Park Orchestra. Conductor Nikolai Malko continued to lead the orchestra for the first half of the decade, and Irwin Hoffman took over in the second half of the decade. There were also frequent guest-conducting appearances by Alfredo Antonini, Leo Kopp, Andre Kostelanetz, Joseph Rosenstock, Julius Rudel, and Erich Leinsdorf.

Among the standout artists of the decade were soprano Beverly Sills, tenor Jan Peerce, and of course, the historic 1958 visit by Van Cliburn. During the decade the Festival also hosted soprano Eileen Farrell (1950, 1952, and 1953); pianists Jorge Bolet (1950, 1954, and 1958), Gary Graffman (1954 and 1959), and Earl Wild (1954); violinists Mischa Elman (1954) and Michael Rabin (1956, 1958, and 1959); and cellist Janos Starker (1958).

Certain programs could still draw immense audiences, as with this 1954 Gershwin program described by the *Chicago Tribune*.

FROM THE ARCHIVES

"Drawn by the combined lure of George Gershwin's music and Andre Kostelanetz's podium personality, 60,000 listeners flocked to the Grant Park Symphony orchestra last night. The crowd filled the entire band shell area and sought places under the peripheral trees. The concert was reminiscent of the pre-television days of the late 1930s, when Grant Park audiences sometimes were numbered in six figures." [9]

Beverly Sills

Soprano, 1956–1958, 1961, 1964, 1967, and 1968

Beverly Sills, an American operatic soprano, made her Festival debut in 1956—the year after her professional debut at the Met—and was a perennial crowd favorite for the next decade, returning six times. Featured on the cover of *Time* magazine in 1971 as "America's Queen of Opera," Sills became the general manager of the New York City Opera and later chairman of Lincoln Center and the Metropolitan Opera after retiring from singing in 1980.

FROM THE ARCHIVES

The *New York Times* described Sills as "more popular with the American public than any opera singer since Enrico Caruso, even among people who never set foot in an opera house."[10]

A 1957 review from the *Chicago Daily Tribune* describes her second performance with the Festival, as Gilda in Verdi's *Rigoletto:*

"The beautiful Gilda of Beverly Sills, a willowy girl with bright hair, a charming voice with promise of riches to come, and a trill without a single chatter." The review also noted that she and the rest of the cast had to overcome assorted outdoor pitfalls: "It is also true that the makeshift stage hampered the performance, that the singers looked cold, and that the audience was cold. In fact, if some of us had attempted to trill along with Gilda, the chattering teeth would have drowned out the hovering helicopter."[11]

Beverly Sills, seen here in glamorous attire, made seven appearances with the Festival in the 1950s and 1960s.

Opposite (from left to right): Gabor Carelli, tenor; Winifred Heidt, contralto; Walter L. Larsen, managing director of Grand Park concerts; Arthur Wisner of Columbia Concerts, Inc.; Antal Dorati, conductor of the Dallas Symphony Orchestra; Frances Yeend, lyric soprano; George London, bass-baritone at the Grant Park concert of July 24, 1948, when Mr. Dorati presented Verdi's *Requiem,* assisted by the two-hundred-voice mixed chorus of the University of Indiana, trained by George F. Krueger, associate professor of choral music at Indiana University.

Van Cliburn

Pianist, 1958 and 1994

Van Cliburn (whose given name was Harvey Lavan Cliburn) is one of the twentieth century's most celebrated pianists and one of the few classical musicians in recent decades who completely transcended the world of classical music and became a household name. Born in Louisiana and raised in Texas, Cliburn gained recognition at a young age, making his Carnegie Hall debut at the age of twenty. Several years later he became an international phenomenon when, in the spring of 1958, he won the First International Tchaikovsky piano competition in Moscow.

This competition, which was held half a year after the launching of Sputnik, was designed in part to highlight Soviet superiority in the world of culture as well as science, but the young, lanky Texan dazzled the judges and won the hearts of hordes of ordinary Russians. Following his magnificent performances, the Soviet judges, hesitating to give the prize to an American, sought Soviet Premier Nikita Khrushchev's permission, to which he reputedly asked, "Is he the best?" The judges concurred, and Khrushchev replied, "Then give him the prize!"

Following his triumph in Moscow, Van Cliburn returned to intense celebrations including a ticker tape parade in New York. Through fortuitous foresight, Van Cliburn had been booked, prior to his victory, to perform with the Grant Park Music Festival in the summer of 1958. His performance in downtown Chicago that summer, at the height of the Cold War, was one of the more unforgettable events in the Festival's history (as was his much-lauded return to Grant Park in 1994).

FROM THE ARCHIVES

Following his triumph at the Tchaikovsky competition in Moscow in the spring of 1958, *Time* magazine, in a cover story, described the intense attachment that Van Cliburn's playing elicited:

"The love affair between Van and the Russians started sizzling when he appeared in the preliminary auditions—and never let up. Wooed by official Russia and by musicians, he was also pursued by adoring teenagers. Total strangers, men and women, hugged and kissed him in the street, flooded him with gifts, fan mail, flowers (one bouquet came from Mrs. Nikita Khrushchev). Women cried openly at his concerts; in Leningrad, where fans queued up for three days and nights to buy tickets, one fell out of her seat in a faint…

"Toward the end of his visit, he confided to a friend what the Russian experience had meant to him. 'I tell you,' he said, 'these are my people. I guess I've always had a Russian heart. I'd give them three quarts of blood and four pounds of flesh. I've never felt so at home anywhere in my whole life.'"[12]

———

Van Cliburn's visit to Chicago in July of 1958 to perform in Grant Park began with a festive serenade by a group of Shriners in the Blackstone Hotel as described by the *Chicago Daily Tribune:*

"A rangy Texan with a mop of hair and a boy's grin loped into Chicago Tuesday night to be welcomed by the Shriners. Van Cliburn, who wowed them in Moscow, strolled into the

Van Cliburn joins several Shriners at the Blackstone Hotel during his 1958 visit to Chicago to perform with the Festival. "Eyes of Texas" and Tchaikovsky get equal treatment.

Blackstone hotel to be greeted by 'The Eyes of Texas Are Upon You' and Tschaikowsky's Piano Concerto No. 1, as interpreted by the brass dance band of Moolah temple, St. Louis. 'I'm honored,' said the somewhat stunned pianist who appears Wednesday and Friday nights at Grant Park."[13]

LOOKING BACK

Jack Zimmerman, author, musician, and subscriber-relations manager for the Lyric Opera of Chicago, recounts his memories of the Van Cliburn concert:

"It was in 1958 when Van Cliburn played at Grant Park. My mother was very captivated by the Van Cliburn story about winning the big Moscow competition. It was really a big deal in America at that time. It was the Cold War, and this kid from Texas goes off and wins the big award. When it was announced that

he would play at Grant Park, my mother said, 'We have to go to Grant Park and hear this guy.'

"We had never listened to classical music before. At the time, I studied piano at an accordion school on the southwest side, but I had never seen a real pianist play before. It was electrifying, of course. But I didn't know enough about classical music to really grasp what was going on. Everybody was there. This was the biggest event in the city.

"I remember he did an encore. I don't remember what the encore was, but he announced it with an opus number. A composer's name and an opus number. As soon as he said the opus number, the audience erupted into applause! It was probably something like Rachmaninoff's C# minor that everyone knew. But I couldn't believe that people knew classical music by opus numbers! It was like another world. It was just unbelievable."

VAN CLIBURN MESMERIZES GRANT PARK

Expectations for his coming performance were intense:

"Weather permitting, the Wednesday-Friday concerts will draw audiences comparable to those in early Grant Park seasons when assemblies of 50,000—or twice that large—were written into the records. If latecomers find space only on the steps of the Museum of Natural History or *behind* the concert shell, attendance records will be close to cracking and the park district traffic specialists can start estimating in earnest."[14]

The actual attendance for Van Cliburn's two performances easily surpassed one hundred thousand and became something of a citywide festival involving fried chicken, Elvis fans, champagne, and much more. The immensity of Van Cliburn's concerts was described by the *Chicago Daily Tribune:*

"Carting babies and blankets and bottles of champagne, 55,000 persons piled into Grant Park last night to hear the phenomenal young man who conquered Moscow with a piano keyboard. They rustled in Christmas Eve anticipation thru the program's first half; then sat in cathedral silence when Van Cliburn, the Texan whose fame was launched with a purse of rubles, sat down to play. He may be Texas' best known export since the longhorns were driven north....In the crowd that spilled to Roosevelt road were teen-age worshippers of Presley. 'Just curious,' they grinned. There were others who admitted they couldn't tell a fugue from a march or a Callas from a boy tenor. But they drove in from Michigan and Indiana, they sat thru a broiling afternoon sun to assure good seats, and they dined on sandwiches and fried chicken partly, perhaps, as one matron put it, 'because that was quite a thing he did in Moscow.'"[15]

Van Cliburn performing with the Grant Park Orchestra in 1958. More than fifty thousand people packed into the south end of the park to hear his performance.

Opposite: Tenor Jan Peerce acknowledges the audience in Grant Park in 1959.

Jan Peerce

Tenor, 1947, 1954, 1959, 1960, 1963, and 1964

New York–born tenor Jan Peerce made his professional operatic debut in 1938 at the late age of thirty-three and went on to become one of the best-loved singers of his era. Many have said that Peerce may have been Toscanini's favorite tenor during the great conductor's seventeen years at NBC. Peerce made his debut with the Metropolitan Opera in 1941:

FROM THE ARCHIVES

Seymour Raven of the *Chicago Tribune* described Peerce's performance in Grant Park:

"As Jan Peerce's singing goes, these are vintage years.... And so when he came to the Grant Park concert site as the week-end soloist, taxpayer listeners to the free music series could know they were this time getting the best. Last night, with Alfredo Antonini conducting, Mr. Peerce offered respective groups of Italian and French arias, music planned to cover a lot of ground in the public park tho its singer made no move toward hamminess."[16]

Decade's End: Cold War Shivers and...

The 1950s ended with a great deal of uncertainty about the future of the Festival, the city, and the world. This was the age of military coalitions, espionage, weapons development, invasions, propaganda, Joe McCarthy's HUAC hearings, and general Cold War angst.

FROM THE ARCHIVES

The following newspaper anecdote about "improvements" in Grant Park provides a reminder of the interwoven sense of optimism about the city's future and dread over potential political conflicts at the end of the decade:

"Chicago may get its first true bomb shelter for the nuclear age, an underground garage capable of sheltering thousands of people from the blast and radioactive fallout of a hydrogen bomb explosion. The Chicago civil defense corps, it was learned yesterday, is studying the possibility of recommending to Mayor Daley that a proposed second underground garage in Grant Park be built as a multipurpose garage shelter and civil defense control center."[17]

This dual-purpose structure was to be located just north of the band shell and was planned to hold eleven hundred cars, helping to accommodate concert crowds. It would also be able to shelter thirteen thousand people in the event of nuclear war with the Soviet Union.

…a Pan American Celebration

Despite such fears, the Festival ended the decade on a positive note when, in August and September of 1959, Chicago served as the host for the third Pan American Games and the Grant Park band shell hosted three special concerts as part of the opening festivities of the games. The games drew 2,263 athletes from twenty-five countries. The games were originally scheduled to take place in Cleveland, but due to a cut in federal funding the city withdrew as a host, and Chicago's Mayor Richard J. Daley quickly offered to take the games instead.

FROM THE ARCHIVES

The *Tribune* described opening ceremony concerts at the Grant Park band shell. Despite the lingering stereotypes, conveyed by the *Tribune* quotation, the Pan American games were a great success and brought back some of the international spirit that imbued Chicago's two great World's Fairs.

"It's true what we've always heard. Latins are just more excitable than other people. The Cuban pianist, Jorge Bolet, and the Brazilian conductor, Eleazar de Carvalho, collaborated Friday evening in a tumultuous performance of Rachmaninoff's Third Concerto. They made the dour Russian composer one of themselves. The predominantly non-Latin Chicago Symphony orchestra was caught up in the general furor. The result was that the throng spreading over the Grant Park acres in front of the band shell tendered an ovation compounded of rapid fire applause and loud 'Bravos.'"[18]

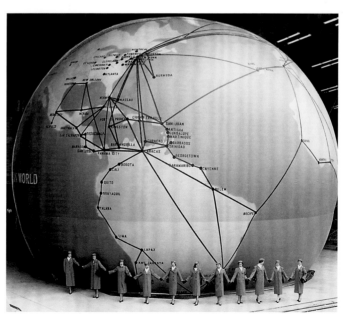

Above: Soldier Field hosts the Pan American Games, which included three special concerts presented by the Festival, 1959.

Below: Pan Am Airlines constructed a massive globe for the games, seen here surrounded by the airline's stewardesses, 1959.

Opposite: A flock of birds is released to help mark the opening of the Pan American Games in Soldier Field in August 1959.

CHAPTER FIVE

The 1960s

Classical Music and Simmering Social Upheaval Share Grant Park

The Grant Park Music Festival was very much influenced by the social upheavals of the 1960s. In fact one of the decade's defining moments—the protests that swept Chicago in August 1968, during the Democratic National Convention—had a focal point at the south end of Grant Park, where the Festival was held. The band shell, which had been the Festival's home for thirty-three seasons, became a meeting area for the protesters.

The 1960s also saw the formation of the Grant Park Chorus, an exciting series of children's concerts, and the presentation of a host of great guest artists.

In the late 1960s the Grant Park band shell was often the site of protests and other social gatherings.

Envisioning the Festival for a New Generation

Another incarnation of a proposed new home for the Festival, a ten-thousand-seat music bowl, which the Chicago Park District unsuccessfully sought to build. Rendering circa 1960.

The Festival changed immensely in the 1960s in many respects. Programming became more adventurous, particularly after 1964, when Edward Gordon took over as manager, and the Festival featured works such as Schoenberg's *Guerrelieder,* Prokofiev's *Alexander Nevsky,* Mahler's *Song of a Wayfarer,* and a season sprinkled with works by Anton Webern.

In addition, the Festival made an important artistic leap when the Grant Park Chorus was formed in 1962 under the leadership of Thomas Peck and an ambitious series of Young People's Concerts began to bring tens of thousands of kids from Park District programs to daytime concerts each summer. The 1960s also featured a host of stellar guest artists who performed with the Festival, including contralto Marian Anderson,

pianists Alfred Brendel and Daniel Barenboim, violinist Itzhak Perlman, tenor Plácido Domingo, as well as a growing focus on presenting dance companies.

The Chicago Park District also made a strong push to build a new, state-of-the-art $3 million, ten-thousand-seat music bowl for the Festival that would have been named after Montgomery Ward. The summer of 1963 was dominated by discussion of the design and possible location. By the winter of that year, however, the plan had been shelved due to opposition from several Michigan Avenue property owners.

Perhaps most importantly, the Festival continued to attract a remarkably diverse audience hungry for adventurous classical music programming outdoors in the heart of the city.

The following portrait from the *Chicago Tribune* in 1961 gives a vivid example of typical Festival audiences:

"In the great melting pot that is Chicago, the free concerts in Grant Park assemble individuals of varied races and languages, as well as different ages, sexes, and occupations. Dr. Sam Johnson (who said, 'He who is tired of London is tired of life') would have enjoyed coming early and watching the crowd gather, rejoicing in the infinite variety of human experience and ancestral background manifest in this cross-section of our cosmopolitan city.

"Behind us, a school teacher was saying that on his way back from the refreshment stand he had just seen one of his truant problem children.... In front of us, a whole row of teen-age girls (except one wearing flats) sat down and promptly took off their shoes. To the right were three gigglers who had come to talk rather than to listen. A memorable young lady who was all of 8, in Sunday best and very dignified, was obviously vastly enjoying herself."[1]

The decade saw a sharp increase in programming by and for kids.

Above: A children's chorus onstage at the Grant Park band shell, 1973.

Left: Groups sprawling on the lawn, 1967.

Right: An improvised hat helps ward off the summer sun, 1965

Daily Life at the Concerts in the 1960s IN THEIR OWN WORDS

The Festival has always functioned as an ideal way for new audiences to develop a curiosity for classical music. The following three stories of young Chicagoans who later went on to play prominent roles in the city's music scene give a sense of how the Festival drew young audiences.

Singin' in the Rain

Chicago Sun-Times classical music critic Wynne Delacoma recollects how the lure of the Grant Park Music Festival brought her and friends to downtown Chicago and unexpected adventures in the 1960s.

"Grant Park was a regular part of my entertainment when I was growing up. It was part of the whole mix of the city. When we talk about the Festival and Grant Park as Chicago's front porch, I think that was definitely the feel. I mean younger people, older people, kids like us by ourselves, and families with babies. I never felt like I didn't belong.

"I remember when it would frequently pour rain, we would drag our completely soaked quilts and bedspreads into the Conrad Hilton lobby. A fair number of people would do that. Then we would line up at phones and call people who were supposed to pick us up and tell them to come early. I remember coming into the Conrad Hilton, and I'm sure they were not at all happy to see me in my shorts and bedraggled look. There were phones there, and we could call someone's dad. It was a safe place to wait and be dry."

May I Take Your Daughter to a Grant Park Concert?

Despite the Festival's open and egalitarian nature, not everyone was given permission to attend. Jack Zimmerman recalls:

"As a teenager, I fell in love with classical music and really started going to Grant Park concerts. I usually went alone,

since none of the girls that I dated would go. I came from a real working-class neighborhood: I lived at 63rd and Western. Girls' parents, in those years, when you said you were driving downtown, they weren't too eager for you to take their daughter. So I went there and really heard a lot of music. For a young person who was finding his way in classical music, there's nothing better than to go hear an orchestra play a couple times a week. Grant Park has always done amazing, diverse repertoire."

Expanding Musical Tastes, Then Pizza

A sense of what the concertgoing experience at Grant Park, as well as post-performance downtown dining, was like for a kid in the 1960s is conveyed by Steve Ovitsky, who later served as the Festival's general manager when he helped reshape the Festival in the late 1970s and 1980s.

"I had gone to Austin High School on the west side of the city. As a kid, occasionally, I'd go down to the concerts, but when I really got interested in music in high school, I can recall many times going a half block from my house and getting on the Jackson Park bus; we'd take the bus down to the old shell on Balbo.

"Everyone knew about these concerts. Even if, for example, my family and I were driving back from visiting relatives on the south side on a Sunday, everybody knew it was there; it was just a matter of taking advantage of it.

"The lovely thing about it was you could go down to the park to hear a concert and then go to a restaurant, and when you added up the total cost, you could go to a nicer restaurant because you didn't pay for the concert. As a high school student in the early 1960s or a college student back home in Chicago for the summer, usually after a concert got out we'd go to a place like Gino's or Due for pizza. It opened up a world to someone who was trying to hear more and more classical music. I got to hear so much repertoire that I would have never heard otherwise."

The Unforgettable Voice of the Festival: Mel Zellman

Few facets of the Festival have been as important in spreading the love of music as Mel Zellman's melodious voice, which from 1964 until 1977 introduced the concerts in Grant Park with a loving balance of folksy wit and historic insight. Zellman was also a long-time announcer for WFMT radio and an important force in Chicago's classical music world.

IN HIS OWN WORDS

"When I started announcing the concerts in 1964, it quickly became apparent that I was not there just to give a strict musico-logical treatise on what was being played, but rather to also leaven it with a few corny jokes. My understanding was that several of the guys who preceded me as commentator were more emcee types, more entertainers. I didn't view the job that way. The way I viewed it, I was there to really tell people something about the music. Depending on what piece of music was being played, whether it was a new piece or one of the warhorses, I just tried to acquaint the audience with something that was less detailed than a printed program note, but still I tried to do something of substance.

"When I first got hired to announce the concerts, I remember I went out to buy some sort of fancy summer tux at some dingy little second-hand store on State Street, before everything was remodeled. I walked in and said, 'I want to buy a summer tux!' and the owner asks, 'What are you? Let me guess: a waiter or a musician.'

"The first time I came out on stage my knees were just shaking, and I was standing at the microphone just terrified. I really wasn't sure. I was used to being on a stage because my major in college was theater, but this was a different kind of presentation.

"Looking at that old band shell from out front, it was impressive. The way the lighting was done, it looked like the Hollywood Bowl. It looked fantastic. But up close, standing on the stage, you could see it was a wreck; it was in dreadful condition. I remember my dressing room backstage was a little room that I shared with all the Andy Frain ushers.

"All in all, doing the announcements in Grant Park was lovely. I had a ball! What James Petrillo did in establishing the Festival is so important culturally to Chicago. It is such a treasure for people who don't have access to music or who cannot afford to buy a ticket to a concert."

Mel Zellman introduces the Grant Park opening concert, June 26, 1976. For fourteen seasons his rich voice, wit, and insight personified the Festival's role in helping to introduce classical music to new audiences.

The Musicians' Perspective

Ted Kaitchuck, violist with the Grant Park Orchestra, 1969–2005, and orchestra personnel manager, 1973–2005: Kaitchuck has played one of the most important behind-the-scenes roles at the Festival with duties ranging from coordinating orchestra auditions to continually rotating the musicians' seating arrangements to handling their payroll. Kaitchuck shares his perspective as an orchestra member and manager.

"The audition process was very different in those years. People would prepare as many orchestral pieces as they could because one never knew what was going to be put in front of one. There was no orchestra list published that you could practice. You just took your chances. I was fortunate to pass the audition.

"Another difference was that the old band shell was so unprotected from the weather. At one point we had to rehearse under the stands of Soldier Field because the temperature was down below the fifties. The woodwinds had to protect their instruments from cracking. Those are certainly conditions that are different from rehearsing in an indoor facility.

"Almost everything that happened over the years at the Festival was very positive, but there were some interesting moments as well."

Pinchas Steinberg, violinist with the Grant Park Orchestra: Steinberg made a sudden career shift to being a conductor in 1968. He has gone on to an illustrious career, with positions at the Vienna State Opera, l'Orchestre de la Suisse Romande in Geneva, the Cleveland Symphony, and other organizations. He reminisces on his learning experience with the Grant Park Orchestra.

"The experience playing outdoors, in Grant Park, for this music-loving public is something I remember very well. Having gone from being a violinist with the Grant Park Orchestra to becoming a conductor is all part of a puzzle of life. Each piece has its unique place. Grant Park is one of the pieces in my puzzle.

A fish-eye view from the choral risers of the Grant Park band shell, circa 1965.

I learned so much. The fact that the concerts happen right in the heart of the city is fantastic. At Grant Park, one of the most exciting things is being able to watch the open rehearsals. It is a fascinating opportunity for audiences. Watching the rehearsals, you know if the dynamics between a conductor and audience will work in the first two minutes. It's like a restaurant. Usually people just eat and don't know how the food was prepared. But if people see how the cooking takes place, they might notice a difference. As a result of having been a violinist with Grant Park, the Lyric, and other orchestras, I have a certain sense of ensemble. It's a tremendous school. A lot of the conductors today have never played in an orchestra, and it helps to know the psychology of an orchestra player and understand how to make each one feel that they are each as important as the soloists. It's all about human relationships and ensemble."

Peanut Butter, Jelly, and Prokofiev CONCERTS FOR THE KIDS

Grant Park concerts had always attracted new and atypical audiences for classical music, and kids could take in the symphony with much greater ease while sprawled on a picnic blanket than sitting in an indoor concert hall. Starting in 1963, however, the Festival took a much more proactive approach to introducing kids to orchestral music when it began presenting daytime Young People's Concerts led by conductor Irwin Hoffman.

FROM THE ARCHIVES

As the *Chicago Tribune* noted, the audiences were immense:

"A crowd of 12,500 persons, most of them children of grammar school age from summer camps, attended the second of a series of three young people's concerts in Grant Park by the Grant Park Symphony orchestra....Park officials said they believed it may have been the largest crowd ever to attend a symphony concert intended for children. Most such concerts are presented in auditoriums where the audience is limited."[2]

The concerts were often interactive, with kids permitted to wield the conductor's baton for a spell, as described in this newspaper account of a 1963 program:

"Four children got unexpected birthday presents yesterday when they got to conduct the Grant Park Symphony orchestra at the second of its three children's concerts this summer at the Grant Park band shell. When Irwin Hoffman, conductor, invited to the stage all children who were observing their birthday about 20 responded....when they finished they scampered off the stage so fast that not even the Chicago park district, which sponsors the children's concerts, got their names. The rest of the birthday celebrants Hoffman organized into a percussion section. Equipped with triangles, tambourines, cymbals, castanets, and wood blocks they got to play with the orchestra."[3]

A sea of kids attending a Young People's Concert in 1964. The daytime programs were attended by over thirty thousand children every summer throughout the decade.

LOOKING BACK

Several decades before she would become a key leader of the Festival as Commissioner of Cultural Affairs, Lois Weisberg experienced the Festival from a mother's perspective.

"During that time when I lived up at Belmont and Lake Shore Drive, we'd take our children and ride our bicycles downtown to the concerts in Grant Park, at the original band shell. We could park our bikes there and go sit on the grass. That is how I became familiar with the free concerts in Grant Park.

"They were just fabulous, always big festive crowds. It's funny, back then we never talked about the fact that it was free. We just knew that that was where we wanted to go. We didn't think about the fact that you were saving money or anything. I think that the crowd has not changed all that much. People were taking their children then just like they do today. It was one of the best things that you could do in the summer in Chicago."

Above: A new classical music fan gets a private serenade, circa 1965.

Left: A ballet performance as part of the Festival's Young People's Concerts, 1964.

Right: A squadron of young violinists fills the stage.

Photos circa 1965.

Great Artists of the 1960s

Duke Ellington and his orchestra performed in the Grant Park band shell in June 1970 as part of a special jazz series that had begun in the late 1960s.

Iconic soprano Marian Anderson, pianists Alfred Brendel and Daniel Barenboim, plus an appearance by Leonard Bernstein were among the guest-artist highlights of the 1960s.

In addition, concertgoers saw and heard pianists Leon Fleisher (1960), Lorin Hollander (1960 and 1962), and Christoph Eschenbach (1969); tenor Plácido Domingo (1967); mezzo-sopranos Marilyn Horne (1962) and Tatiana Troyanos (1964); sopranos Martina Arroyo (1963–1969) and Roberta Peters (1960 and 1962);

violinists Itzhak Perlman, who debuted at the age of twenty (1965), Ruggiero Ricci (1961), Charles Treger (1963), and Jaime Laredo (1962 and 1964); and cellist Leonard Rose (1961). The Festival also began to feature dance companies on a regular basis, including the American Ballet Theater (1965), the Maria Alba Spanish Dance Company (1966 and 1969), and the Joffrey Ballet (1969), performing Gerald Arpino's *Fanfara* and excerpts from Balanchine's *Donizetti Variations*.

Marian Anderson

Contralto, 1966

Marian Anderson appeared at Grant Park in 1966 with her nephew, frequent Festival guest conductor James DePriest. By this time she had "officially" sung her farewell performance at Carnegie Hall in 1965, but she still occasionally continued to give concerts. Anderson was one of the most celebrated singers of the twentieth century. As an African American, Anderson became an important figure in the struggle for black artists to overcome racial prejudice in the United States. She performed a groundbreaking concert in 1939 on the steps of the Lincoln Memorial, and she was the first African American to sing at the Metropolitan Opera, in 1955.

FROM THE ARCHIVES

The *Chicago Tribune* wrote of Anderson's soaring performance.

"When Marian Anderson sang at Grant Park last night, no one left during intermission. Quite the contrary! The crowd continued to swell, probably up to the time of Miss Anderson's concluding spirituals....

"They had come to hear and honor—to hear and honor what, in its prime, was one of the most glorious voices of the century, and a woman whose very name can be an inspiration.

"That it is no longer the voice of 10 or 20 years ago cannot be denied. And, yet, many must have left the park yesterday with a lump in the throat, signaling the highest and most moving experience....

"Certainly, there are better singers on the stage now than Miss Anderson. But none has her pioneering career and few have her high seriousness of purpose.

"All those present last night knew this. All had come to honor this...Honoring the cheers and devoted applause, Miss Anderson responded with the familiar Schubert 'Ave Maria' as an encore.

"In keeping with the festive atmosphere of the event and its official program, 'A Tribute to the United Nations,' the concert began with Aaron Copland's 'Preamble for a Solemn Occasion.' The short work commemorating the U.N. Bill of Human Rights was composed on commission in 1949.

"In itself, it is rather innocuous; with Miss Anderson narrating, it struck home and made its point."[4]

Legendary contralto Marian Anderson with her nephew, conductor James DePriest, backstage after her 1966 concert at Grant Park.

Daniel Barenboim

Pianist, 1964

Renowned pianist and conductor, Daniel Barenboim, made his first (and only) Grant Park appearance in 1964 at the age of twenty-two as a pianist on opening night. Chicagoans know him as music director of the Chicago Symphony Orchestra from 1991 to 2006. He is now conductor-for-life at the Berlin State Opera and principal guest conductor of the La Scala opera house.

FROM THE ARCHIVES

Tribune critic Thomas Willis described the performance:

"There was a gentle breeze to cool the scene, a quiet night relatively free from trains and planes, the Grant Park Symphony Orchestra doing some good playing under its talented veteran conductor, Irwin Hoffman, and a gifted young pianist, Daniel Barenboim, playing his first concerto in this vicinity....

"Mr. Barenboim, still only 22, has been heard several times here in recital, tho never with orchestra. He remains a puzzle.

In the 'Emperor' Concerto, he seized attention with a commanding opening arpeggio, then blurred the effect by harshly overplayed bravura and obtrusive accents. There is no denying his musical understanding, however, nor his interesting tonal palette. Stunning soft passages of balanced line and impeccable rhythm flow into subtle accompaniment figures or grow into broad singing lines direct and to the poetic point. When he is at the quiet heart of the music, it speaks and we listen."[5]

A youthful Daniel Barenboim takes the stage before his performance at Grant Park in the summer of 1964.

Alfred Brendel

Pianist, 1966 and 1967

Famed Austrian pianist (born in Moravia) Alfred Brendel appeared at Grant Park in both 1966 and 1967. Brendel is largely self-taught and considered one of the foremost interpreters of Germanic composers such as Mozart, Beethoven, and Schubert.

FROM THE ARCHIVES

The *Chicago Tribune* recognized Brendel's gifts:

"Quiet joy and dynamic range mark his playing…Within his subdued articulate Mozart style, he manages maximum interpretative freedom, varying returning melodies in subtle ways which serve to implant them more strongly in our minds. This is the sort of playing one does not find often; it is to his credit that he refused to compromise with the band shell drawbacks and insisted on playing music all the way."[6]

LOOKING BACK

Mel Zellman, long-time festival announcer, recalls meeting Alfred Brendel backstage of the band shell: "I met lots of great guest artists. My favorite story concerns Alfred Brendel, the great pianist. He was a tall, aristocratic Austrian. The first evening, he gave a knockout performance, but he was very serious. The second evening, he showed up backstage at the band shell, and he was grinning from ear to ear and carrying a brown paper bag. He had been out shopping somewhere in Chicago. He had never been to Chicago before, and he was buttonholing every girl he could backstage to show them this 'magnificent thing' he had found while shopping.

Renowned pianist Alfred Brendel made two memorable appearances with the Festival in the 1960s.

"Then he showed me. He withdrew from the bag this little plastic box. It was one of those novelty devices where you flip a switch, and then a little door in the top of the box opens, and up comes a wrinkled green hand. Next, the hand flicks off the switch and goes back in the box. He was delighted by it. I learned subsequently that he has a huge collection of these sorts of kitsch gag items. He was just in love with them. It was so startling to see the change in his demeanor from the night before."

Opera in the Park and a Bernstein Visit

Beginning in 1964, the Festival embarked on an ambitious initiative to present operas in concert or semi-staged versions, often with all-star casts. Some of the highlights of the decade included: 1964—*The Tales of Hoffman* with John Alexander, Beverly Sills, Tatiana Troyanos, and Norman Treigle; and *Madama Butterfly* with Martina Arroyo; 1965—*Tosca* with Sherrill Milnes; 1966—*Il Trovatore* and *La Cenerentola;* 1967—*The Abduction from the Seraglio,* with Beverly Sills and John Alexander; 1968—*La Traviata* with Beverly Sills; *Carmen* with Beverly Wolff; and *Candide.*

FROM THE ARCHIVES

Among the opera highlights of the decade was a 1968 production of Leonard Bernstein's *Candide,* which the composer attended in person. The *Chicago Tribune* described the event.

"Leonard Bernstein joined an estimated 15,000 people last night in Grant Park to hear a new concert version of his 1956 operetta *Candide*…The new production proved superb, which is fitting, for despite its dismal opening run of 73 performances, the American musical stage now is ready for *Candide,* having become acclimatized to musicals more musical than the standard Broadway vehicle-laden fare by works like Mr. Bernstein's own *West Side Story.* Mr. Bernstein, accompanied by his 13-year-old son, Alexander, bounded on stage for a bow with the cast. Deservedly."[7]

Soprano Martina Arroyo during one of her six appearances with the Festival in the 1960s.

Creating a Chorus

In the early 1960s, the Festival made another musical leap when it formed its own chorus. More than forty years later, the Grant Park Chorus has grown into one of the most respected choruses in the country (having won the 2006 Margaret Hillis Award for Choral Excellence, a national award given to only one professional chorus every three years). The existence of a professional chorus as part of a summer music festival, partly funded by local government is a remarkable anomaly and has long been one of the Festival's greatest strengths.

The Grant Park Chorus was organized in 1962 by Thomas Peck, who directed the chorus until his death in 1994. Peck had joined the Chicago Symphony Chorus as a singer and was mentored by CSO Chorus–founder Margaret Hillis. Peck later went on to found the St. Louis Symphony Chorus.

FROM THE ARCHIVES

The Grant Park Chorus quickly began to draw strong reviews. Several decades later, music critic John von Rhein summed up Peck's achievements:

"Perhaps no Chicago musician knows more about working under the deadline gun than Thomas Peck, founder and director of the Grant Park Symphony Chorus. And few are better equipped to turn the often impossible conditions under which these summer concerts are produced to the actual benefit of the music....

"Peck's central achievement is having built the Grant Park Chorus from an essentially volunteer ensemble into one of the most respected professional choral organizations in the Midwest. It has been a slow process...fraught with...sporadic shifts of management, and, most frustratingly, with the fickle storm gods deciding which music gets heard and which music never makes it beyond the park-district cafeteria where the chorus holds its rehearsals....

"'When you can get more than 100 choristers together at the end of May and by the beginning of July they all love each other, that's something very special,' said Peck, looking benignly Buddha-like during a recent rehearsal break despite blanketing heat that had sent the temperature inside the music shell shooting up past 100 degrees. 'There is incredible camaraderie here. These people are troupers who care about music. They have performed under every condition imaginable. So being able to hack it in this city is a point of honor.'" [8]

The Grant Park Chorus in 1962. Led by Thomas Peck for more than thirty years, the chorus quickly developed an excellent reputation and became one of the great strengths of the Festival.

The 1968 Democratic Convention

Some of the most gripping images of the protests that swept the world in 1968 were those of confrontations between Chicago police officers and protesters in Grant Park during the Democratic National Convention that summer. Many of the most heated and violent clashes occurred in the southwest corner of Grant Park in the area immediately adjacent to the Festival's home, the band shell, because many of the delegates to the convention were staying at the Hilton Hotel directly across from the park. Anger erupted over the Democratic Party's choice of a candidate who was not a strong advocate of ending the war in Vietnam.

The Festival's season ended just a few days before the convention began, and concert audiences were already sharing the south end of Grant Park with a steadily building protest movement. The final performance of the summer was a concert production of Verdi's *La Traviata,* featuring Beverly Sills as Violetta. While Verdi's gypsy chorus "Noi siamo zingarelle" was being sung on closing night, Grant Park had already begun to fill with thousands of protesters gathering in advance of the convention.

A few days after the final concert, Mayor Richard J. Daley and the Chicago city government, in an attempt to prevent the protesters from marching to the Chicago Amphitheater where the convention was taking place, offered them several alternate protest routes, all of which aimed to have the protesters instead march to the aging Grant Park band shell and hold their rally there. The battered thirty-five-year-old band shell was eagerly being offered up as a sacrificial lamb. The protesters, however, rebuffed the city's offer and instead stuck to their plan to march directly to the convention itself.

The climax arrived on Wednesday, August 28, when a full-fledged conflict between at least ten thousand protesters and more than twenty-three thousand police and National Guard members erupted in Grant Park just north of the band shell and quickly spread into downtown Chicago. Tear gas wafted through the city, producing archetypal images that would contribute to defining the 1960s.

More than five hundred protesters were arrested, and hundreds of protesters and police were injured, but the band shell survived the melée relatively unscathed, with just a few crushed wooden benches. It would put in another ten seasons as the Festival's home, until its demolition in 1978.

During subsequent decades, Grant Park and the 1968 protests would be intrinsically linked. That association was only to be upstaged forty years later when another pivotal moment in presidential politics took place in Grant Park: just a few hundred feet from where the protests occurred and the concerts were held, an election night rally for president-elect Barack Obama drew a crowd of nearly a quarter of a million people and again made Grant Park a name known around the world.

Protestors gather at the Grant Park band shell. The venue was a frequent gathering place for many political events, most notably during the Democratic National Convention in August 1968, when Chicago's lakefront was gripped by massive protests that drew the attention of the world.

CHAPTER SIX

The 1970s

Building a Better Band Shell and Other Adventures in Urban Renewal

In the 1970s the Grant Park Music Festival remained a beacon of outdoor, public art in Chicago during a period when many people were skeptical about the future of cities in the United States. Although audiences for the Festival grew smaller in the face of a struggling economy and a rise in crime, an important seed in the revival of the downtown was planted toward the end of the decade, and in 1978 the Festival celebrated the opening of its second home, the Petrillo Bandshell.

During the Petrillo's first season, the Festival began producing the annual Independence Eve fireworks concert, which brought together hundreds of thousands of people from all walks of life and helped to create a further sense of optimism about a possible downtown renaissance. A quarter of a century later the opening of Millennium Park helped to fulfill this early promise.

A dancer from the Ballet School of the Lyric Opera of Chicago performs on the stage of the recently inaugurated Petrillo Bandshell on August 3, 1978.

A New, Removable, Band Shell

By the late 1970s, the original Grant Park band shell had been active for more than forty seasons and was by all accounts well past its prime. The *Chicago Tribune* reflected on its tattered state in an article a few years after its demise in 1978.

The Petrillo Bandshell, which opened in the summer of 1978, was designed to be disassembled in order to adhere to stipulations that permanent buildings not be erected in Grant Park. The band shell served as the home of the Grant Park Music Festival for twenty-six seasons. Photo circa 1980.

FROM THE ARCHIVES

"Meanwhile, the old shell continued to deteriorate. Conductor David Zinman once likened it to 'the 57th Street men's toilet in New York City.'

"Musicians kidded each other about wearing hardhats with their tuxes, but then came several mishaps—a piece of ceiling fell on the violin section; during one unforgettable rehearsal, a steel cable ripped loose and ripped across the stage narrowly missing the players; a grand piano once crashed through the floor. In 1977, the city spent $77,000 renovating the shell, but the players and management wanted out. 'If the park district hadn't pushed the new facility,' Steven Ovitsky says, 'there was a strong chance that the season would have been canceled in 1978. Fortunately we made it, and Grant Park's been on the upswing ever since.'"[1]

PRESERVING THE OPEN LAKEFRONT

Debates about building a new band shell for the Festival in Grant Park had been raging since the 1940s, but a variety of factors kept the project at bay. Financing the project was always an issue.

Equally significant, however, was the famed 1836 stipulation (originally recorded on an early map of Chicago) that the Grant Park area "remain forever open, clear, and free of any building or obstructions whatever," a status that Chicago department-store owner Aaron Montgomery Ward vigorously helped lead a campaign to preserve starting in the 1890s.

The Petrillo Bandshell was named for James C. Petrillo, a key figure in the founding of the Festival and president of the American Federation of Musicians. When it opened in 1978, the band shell slipped around the "open, clear, and free" prohibition by being "semi-permanent:" it had been designed with the potential to be dismantled after each summer season. The costs of doing so were steep, however, and the band shell was never actually taken apart.

Plans for a new band shell reached the design stage several times before the building of the Petrillo. In 1946, a twenty-five-thousand-seat, $1.5 million "music court" with a retractable roof was being discussed, to be located between Monroe Street and Jackson Boulevard.

FROM THE ARCHIVES

In 1972, a $31 million band shell was widely touted, and designs were created by C. F. Murphy Associates. The design sparked discussion of a larger plan to try to help stem the decline of downtown Chicago. As one critic noted at the time:

"A downtown band shell may be even more important from a social point of view as Chicago becomes increasingly a 9-to-5 city during the week, and just about moribund on the weekends. Band shell proposals have been grandiloquently announced for poor Grant Park since the conclusion of World War II. Like some hardy biennial which refuses to be discouraged by any lack of attention, they've popped up—in theory—all over that ravaged parkland. Retractable roofs, open air gizmos, amphitheatre style (whether Grecian or otherwise, sunk or not)—well, you name it, and we've seen variations on the theme in architectural model form for what seems like eons."[2]

While the Petrillo was in many ways considerably more modest than some of the other proposed but unbuilt band shells, it was built with a strong sense of pragmatism.

Left: A 1972 proposal for a new venue for the Grant Park Music Festival designed by C. F. Murphy Associates. This was at least the fifth seriously considered proposal in the decades between the Festival's birth and the creation of the Petrillo Bandshell in 1978.

Right: The original Grant Park band shell in its final moments, 1978. The band shell was the site of more than two thousand Grant Park Music Festival concerts, plus numerous other events, between 1931 and 1978.

The new Petrillo Bandshell had a stunning view of the magnificent Michigan Avenue skyline, featuring works by Daniel Burnham, Louis Sullivan, and other Chicago architects. Photo circa 1980.

Ed Kelly, Park District General Superintendent, 1972–1986:
"The original band shell on the south end of Grant Park was in very bad shape by the 1970s. Structurally, it was so dangerous that I wanted to build a new band shell further north, over on Monroe Street. The only way I could do it was to meet with Mayor Richard J. Daley. So, in the early 1970s I went to lunch with the mayor, and on the way back, I asked the driver to take us down Monroe Street. As we got down there, we pulled up, and the mayor was wondering what I was doing. I started explaining that I had to move the band shell and I was wondering if he could give me the money to help me pay for the new structure.

"When you talked about getting money from Mayor Daley, he sometimes developed a case of amnesia. He asked, 'Why do you want to put the band shell here?' I gave him several reasons: the existing band shell was at a very bad location; there was no parking; the music conflicts with any events going on at Soldier Field; and there was a general sense of chaos there.

"But I saved my real argument for last: the seniors. I said, 'The seniors can come over by bus and just walk a block over here to the band shell, whereas there is no city transportation to get them to the original place.' The mayor said, 'I think it is a great idea. Why don't you just go ahead and do it?' So I asked him, 'You can't help me with the financing?' And then the mayor said, 'I know that you have the money, otherwise you wouldn't be asking me.' And I did have the money.

"When the new band shell was built, the Petrillo, it wasn't a permanent structure because of the Montgomery Ward law that didn't allow us to build new permanent facilities under the Burnham plan. As it turned out, the new location proved to be very popular. As for the importance of the Grant Park Music Festival to me, I am not a classical music aficionado. However, I think the idea of having free concerts for people without funds to go elsewhere was a great idea. I wanted to attract people into the parks at no cost to them. In fact, Mitch Miller came in from New York, and I was given an award for being supportive of the musicians. I was very proud of that."

Ed Uhlir, architect and director of design for Millennium Park:
"I started at the Park District in the early 1970s. At the time, the head of the Park District was Ed Kelly. One of my first connections to the Grant Park Orchestra was being asked to design a 'fly' that would shade the orchestra during rehearsals at the first band shell because it was facing south. When my boss, who was the head architect and in charge of engineering, was promoted up the line, I became head architect for the Park District. We were exploring the idea of creating a new music pavilion, which would eventually become the Petrillo Bandshell.

"There was a big battle going on between the Park District and the civic leaders about whether the new band shell should be situated in the new site where the Monroe Street parking lot was located. The Park District wanted to build it in Butler Field, which was a big open field. I had the job of looking at the estimates that Skidmore, Owings & Merrill had done for the Lakefront Arts Project. They asked me to estimate the cost of that particular project, and I came up with a number around $50 million. A key issue was the need to gain control of the property from the railroads, who were claiming control of the air rights, and the property itself because the parking lot was there.

Turkeys and candelabras were part of the celebration for the opening of the new Petrillo Bandshell, named for the Festival's indomitable founder, James Caesar Petrillo, in June of 1978.

"The board of the Park District decided that we weren't going to spend $50 million; we were going to spend $3 million, including $1.4 million for the facility and the building and another $1 million for the site work and the landscaping. So, we designed it with the objective of being able to remove the band shell and store it. If you look at that facility, it is a simple, off-the-shelf system that can be bolted together and then taken apart and stored. It had to be a temporary facility. It was done really inexpensively compared to the SOM plan, but it served its purpose for quite a while. It was only designed for symphonic music, and it wasn't until later that it hosted all the other festivals."

Daily Life at the Concerts in the 1970s IN THEIR OWN WORDS

Life at the two band shells in the 1970s (the original Grant Park band shell and the Petrillo) was certainly somewhat different. Although the Petrillo Bandshell always drew mixed reviews for its sound system, comfort, and aesthetics, it did foster an air of inclusiveness. The band shell was originally built with the Grant Park Music Festival in mind; however, it quickly became the centerpiece of other music events and city festivals, including the Taste of Chicago, Blues Festival, Jazz Festival, Chicago Outdoor Film Festival, and many others. The Petrillo Bandshell helped Grant Park fulfill its function as Chicago's front yard.

Growing Up at the Concerts

Jack Zimmerman, musician and arts administrator, recalls the experience of bringing his children to the Petrillo Bandshell in the 1970s.

"In the early years at the new Petrillo Bandshell, we sat on the lawn. My wife, Char, started playing second clarinet with the Grant Park Orchestra a few years before, and we really got into being a Grant Park family. The great thing about Grant Park was that you could really expose your kids to music. People always say you should start by taking kids to something with a melody, but I would just take my kids down there to the Petrillo, and I didn't care what they were playing. My kids, they learned to appreciate all kinds of music, even twentieth-century music. It was no big deal with them; they came to understand it just fine.

"And you know what? Today one of my kids is the artistic director at the Caramoor Festival in New York. So he's in the summer festival thing. The other one is a jazz musician living on the West Coast. The jazz musician, when my wife was pregnant with him, Grant Park was playing some big percussion piece at the Petrillo. She was on stage, and the percussion started playing, and the baby started kicking like crazy. She came home and said, 'I think we got a musician.' Today he plays tenor sax. He's a natural musician. That's the great thing about Grant Park: you can go there and be educated."

Left: Members of the Grant Park Orchestra behind the scenes at the original band shell, including long-time violinist, Norman Schoer, center, 1972.

Right: The Festival has always attracted an abundance of kids and families, introducing hundreds of thousands of people to classical music. Photo circa 1970.

Opposite: A blanket on the lawn of a Grant Park concert becomes a home away from home, 1974.

Tailgating with the Chorus

Jan Jarvis, a long-time chorus member shares some memories of the musicians' culinary adventures at the Petrillo.

"In the 1970s, we started this tradition of post-rehearsal cook-outs: sort of tailgate parties with the chorus. At first we used to bring little coolers of beers and just drink after rehearsal. Then I started to bring a little grill, and little by little, it snowballed until it was a regular party, once a week or so, every Thursday, because there were no performances after. Hamburgers and beer. Everyone paid by contributing a dollar here or there. If someone wanted cheese on their hamburger, I'd tell them to give a little extra. It was all on the honor system. That was the way things were in those days—casual. It's the kind of thing that maybe now, in the new band shell, couldn't happen quite the same way."

Flamenco and the Rats

Mike Geller, principal bassist with the Grant Park Orchestra, shares the memory of one of the original band shell's more frightful moments.

"When the Maria Alba Dance Company came to the old band shell in the 1970s, they launched into this solo dance thing with all this flamenco tapping of their heels on the stage. Well, all of a sudden, just as they got started, a group of rodents scurried out from underneath the stage and dashed out into the audience. It was a stampede of rodents, and it was hysterically funny. The audience had a noticeable reaction."

Great Artists of the 1970s

The Festival offered the public the chance to see an array of world-renowned artists and first glimpses of up-and-coming performers who would later go on to great acclaim during the 1970s. Below are just a few of the highlights of the decade.

In addition, this decade included soprano June Anderson (1979); vocalist Gordon MacRae (1971); pianists Dave Brubeck (1971), Alicia De Larrocha (1971 and 1972), Jerome Lowenthal (1973 and 1975), and Sheldon Shkolnik (1970 and 1977–1983); violinist Elaine Skorodin (1976); and dancers from the Chicago City Ballet (1977 and 1978) and the New York City Ballet (1970 and 1977).

Mitch Miller

Conductor and Music Director, 1974–1985 and 1987–1988

Few musicians did as much to help popularize classical music—or wore as many musical hats—as Mitch Miller. He has been a conductor, singer, director of artists and repertoire at Columbia Records, and oboe- and English horn–player. (He toured with George Gershwin's orchestra.) Miller became a household name, thanks in part to his widely watched television show, *Sing Along with Mitch* (1961–1964), with its famous admonition to "follow the bouncing ball." In the 1970s and 1980s he was a regular conductor with the Grant Park Music Festival, leading some of its most popular programs and drawing swarms of new audiences to the concerts.

FROM THE ARCHIVES

"It's always a grand night for singing when Mitch Miller comes to town," wrote John von Rhein, *Chicago Tribune* music critic in 1978. "The bearded bandleader dropped in on his musician friends of the Grant Park Symphony for the fifth consecutive year, leading the orchestra in one of those lightweight but ingratiating programs for which cool summer nights, picnics on the grass, and Cinemascope cityscapes must have been invented.

"There was no bouncing ball, no wheezing theater organ, only the orchestra pouring out some sweet old standards and Mitch presiding over the whole songfest as if it were the musical equivalent of a Friar's Club roast. Once again he proved you don't have to be eligible for Medicare to feel like dusting off your vocal cords for such vintage oldies as 'Baby Face,' 'Singin' in the Rain,' or 'Tiptoe through the Tulips.' A young couple out on the lawn even got up to dance (cheek-to-cheek, of course) when Miller launched into 'Now Is the Hour.'" [3]

Thanks in part to his presence on television (and his "follow the bouncing ball" sing-along trademark), Mitch Miller was an immensely successful ambassador for classical music and an ideal presence at Grant Park, drawing countless newcomers to orchestra programs.

Opposite: Mitch Miller, legendary conductor and promoter of classical music, pours his soul into one of his fourteen performances with the Festival in the 1970s and 1980s.

Photos circa 1980.

Leonard Slatkin

Conductor and Music Director, 1974–1975, 1977–1982, 1985, 1986, 1988, and 1994

The Grant Park Music Festival has a long history of engaging first-rate conductors, and Leonard Slatkin was among the key conductors in building the orchestra and shaping its sound. He went on to become music director of the St. Louis Symphony and more recently of the Detroit Symphony Orchestra.

Leonard Slatkin (seated) with the Festival's Manager, Stanley Ackerman, became principal conductor in 1974.

FROM THE ARCHIVES

The *Chicago Tribune* was quick to embrace Slatkin's appointment as the Festival's principal conductor in 1974:

"Slatkin, who is associate principal conductor of the St. Louis Symphony, is a find, and congratulations to Grant Park for engaging him as principal conductor for the next summer. Around 30, he has a direct, music-oriented competence which shows the thoroughness of his training and his concentration on things which matter."[4]

Several years later, in 1978, the *Tribune* continued to offer praise of Slatkin's prowess as both a conductor and programmer:

"Assembling a symphonic program that is challenging enough to engage an orchestra's full faculties, appealing enough to bring an audience downtown whatever the weather, and unusual enough to please persnickety critics is a juggling act which few conductors manage to achieve very successfully, and fewer still deem all that important to begin with. Leonard Slatkin is one of the more prominent exceptions to this rule, as he has proved in numerous exceptionally interesting programs."[5]

Aaron Copland

Composer and Conductor, 1972

The iconic American composer of *Appalachian Spring, Lincoln Portrait,* and *Fanfare for the Common Man* was less known as a conductor, but he joined the Festival for a July 3rd concert, conducting Tchaikovsky's *Romeo and Juliet,* Leonard Bernstein's Overture to *Candide,* the Adagietto from Mahler's Fifth Symphony, as well as several of his own works.

FROM THE ARCHIVES

As the *Chicago Tribune* noted, Copland's performance at Grant Park had a great historic resonance:

"According to Grant Park spokesmen, somebody said, 'It's time we honored Aaron Copland,' and the composer joked, 'It certainly is.' The composer of *Fanfare for the Common Man,* who taught many what to listen for in music—from the book of the same name—and who helped mold the United States version of socialist realism called Americana, has a special place on the podium of a free concert series. One suspects the orchestra of doing more counting than swinging in *Rodeo* and *Music for a Great City.* Considering the problems in the band shell of the great and Windy City—all that sheet music flying around the stage—who could blame the players for counting to 10?" 6

Composer Aaron Copland conducts the Grant Park Orchestra beneath the majestic, curving lines of the Grant Park band shell in 1972.

David Zinman

Conductor, 1976–1983

In the mid-1970s, David Zinman became the principal guest conductor of the Grant Park Music Festival. Zinman went on to become music director of the Baltimore Symphony, the Tonhalle Orchestra in Zurich, and the Aspen Music Festival.

FROM THE ARCHIVES

The *Chicago Tribune* commented on Zinman's capacity to deal with the many unique challenges of conducting outdoors in Grant Park, and he himself offered some reflections on the sometimes daunting task of concentrating amid the noise of the city.

"Zinman, who this week conducts the final five concerts of his three-week engagement at the Petrillo Music Shell, is no stranger to the wonderful world of bawling infants, meandering adults, Frisbee-tossing teens, sputtering loudspeakers, sirens, whistles, planes and other extramusical distractions at Grant Park. This is his sixth consecutive year as guest conductor. And despite the festival's built-in problems, he does not seem inclined to trade his situation here for all the hermetically sealed concert halls in the world. Not yet, anyway.

"The relatively relaxed program format of Grant Park allows him, within limits, to try music he would not otherwise be able to venture with his other orchestras.

"'Still, I have to think very carefully about what can be done in two rehearsals,' Zinman explained. 'You can't decide to do kooky things all summer, even though your core audience…may want that sort of music….Working at Grant Park is the best kind of discipline for a conductor. You learn to work very fast because you don't have time for detail. And working against the clock, against the elements, builds your concentration and technique. I've gotten so that now, when I'm on the podium, I can shut out everything but the music. If—God forbid—a bomb went off three feet from the stage, I'm sure I wouldn't hear it.'"[7]

David Zinman, the Festival's principal guest conductor for nearly a decade. Photo circa 1980.

Edward Villella

Dancer, 1967–1971, 1973, and 1974

Edward Villella was regarded as the preeminent American male ballet dancer of his era. He danced at John F. Kennedy's inauguration and founded the Miami City Ballet.

FROM THE ARCHIVES

The *Chicago Tribune* described Villella's 1973 performance: "Thirty-four thousand dance fans swarmed back to the band shell Saturday and last night to see Edward Villella leap his annual pas de deux. His partner for 'Le Corsair' and 'Don Quixote' was Anna Aragno of the Metropolitan Opera Ballet.... Villella was the amiable speeding bullet we come to expect from America's superdancer."[8]

Kathleen Battle

Soprano, 1974 and 2000

A year before her professional operatic debut, rising star Kathleen Battle was engaged to perform with the Grant Park Music Festival and sang arias by Puccini, Bizet, Donizetti, and Gershwin, with James Levine conducting.

FROM THE ARCHIVES

Music critic Alan Artner was quick to note Battle's potential, writing of the concert, "Young Kathleen Battle, who is just at the start of a promising career, brought a crowd to Grant Park yesterday. The voice is as slender as Miss Battle herself. Her platform manner is natural, and....allowed the lines to float from Bizet's 'Je dis que rien'...and Puccini's 'O mio babbino caro.'"[9]

Left: Celebrated dancer Edward Villella warms up at a rehearsal at the Grant Park band shell. Villella appeared with the Festival six times in the late 1960s and early 1970s. Photo circa 1980.

Right: Soprano Kathleen Battle, surrounded by admiring donors to the Grant Park Music Festival, following her first appearance with the Festival in the summer of 1974, a year before her professional opera debut.

Fireworks + the 1812 Overture and Howitzers = A Chicago Lakefront Tradition

The creation of the Petrillo Bandshell also helped initiate a citywide Independence Eve fireworks concert featuring the Grant Park Orchestra, which became an annual tradition that drew hundreds of thousands of people to the lakefront. The Independence Eve concerts were especially important in drawing audiences that might not usually attend Grant Park Concerts.

IN HIS OWN WORDS

Jack Zimmerman, musician and arts administrator, recalls the first fireworks concert:

"I went to the very first July 3rd fireworks concert in 1978. It was the consecration of the new band shell, the Petrillo. July 3rd was a workday that year. My mother used to work at Sears as a copywriter. I didn't know how many people would be there so I called her and said, 'Just meet us there.' We got over there around 4:30 or so, and there were already a couple thousand people, and the crowd was huge by 7:00. It was unbelievable. I've never seen so many people.

"What was most unbelievable about that first July 3rd concert was the spirit of civic togetherness. The concert was pure classical, and there was such enthusiasm about the new shell. Wow, it was a great evening. The weird thing was, despite the huge crowds, I found my mother. My mother was Irish. My mother was the luckiest person that ever lived.

"From the first July 3rd concert, I felt the start of a new Chicago. See, living in a neighborhood in Chicago in those days was a much more insular experience. You didn't trust people from outside your neighborhood that much. You didn't make friends right away with people and north-siders. If you were a south-sider, you wouldn't visit them. But on that first July 3rd concert, I really felt that that was the start of a new Chicago."

Opposite: The beaming faces of the audience at the Petrillo Bandshell are a reminder of the affection felt toward Chicago's free "people's music festival," 1974.

FROM THE ARCHIVES

The *Chicago Tribune* noted that the first July 3rd concert brought together a wide and democratic cross section of the city:

"It was a Fourth of July celebration that Chicago hasn't seen in years, or perhaps ever. There were 125,000 celebrants happily picnicking on muddy grass, drinking wine and beer, and trying—mostly in vain—to hear the free concert being performed from Grant Park's new outdoor band shell.... a spectacular fireworks display, cannon booms, and the ringing of church bells throughout the city, all timed to coincide with the rousing end of Tchaikovsky's *1812 Overture,* which was being performed by the Chicago and Grant Park Symphony Orchestras. 'I guess you could say it was a smashing success,' said Mayor Bilandic as he left the park."[10]

The galvanizing quality of Chicago's lakefront fireworks celebration was vividly captured by visiting journalist Marco d'Eramo in his fascinating history of Chicago, *The Pig and the Skyscraper:*

"On a calm summer's night they come in tides to see the Fourth of July fireworks...they come from the far-off suburbs, from Cicero and Calumet, Gary and Evanston, and they pour into Grant Park, on the shores of Lake Michigan opposite the Art Institute, beneath the giant silhouettes of the skyscrapers. Fantastic flowers of multicolored light burst into bloom in the night sky, and an immense wave of heat emanates from the crowd, from those millions of human beings who are gathered here together, conveying the feeling of stubbornly cheerful hope, intense participation, enormous pride or simply satisfaction in being here, and filling you with an inexplicably moving sense of faith in the future."[11]

CHAPTER SEVEN

The 1980s

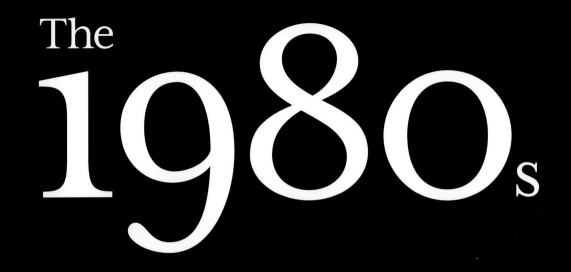

The Music Festival's Innovations in the Era of 'Beirut by the Lake'

During the 1980s the city of Chicago underwent immense changes. Perhaps none was more profound than the 1983 election of Harold Washington, Chicago's first African American mayor, which shattered the status quo. Washington's election, combined with the subsequent city council wars that gripped the city, provoked both optimism and tension and set in motion transformations that ripple into the present.

During the decade the Grant Park Music Festival, among other achievements, developed a reputation for presenting more new works and pieces by American composers.

The Independence Eve fireworks concerts, in which the Grant Park Music Festival participated since 1978, became an important annual event and a key reason for many people to gather downtown in the summer. Photo circa 1980.

An Air of Harmony for Fireworks on the Lakefront

The Grant Park Music Festival concerts were, in their own way, a barometer of the city's mood. The ambiance of the Festival's Independence Eve fireworks concert had begun to change.

FROM THE ARCHIVES
In the summer of 1983, shortly after Mayor Harold Washington's victory, the *Chicago Tribune* described the scene at the Festival:

"The same park where 15 years ago this summer headlines were made around the world. It began at the park's band shell, where the crowd became a mob. Where the American flag was ripped down in anger, where police and demonstrators fought. Where heads were cracked open and people used bottles and rocks on each other....The image projected around the world was one of a country split in two, at war with itself. The way those days of the 1968 Democratic National Convention are remembered by Americans usually is one place: Grant Park.

"But nowadays, on a warm summer July night filled with music and families, with children's laughter coming from somewhere in the dark, with couples cooing in the grass, old people leaning back in lawn chairs and teenagers trampling through the crowd so curious about life they can't sit down, Grant Park is different. You'd never know it was the same place. For it is the 4th of July celebration in Chicago, and Grant Park, as well as America, has changed.

"It is the most popular single event in Chicago: the evening concert by the Grant Park Symphony Orchestra that ends with the *1812 Overture*, the boom of howitzers and a crescendo of fireworks that bang their way up into the dark and then break out into iridescent blooms across the night sky. It is the one night, the one American holiday, that is for everyone. And in Chicago, everyone is there. Suburbanites and even small-town folk whose ancestors might have arrived here 200 years ago, come into

Chicago and settle onto the wet grass to mix with those so new to this country that their accents are thick and weighted.

"Scores of foreign tongues can be heard in this crowd of America's people. Blacks and whites, Orientals and Asians, Hispanics and mulattos. For those with no summer home and no money to leave town for the weekend, Grant Park is the place to go, too…For those who can afford to get out of town but choose to stay, Grant Park is the place to go…Despite all their differences, there is no disunity in the air. The American flags, often waved by little children, are not made fun of or ripped away. The police are easygoing and chat with people they know.

"There are people shoulder to shoulder as far as the eye can see. People camped on every inch of ground for blocks. People lined up along the lake boulders for miles south and north. People holding their babies on their shoulders, drinking beer from a cooler, eating chicken from a picnic basket, drinking martinis from a flask….There is no fear on this night in the park. No anger. No violence. No swelling of a crowd into a mob. There is, unlike any other night in Chicago, an air of harmony. It is an experience shared by hundreds of thousands of people who do not know each other yet do not feel like strangers. In unison their faces turn skyward for the fireworks, and altogether their hundreds of thousands of voices rise to cheer as the fireworks burst into shimmering explosions over the lake."[1]

NEW SOUNDS ON THE LAKEFRONT

Despite the bucolic description, Chicago in the mid-1980s was not so entirely amiable. The city had recently been dubbed "Beirut by the Lake" by the *Wall Street Journal* because of the city council battles that nearly paralyzed the city's political process as many members of the political establishment sought to block initiatives by Harold Washington's administration. After Washington's sudden death in office in 1987, Eugene Sawyer served for a year and a half, and then in 1989 Richard M. Daley was elected mayor, taking the office that his father had once held for more than twenty-one years.

In the midst of such flux, the Grant Park Music Festival made a shift toward more innovative programming. This change was due in part to Steven Ovitsky, who served as concert manager for the Festival from 1979 until 1990 and whose priorities included, among other things, a strong vision for presenting new American works. The decade was filled with pieces by living American composers such as William Bolcom, John Adams, Michael Torke, and Paul Freeman, who often came in person and conducted.

The decade of the 1980s was a period of first-rate conductors including principal conductor Zdenek Macal, Leonard Slatkin, Hugh Wolff, David Zinman, and Robert Shaw. The Festival also embraced adventurous projects that were well suited to the times, such as a performance with Maria Tallchief's Chicago City Ballet (1980); collaborations with National Radio Theatre of the George Gershwin musical *Of Thee I Sing* (1984) and Benjamin Britten's *A Midsummer Night's Dream* (1985); a lavish Leonard Slatkin–led concert version of Puccini's *Turandot* (1984), and a semi-staged version of Kurt Weill and Bertolt Brecht's experimental opera, *Rise and Fall of the City of Mahagonny* (1980), with its whiskey-soaked satirical lyrics, onstage boxing ring, and sly skewering of blind faith in reckless financial speculation.

A musician's-eye view of a rehearsal at the Petrillo Bandshell.

Opposite: The Taste of Chicago, which began in 1980 during the mayoral administration of Jane Byrne, is by some accounts the world's largest food festival. In recent years more than three and a half million people have attended the ten-day event.

Photos circa 1980.

New Management and Creative Programming

Following in the footsteps of Walter L. Larsen, Edward Gordon, and Robert Wilkins, Steven Ovitsky served as concert manager for the Grant Park Music Festival from 1979 until 1990. Ovitsky describes what it was like to take over a Festival that already had a storied five-decade history and the challenges of reshaping its artistic programming.

IN HIS OWN WORDS

"When I began as concert manager for the Grant Park Music Festival in 1979, most of that first season was already programmed, and a big part of the challenge was learning to operate within the Park District's very unique system. At times it was a wonderful safety net, and at other times it could be frustrating. Jane Byrne had just come in as mayor, and one of the first things she wanted to do was to eliminate the big Independence Day concert because of all the money spent on fireworks. She didn't want to be connected to stuff that had gone on before her. They were all part of the new blood that was coming into the city, and they didn't want anything to do with the old. But I met with them, and we worked it out that we would continue the July 3rd concert.

"Back then, the Taste of Chicago was on Michigan Avenue. Because the Independence Day concert was so successful and there were so many people attending, they decided to move the Taste of Chicago into the area around the Petrillo Bandshell during the same weekend. It was our concert that pulled the Taste of Chicago into the location on Jackson and Columbus. The problem, of course, was trying to produce a concert series.

"As for the musicians, the orchestra really believed in what it was doing, and it really added to the quality of life in the city. I think there was a good attitude. And the chorus was incredible. The thing that is wonderful about Grant Park is that the chorus is so identified as part of the operation; it's very integrated. I always felt that the choral programs were some of the highlights. Tom

Peck ran such an unbelievably great chorus; we were able to do spectacular, large pieces. Tom and I were both big fans of the major masses. We were able to do Janáček's *Glagolitic Mass*. And then we did Vaughn Williams's *Sea Symphony* a couple of times, which I think was one of our great all-time productions.

"I also tried to develop the concept that we didn't have the money to commission new works, but we could always ask to do the *second* performance of something once it had been premiered—which is just as important in terms of getting something into the repertoire. We did John Adams's *Harmonium* in 1983 in its second performance after the San Francisco premiere. The audience really ate it up. This was when John's music was just beginning to really become known.

"I think the brilliance of the Grant Park Music Festival, and the reason why it is in some ways the most creative place around, is because it is a place that can balance the artistic, the financial, and management all together. Because the concerts are free, box office receipts are not the barometer of a successful program."

Steven Ovitsky, here speaking to the audience at the Petrillo Bandshell in 1978, led the Grant Park Music Festival throughout the 1980s and deepened the Festival's reputation for presenting new and unusual works.

Backstage Philosophy from the Broom Closet

For over four decades, John Daniel served, uncelebrated, behind the scenes at the Grant Park Music Festival. As a janitor and stage manager at the original band shell and then at the Petrillo, he saw and heard perhaps more than anyone. This 1987 profile gives an image of a man few in the audiences may have known, but whose commitment and artistry was a quiet embodiment of what the Grant Park Music Festival is all about.

FROM THE ARCHIVES

"John Daniel…sits in his 'office' in the basement of the Petrillo Music Shell. Surrounded by mops, brooms and other tools of the maintenance trade, Daniel waxes philosophic on life, work and the human condition…. At 68 and counting, Daniel is a self-made philosopher, Chicago-style….

"There's just common sense and uncommon humanity developed through 28 years of service to the city and its patrons of the arts. Since 1959, Daniel has served as stage manager and maintenance man at both the old Grant Park Band Shell and the new music shell, and has catered to the caprice of temperamental artists and their adoring fans. Fellow workers, bosses and artists agree that Daniel is 'one of a kind.'

"'You see,' said Daniel, 'a lot of people in the arts have a lot of problems. But they come down here and talk to me some, and after a while they smile. When they are happy, the audience will be happy. Then we all happy.' Daniel's outlook has made the Chicago music scene his oyster, within the half-shell confines of the music shell and the artists who have played there. And they are legion.

"There's Duke Ellington and the time Daniel helped Ellington's freezing posterior. 'Yeah, Duke was a regular. A real right on, right on guy,' said Daniel. 'When he played one night, he said, "Damn, that stool is cold." When I got him the blanket, I asked him if he was goin' to play the "A Train" for me. He said, "Yeah, I'll play the 'A Train.' I'm warm now."'

"But it's all in a day's and night's work for a man who came from Macon, Ga., at 14 and lived in La Grange, where he earned money cutting grass. After being wounded in World War II, Daniel was discharged and returned to Chicago's South Side, landing a job coaching kids for the park district. Later, he was transferred to the old band shell.

"Although the new shell has its advantages, there's regret in his voice when he says, 'The old band shell was a beautiful place, a lovely place. It was like a knight on a white horse that I would visit every day…. Artist? Yeah, I guess I'm an artist. You need to be an artist at life and at work.'" [2]

An empty stage awaits the musicians, 1989. The behind-the-scenes preparation at the Festival involves dozens of skilled staff.

Daily Life at the Concerts in the 1980s TIDBITS FROM THE ARCHIVES

The ambiance at Grant Park concerts has often been a balance of elegant and casual, as in this shot of open-air dining in 1984.

Slipping Past the Sword Swallowers and SWAT Teams

"I went to a Grant Park Symphony concert not long ago. How different from the 'tastes' and festivals held earlier this same summer at the very same spot. This is true even though inside every festival there is a concert trying to get out … It's agreeable to have an event at which you don't have to arrive early and leave late to beat the traffic, and which you can get to without slipping past sword swallowers and SWAT teams. It helps keep you from feeling like a tourist in your own hometown." [3]

Float Like a Butterfly, Sting Like a Handel Suite?

"Making his first appearance at a Grant Park Independence Day celebration was Muhammad Ali, who sat next to Mayor Byrne… 'I came to be the grand marshal of the Patriotism Day parade…, I came to see the mayor, and I came to see this,' said Ali, pointing to the sky as a roman candle burst open to the accompaniment of Handel's Royal Fireworks Suite, played by the Grant Park Symphony and conducted by Leonard Slatkin. 'It's terrific,' said Mrs. Byrne. 'Just look at the crowds of happy people.'" [4]

Going Head-to-Head against the CSO—in Softball

Laura Miller, violinist 1988–present, remembers a big win over the CSO. "We've always been used to being the underdogs, and I think that our Grant Park Orchestra softball team was a reflection of that. We had a lot of good players on the team. Every year we held a tournament, and we'd play the Chicago Symphony Orchestra, people from the radio—WFMT—and the stagehands. There were usually three games, and we would always get creamed. The CSO would just pound us. But then suddenly, somehow in the mid-1980s, we finally got on a winning streak. I remember I was pitching. I tried to pitch once before against the CSO, and I was just so stiff that the ball went up into the air. I think I practiced a little bit and loosened up my arm. It is my bow arm, and you would think that that wouldn't be a problem. And we beat them. They were pretty surprised by that. Two years in a row we beat them."

Parents' Debate: Shortstop or the String Section

"Two-year-old Erez Cohen, who 'just loves opera,' was dancing on his dad's shoulders Saturday night at Grant Park as the orchestra played 'Carmen.' The boy, his parents and about 20,000 others were attending the opening of [the] 55th annual Grant Park Concerts series at the Petrillo Music Shell. 'He just loves opera music, and I must be the reason,' said Judith Cohen, of Skokie. Before Erez was born, she said, she would feel her son kicking when she listened to opera....

"Later, Avi Cohen, Erez's father, didn't mind the dancing on his shoulders, but doesn't want his son to become an opera singer—he wants him to be a baseball star. He should still love the opera though, said Judith, 'especially "Carmen."'"[5]

Above: Members of the Grant Park Orchestra softball team in 1988. For many years on the lawn of the Petrillo Bandshell, there was a spirited softball rivalry, featuring games between Grant Park musicians, members of the Chicago Symphony Orchestra, WFMT radio personnel, and Festival technicians.

Below: Buckingham Fountain rises above the crowds heading down to a Grant Park concert in the 1980s.

Experiments in New Music

It may seem unlikely for a free, outdoor, park district- and city-supported summer music festival to be a hotbed of new music and world premieres, but the Grant Park Music Festival was teeming with new sounds in the 1980s. Below are two of the more memorable examples.

William Bolcom

The American composer, William Bolcom, whose operas *McTeague, A View from the Bridge,* and *A Wedding* (created in collaboration with filmmaker Robert Altman) have been among the most acclaimed new American operas in recent decades, also won the Pulitzer Prize for his vast song cycle, *Songs of Innocence and Experience,* based on the poems of William Blake. The work received its American premiere at the Grant Park Music Festival in the summer of 1986 and received the following review:

"Bolcom attempts to meet the poet [William Blake] on his own, wildly eclectic terms, by casting his magnum opus (25 years in the making) as a largescale synthesis of musical styles—from Mahlerian Romanticism and modernist idioms, to country, folk, swing, bluegrass and, in his grand choral finale, reggae. The performing palette is similarly vast, involving some 250 musicians, including rock singer. At three hours' duration, 'Songs of Innocence' may be the longest song cycle in music history....

"What makes the score finally successful—indeed, I would be willing to call it one of the finest and most important new American works of the decade—are two factors. First, [Bolcom] has the facility to write well in every idiom—he's no pasticcheur. Second, his ideas are so effectively (indeed wittily) juxtaposed that the listener is kept in more or less constant expectation, despite some weak pages in the latter two-thirds of the piece. 'Songs of Innocence' ultimately is far more than the sum of its crazy-quilt parts.

"It remains only to say that this poignant, moving, exhilarating, thought-provoking piece is typical of the enterprise and imagination of Grant Park Concerts' artistic director, Steven Ovitsky. His faith in the evocative power of Bolcom's score was borne out by the accomplished performance. The singers and instrumentalists made an impressive ensemble and they rose to every musical challenge with skill and dedication." [6]

John Adams

A regular presence at Grant Park concerts since the early 1980s, Adams has been a major force on the American classical-music scene, with groundbreaking works such as his operas *Nixon in China* and *Doctor Atomic.* His Pulitzer Prize–winning piece, *On the Transmigration of Souls,* a choral work commemorating the victims of September 11, was performed by the Grant Park Music Festival in 2005. The performance of his work *Grand Pianola Music* was reviewed by John von Rhein in the *Chicago Tribune:*

"Adams, a young San Francisco–based composer, was introduced to Grant Park last year with his big chorus-orchestra piece, 'Harmonium.' 'Grand Pianola Music' extends the minimalist gestures and techniques of that absorbing work, using slightly smaller forces…'Grand Pianola Music' (a great title by the way) begins in the blissed-out style of one of Steve Reich's trance pieces, with the gentle, rhythmic pulsing of keyboards and winds. But then the women start vocalizing wordlessly, Swingle-style; slow ripples of tonic-dominant spread outwards across the brasses and percussion; long crescendi and decrescendi build dramatic tension and release, like inexorable ocean tides; climactic sprays of piano arpeggios finally signal what Adams calls 'The Tune.'…'Grand Pianola Music' is refreshing evidence that there is still a world of creative possibility lurking in the good old major triad." [7]

Opposite: The Petrillo Bandshell offers dramatic views of Chicago's continually evolving skyline, seen here in 1989, with Two Prudential Plaza under construction to the right of the original Prudential Building and left of the Aon (former Standard Oil) Building. The city's innovative architecture helps set the mood for audiences to hear new and experimental music, such as key new works by William Bolcom and John Adams presented by the Festival in the 1980s.

The Musicians Talk Shop

Nothing compares to hearing directly from the members of the Grant Park Orchestra and Chorus about what it is like to put the Festival together over the years.

Alexander Belavsky, violinist, 1979–present: "I think the orchestra can be best described as a multicell organism. We can easily adapt to so many conductors and pieces, and our success comes because we are extremely flexible. We can easily translate different styles and emotions, and that's why we succeed."

Andrea Swan, principal keyboards, 1983–present: "Every year at Petrillo, we would inevitably have an extremely hot and humid stretch of weather, the typical Chicago summer heat. During concerts, small bugs would be flying around in the heat of the stage lights, die, and land by the thousands on the piano. I can remember several performances where I literally had to brush off the keys during the rests because they were covered with bugs!

"We discovered that using a harpsichord wasn't always the best idea at Petrillo. I remember playing Vivaldi's *Four Seasons* with Joseph Silverstein, who was the conductor and soloist. When I played the A for the orchestra to tune, it was literally so flat that everyone gasped, and I ended up leaving out large parts of the harpsichord part because it sounded so bad. After that, we rented a keyboard and used the harpsichord setting!"

Fritz Kaenzig, principal tuba player, 1984–present: "It has always been a great group to get together. At the beginning of the summer, everyone is so excited to see each other. You are excited to see your buddies back again for the summer festival, although it is definitely an intense schedule. The biggest difference is the amount of music. It's incredible, the amount of music that we go through in a summer. As a tuba player, when I get all my music, I have a pretty thick pile. Then I look at what the woodwinds and the violinists have, and I feel glad that I play

Left: Members of the Grant Park Orchestra cello section (clockwise from top left): Michael Geller, Linc Smelser, and Dale Newton.

Right: Percussionist Michael Green performs Carl Vine's *Percussion Symphony.*

tuba. I am pretty amazed at what they are able to do, even when we rehearse programs out of sequence. I can't think of anyone that just goes in and puts in their time. This group has a lot of pride.

"Thinking back to Leonard Slatkin, when he was the principal conductor with the orchestra, I could really tell that he learned his craft of rehearsing with the Grant Park model. Conductors and musicians both have to go in and be very efficient and not waste time because there is not a lot of time to get things prepared.

"I remember one time in the Petrillo, we had an invasion of bugs. We would usually get it once a season, and this particular time was a bit much. I was chairman of the orchestra committee at the time. We were trying to warm up, and with every breath we would take in a mouthful of bugs. It was like it was raining bugs!"

James Paul, principal guest conductor, 1999–2004; he first conducted at Grant Park in 1986: "The first time that I came to Grant Park to conduct, I came early enough to hear a rehearsal of the chorus. I always ask the chorus master to take the first part of the rehearsal so I can really listen to the chorus and see how they have been trained. It gives you a really good insight on how to approach the group. Choruses tend to bond with their conductors. Orchestras may or may not like conductors, but choruses tend to bond very much with their conductors.

"I remember that they were rehearsing a Vaughn Williams piece, and all of the sudden Thomas Peck said to me, 'Would you like to lead the chorus?' I didn't expect to conduct that night, but it would have been impolite to not accept the invitation. I remember watching the chorus, they sang very beautifully, but I could see them watching Tommy to see whether he agreed with what I was doing or not. He nodded his head, and everything was fine, and I remember that I breathed a huge sigh of relief."

A brass ensemble plays on the lawn of the Petrillo Bandshell, circa 1985.

Great Artists of the 1980s

During the 1980s the Festival presented pianists Walter Klein (1980 and 1981), Lorin Hollander (1987), Andre Watts (1988), and Garrick Ohlsson (1989); clarinetist Richard Stoltzman (1987); the Vermeer Quartet (1984); baritone Robert Merrill (1984); bass Paul Plishka (1982, 1984, 1985, and 1989); soprano Arleen Auger (1983 and 1985); and harmonica player Corky Siegel (1981 and 1985).

Zdenek Macal

Conductor, 1983–1991

This Czech-born conductor became the principal conductor of the Prague Symphony Orchestra but left a promising career there after the Soviet-led invasion of 1968. He made his American debut with the Chicago Symphony in 1972, but the Grant Park Symphony gave him his first permanent position in the United States. Subsequently, he became the music director of the Milwaukee Symphony Orchestra from 1986 to 1993.

Zdenek Macal, who became principal conductor with the Grant Park Music Festival in 1985, leads the orchestra as renowned clarinetist Richard Stoltzman performs Mozart's Clarinet Concerto in 1987.

FROM THE ARCHIVES

The *Chicago Tribune* described Macal's effect on the orchestra:

"Euphoria seems to be typical of the reaction of most orchestra members wherever Macal conducts. 'Denny is a genuinely nice man who really knows his music—there is no faking whatsoever,' reports a violinist of the Grant Park Symphony. A veteran of the world's podiums—he has conducted more than 135 orchestras on nearly every continent—the 49-year-old maestro possesses the elusive combination of personality and musicianship that earns respect on both sides of the footlights.

"'If you can create a sense of "family" among, say, 10 of the 100 musicians, this is the nicest prize your work could receive,' says the well-traveled maestro. Macal...is busy putting his reputation as a sort of musical Dale Carnegie to productive use, here and abroad." [8]

Robert Shaw

Choral and Orchestra Conductor, 1985–1987

In a career that spanned sixty years, Shaw transformed choral conducting into an art and raised its standards to a new level. He founded the Robert Shaw Chorale in New York in 1948 and conducted it for twenty years, then served as music director of the San Diego Symphony Orchestra. Shaw was then recruited by George Szell to conduct the choral section of the Cleveland Symphony Orchestra, where he reshaped its chorus. He then accepted the directorship of the Atlanta Symphony Orchestra in 1967.

Robert Shaw conducts the Grant Park Orchestra in 1986.

FROM THE ARCHIVES

Chicago Sun-Times critic Robert Marsh praised Shaw's appearance with the Festival in 1987:

"Shaw is two years older than Leonard Bernstein, although he doesn't look it, and he might be called the dean of American conductors, except that he probably would hate the idea. He is one of the elder statesmen of American music, and he brings to whatever he does the authority that comes with years of study and experience. The Grant Park Symphony plays for him with the enthusiasm and complete cooperation that come from respect, and he, in turn, leads it with complete dedication to the task at hand. His back inspires confidence.... Shaw's extraordinary gifts as a choral conductor were conspicuous in his phrasing, his shaping of long lyric line and his wonderfully expressive touch with a good tune."[9]

Andre Watts

Pianist, 1988

Born in Germany, Watts studied music in Philadelphia where he appeared with the Philadelphia Orchestra at age nine. In 1963, at the age of sixteen, he appeared in a televised performance of a Young People's concert with Leonard Bernstein and the New York Philharmonic. He has since performed on the most prestigious concert stages with many of the world's best-known orchestras and conductors.

FROM THE ARCHIVES

The *Chicago Sun-Times* wrote of Watts's appearance:

"Andre Watts, one of Ravinia's long-established superstars, made his Grant Park debut Wednesday with his friend George Cleve conducting the Grant Park Symphony. It was an event that gave you a variety of things to think about. Watts' reputation drew a large audience, and the festive mood of the holiday weekend still prevailed.

"If you wanted to turn philosophical, the concert might be taken as the food for the spirit booth among the rival offerings of food for the stomach. Basically, the park concerts and Taste of Chicago are at odds with one another. The concert generates sweet harmonies, the festival of food produces noisy distractions—like the off-stage tambourine band that seemed to be driving the musicians slightly daffy during the opening part of the piano concerto....

"Watts, who is one of the most completely relaxed and professional pianists in the business, played beautifully. The opening bars of the concerto were punctuated by an indignant woman nearby telling a guard she belonged to the Grant Park Concerts Society and was entitled to a seat, but Watts and Beethoven were in another world.

"That is the essence of what happened. Watts, Cleve and the orchestra built a little world of the Beethoven Fourth Piano Concerto, retreated into it through concentration, and invited you to join them. It was a world of refined lyric drama in which Watts' playing was truly elegant and impassioned. The real test of the soloist in this work is the slow movement which must be sustained and carried to a climax with very little assistance from the orchestra. Watts managed this easily." [10]

Pianist Andre Watts's 1988 Grant Park performance drew enthusiastic reviews.

They Don't Have This in Iowa: Urban Edge

Prominent Chicago journalist Richard Longworth, who among other subjects covered the tearing down of the Berlin Wall and the collapse of communism for the *Chicago Tribune* in the 1980s, talks about discovering the appeal of urban concertgoing in Grant Park during the same decade.

LOOKING BACK

"When the kids left home, we sold the house in Evanston and moved back down to Chicago, to an apartment near Wrigley Field. That was pretty much the time when I first became aware of the Grant Park Music Festival, and we became regular concertgoers at the old Petrillo Bandshell. I loved that band shell because of the whole experience. It was a little bit like going out to Wrigley Field on a nice summer afternoon and sitting in the upper deck. It was the whole urban experience.

"You go to Grant Park at the old Petrillo Bandshell or to the new Pritzker Pavilion today, and you are sitting there in the midst of the city and the city noise, including cars honking and the occasional siren as part of the experience. You see this sensational stage set, backdrop, and skyline darkening, combined with the lights in the skyscrapers nearby, all the while being surrounded by the city, and you are listening to this wonderful music. I'm still a small-town boy, and I think to myself, they don't have this in Iowa. So, the only way to describe it is that it is the full urban experience.

"As a journalist, it's important to remember the history of Grant Park's free concerts, because it was a civic idea. It does go back to Julius Rosenwald and to the original thought of preserving the lakefront. Grant Park is Chicago's front yard, and the importance of this piece of real estate to the city, and how Millennium Park grew out of this idea is completely separate from the music. Would we have free concerts in Chicago for seventy-five years if they weren't held in Grant Park, if Grant Park hadn't been there?

A cheerful group gathers for a photo on the Petrillo lawn, circa 1985.

What is the connection between this musical institution and this geographical institution?

"There is now a city population in Chicago, following the period of white flight that has begun to be reversed as older people have come back into the city, and people are raising their kids here because they want to be city people. And there is a city sensibility, sort of an edginess to taste that you don't find in the suburbs. You get storefront theaters in Chicago and dinner theaters in the suburbs. Grant Park programming reflects what people in the city want, and it is edgy, more modern, and more experimental. There is a challenge to it and an intellectual capacity with music that you haven't heard before. There is the new immigrant population who want to be part of this, who want to give their kids the experience of hearing quality music."

CHAPTER EIGHT

The 1990s

New Names, New Works: Stirring Things Up before the Millennium

Since the Festival began in 1935, each decade has brought its own unique set of changes to Chicago's lakefront and the Grant Park Music Festival. But perhaps no decade has seen such a stirring up of the way things are done as the 1990s. During the 1990s, the Festival gained a new name, a new long-serving principal conductor, and chorus director, and a transformed leadership structure. And finally, after six decades of debate and declarations about the need for a truly first-rate band shell, plans moved ahead on the construction of an ambitious new music pavilion in a state-of-the-art park for the coming millennium.

A crowd gathers on a warm summer evening to hear the music radiate through the city.

The Transformation of Grant Park

The city of Chicago as a whole was in the throes of a dizzying transformation and beguiling contradictions during the 1990s. The rising economy and the technology boom spurred a burst of ambitious urban planning.

FROM THE ARCHIVES

Capturing the ethos of the era, Chicago historian Donald Miller described the city's state of flux at the turn of the millennium:

"Chicago has changed. No longer Carl Sandburg's brawny 'hog butcher to the world,' it is now the globe's candy capital, where more sweets are made than in Hershey, Pa. A cholera-infested mud flat in its early days, it has been transformed into one of the world's handsomest cities. Yet to a remarkable degree, Chicago is what it was, its character forged by its lusty origins. A magnet for hustlers and visionaries, the city has been forever in flux, always re-inventing itself, as new groups—Syrians, Mexicans, Serbs and Vietnamese—continue to gather to its promise.

"It's a tough, straight-talking town, 'too impatient for hypocrisy,' as Norman Mailer famously described it, 'in love with honest plunder.' And it remains a city of deep contrasts, renowned for its reckless cupidity and monumental corruption. No other metropolis has a stronger civic spirit; its business barons are modern Medici in their public largesse and self-promoting splendor. Chicago's new immigrants, like those who came before them, feel the sting of prejudice, but many of them embrace their new homeland with heart-stabbing fervor.... In its short, explosive history, Chicago has built some of the world's most spectacular engineering and architectural achievements and has been the nurturing ground, as well, for far-reaching experiments in social justice. This tradition of doing things in a big way endures. Millennium Park, the city's new lakefront pleasure ground, with works of eye-popping audacity by Los Angeles architect Frank Gehry and London sculptor Anish Kapoor, has reaffirmed Chicago's reputation as a center of architectural experimentation."[1]

INVENTIVE PROGRAMMING

Vitality was a hallmark of the Festival as well. Artistically, the Festival wove together disparate strands while maintaining a deep commitment to an ambitious classical-music core. The decade opened with the 1990 season kickoff, a three-hour concert version of the formidable and seldom performed Russian opera *Prince Igor.* It saw visits from mezzo-soprano Frederica von Stade, balanced by Rosemary Clooney, while Chicago Cubs announcer Jack Brickhouse's narration of *Casey at the Bat* performed with the orchestra was juxtaposed with visits by Maxim Shostakovich, who conducted works by his father, Dmitry Shostakovich.

Trumpeter Doc Severinsen and the funk band Poi Dog Pondering took the same stage as soprano Deborah Voigt and violinist Joshua Bell. Throughout the 1990s, as the Chicago Bulls charged to six NBA basketball championships, the Festival's home, the Petrillo Bandshell, became the gathering place for nearly annual frenzied victory celebrations.

To help celebrate the Festival's sixtieth season, a beloved pianist returned, bringing with him some of the frenzied fascination—and immense crowds—of his historic appearance four decades earlier.

FROM THE ARCHIVES

"Cliburn...was emerging from semi-retirement to open the 60th anniversary season of the Grant Park Music Festival...Playing the same concerto he had performed at his Chicago debut at Grant Park in July 1958—three months after winning the gold medal and the hearts of millions at Moscow's Tchaikovsky Competition—the lanky Texas pianist proved that, whatever problems had forced his withdrawal from the concert stage two decades into his career, he was well-prepared to compete with the Van Cliburn who once so captured the American imagination.

"The important thing was that the Van Cliburn the piano world remembers so fondly was back in form....[He] sent the crowd (official estimates put the attendance at just below 350,000) home happy."[2]

Left: Following a rehearsal for the 1990 opening-night program, the cast of a concert version of Borodin's opera *Prince Igor,* poses for a photo. From left to right, vocalists Dimitri Gnatiuk, Oksana Yatsenko, Paul Plishka, conductor Zdenek Macal, and Svetlana Kislaya.

Right: A musician's-eye view of a concert in the Petrillo Bandshell, circa 1990.

Great Artists of the 1990s

Besides Van Cliburn's triumphant return in 1994, Festival audiences in the nineties were treated to appearances by Rosemary Clooney and Joshua Bell, among many others.

Rosemary Clooney

Vocalist and Actress, 1996

The spirited and resilient singer, who shared the stage with the likes of Bing Crosby and Marlene Dietrich during her storied career, performed with the Festival during the last decade of her life.

FROM THE ARCHIVES

Clooney received a glowing review from the *Chicago Sun-Times's* Bill Zwecker:

"Interspersed between such Clooney classics as 'Foggy Day,' 'Come Rain or Come Shine' and her first novelty hit, 1951's 'Come On A My House,' the 68-year-old singer shared amusing anecdotes about everyone from her longtime arranger Nelson Riddle to Judy Garland to Ira Gershwin. But it was Clooney's musical gift— a voice that remains rich and glowing, even as it has narrowed in range—that provided a program as uplifting to the soul as the evening's balmy weather was soothing to the body....

"It is not easy to turn Grant Park into an intimate cabaret, but Clooney did just that Friday as she gracefully shared her music, humor and personal insights with an audience that had witnessed her 50-year transition from big band 'girl singer' to pop sensation to 'the woman who is delighted to be known as George Clooney's aunt.' Rosemary Clooney also knows something else. She understands that a true balladeer tells a story as much as he or she sings it. The contemporary Clooney's voice has been finely seasoned by a life that has known sadness, despair as well as triumph and joy." [3]

Singer Rosemary Clooney brought a cabaret ambiance to Grant Park during her highly lauded 1996 performance with the Festival.

Joshua Bell

Violinist, 1997

Violinist Joshua Bell's 1997 opening-night performance was a triumph, although his appearance was a result of inventive, last-minute scheduling.

The American-born violinist began taking violin lessons at the age of four. By age fourteen Bell had appeared as a soloist with the Philadelphia Orchestra under Riccardo Muti. He has since performed with almost all of the world's major orchestras and conductors. He performed the solo part on John Corigliano's Oscar-winning soundtrack from the movie *The Red Violin*.

FROM THE ARCHIVES

As an example of the Festival's constant capacity to adapt to change, Joshua Bell, one of the decade's biggest guest artists, came to Grant Park as the result of a mad scramble to replace the last-minute cancellation of another renowned artist, Russian baritone Dmitri Hvorostovsky, just days before the gala concert at the beginning of 1997. The frenzy was recounted in full in a contemporary newspaper story:

"The head of the Grant Park Music Festival started calling for a little help from his friends in the music business last Tuesday, and by Friday night, a young virtuoso was winging his way from New York to the rescue. It's the kind of situation that gives concert managers ulcers.

"James Palermo, artistic and general director of the Grant Park Music Festival, received a phone call Tuesday from the London-based managers of Siberian baritone Dmitri Hvorostovsky. The young baritone, scheduled as the big-name centerpiece of the Grant Park Symphony's gala season opening concert on Saturday, was ailing. It was an upper respiratory problem, his managers told Palermo, and he had a doctor's appointment on Wednesday.

If the news was bad, Hvorostovsky might have to drop out. After his doctor told him to rest his voice for a week, Hvorostovsky canceled his Grant Park engagement.

"Grant Park had exactly two days to line up a suitable big-name replacement. But fate smiled on the festival, and at the last minute, Palermo was able to book young virtuoso Joshua Bell, who agreed to perform the Mendelssohn Violin Concerto at the Saturday gala opening-night concert.

"Cancellations are an unwelcome but common problem in the classical music business, which schedules its seasons years in advance. Some unreliable artists cancel at the appearance of a hangnail. But even the most conscientious artists are prey to flu bugs and other germs that care little for full calendars.

"The Grant Park performance created a mad time crunch for Bell, who is performing in London this week. Before Palermo's call, he was planning to leave New York on Saturday and rest up a day in London.... By all accounts, Saturday night's gala went off beautifully. The weather was mild and fireworks at Navy Pier began just as the concert's final note was fading away."[4]

Behind the Wheel:
Changing How the Festival Is Run

The complex question of who "runs" the Festival underwent major changes in the 1990s. Since the 1930s the Chicago Park District had provided the majority of the funding for the concerts, following the arrangement that James Petrillo had helped to negotiate. The Park District not only paid the musicians but provided the marketing, oversaw orchestra auditions, and approved each season's schedule and list of guest artists.

Beginning in 1977 a new organization, The Grant Park Concerts Society, was formed. For twenty seasons it served as the fundraising arm of the Festival; it also produced much of the Festival's marketing and oversaw the membership program. The Concerts Society hosted fundraisers and sold Festival memberships to help supplement the Park District's funding (which hovered between $1.5 and $2 million per year). In the spring of 1996, Park District and Festival staff made the decision to cut ties with the Grant Park Concerts Society and bring all the marketing and fund-raising in-house, a decision that created a burst of debate in the newspapers.

Behind the scenes the Festival was consumed with other crucial changes as well. On the leadership front Catherine Cahill was hired as general manager and artistic director in 1991, followed by James W. Palermo in 1995, both of whom daringly embraced change. Artistically, Hugh Wolff served as principal conductor from 1994 to 1997, followed by a long, meticulous search and the naming of Carlos Kalmar as principal conductor in 2000.

One of Cahill's first initiatives was a name change: after six decades, the Festival officially became a "Festival." For much of its history it had been referred to as simply the Grant Park Concerts, but in the spring of 1992, the series officially became the "Grant Park Music Festival, Summer Home of the Grant Park Symphony

Hugh Wolff served as principal conductor from 1994 to 1997.

Orchestra and Chorus," although the "Summer Home" epithet soon fell by the wayside.

By the end of the decade, the Park District sought to broaden the governance of the Festival. The Park District reached out to the Chicago Department of Cultural Affairs under the leadership of Commissioner Lois Weisberg and developed an arrangement whereby that city department would help to oversee some of the artistic and administrative facets of running the Festival. At the same time, the Festival gained legal non-profit status. The result was that the Festival became a distinct non-profit arts organization that continued to receive funding from the Chicago Park District; raised most of the rest of its funding through memberships, corporate and individual donations, sponsorships, grants, and broadcast fees; and received logistical and in-kind support from the Chicago Department of Cultural Affairs.

Putting a Stamp on the Festival

Catherine Cahill

As manager and artistic director of the Festival from 1991 to 1994, Catherine Cahill sought to bring a number of changes to the Festival, many of which are described in this *Chicago Sun-Times* article:

"'I'm trying to do a variety of things with the repertoire this season,' said Cahill, who came to Grant Park after five years as associate artistic director of the Santa Fe Chamber Music Festival. 'I wanted to tempt a number of different palates. I have a strong commitment to American music, but there has to be a healthy balance maintained between new, contemporary repertoire and the standard warhorses that people know and love and come to expect.'"[5]

"Cahill's improvements to the festival during her three-year stay have been many and varied: flower boxes now add color to the stage, the trees surrounding the concert site are festooned with lights, and the public seating is freshly painted. Cahill also worked with the festival's catering company to create a sit-down restaurant in the park where once there were only trailers and booths dispensing food. And she says the festival will get a newly designed and more attractive program book this year. But perhaps her biggest coups have been on the programming front: She spent most of her tenure at the festival wooing the Saint Paul Chamber Orchestra's respected young music director and conductor Hugh Wolff, and earlier this year she succeeded in signing Wolff to a three-year contract as principal conductor of the Grant Park Symphony Orchestra. Furthermore, she nabbed famed pianist Van Cliburn to join conductor Leonard Slatkin in kicking off the festival's 60th season. Cahill also broadened the spectrum to include theater and dance events where budgets would allow."[6]

Members of the Boitsov Classical Ballet perform at a Concert for Kids at the Petrillo Bandshell in 1991.

James W. Palermo's Long-lasting Touch on the Festival

James W. Palermo came to the Grant Park Music Festival in 1995, after having helped lead the Louisville Orchestra and the Evansville Philharmonic. He became the longest-serving leader of the Festival since Walter L. Larsen who served from 1944 to 1964.

FROM THE ARCHIVES

The Grant Park Music Festival never fails to provide surprising logistical challenges, and the *Chicago Tribune* describes one of Palermo's first big feats in overcoming obstacles as the artistic and general director.

"Although Palermo has occupied his post for little more than a month, he already has undergone his baptism by fire, having presided over the city's record-busting blues and gospel festivals. Thus far, he says, he feels more like a facilities manager than a general director. But he's not complaining....

"Of course, Palermo is well aware that Grant Park, being an outdoor facility with no covered seating, is wholly at the mercy

of the storm gods—not to mention the traffic noise of a busy urban setting. The trick, as he sees it, is to minimize these disadvantages by making the concert experience as attractive to as many kinds of listeners as possible." [7]

IN HIS OWN WORDS

Palermo recalls his goals for the Festival:

"One of the things that I've tried to do, that not many organizations do, is to develop programs that are very site specific. For example, one that was really exciting to me to put together was the Brazilian jazz singer Luciana Souza with the Chicago Latino dance company Luna Negra and the Grant Park Orchestra for the 2009 season. Anytime you collaborate with an organization in town, I think it is great for both organizations because what you are doing is saying we aren't competitive, we're collaborative. As a city and Park District program, you have to be collaborative.

"Another great example was working with the Joffrey Ballet to help celebrate their fiftieth anniversary in 2006—that was

Looking out at the crowds at the Petrillo Bandshell. The Petrillo served as the Festival's home for twenty-six years, from 1978 to 2004. Photo circa 2000.

a fantastic thing for both of us. Likewise, pairing the Tibetan Monks with Mozart's *Requiem* in 2005 was a provocative project; some people loved it and some people didn't like it at all. The point was that we tried something, and it resonated currently with what's happening in Tibet, with China and with the role of spirituality in our lives today. It's interesting now to look at Barack Obama and what he is doing to embrace other cultures and religions. It takes a certain amount of courage to do that, and also you realize you are serving a larger social cultural goal than just putting on a concert.

"The music festival has been supported by the Park District for seventy-five years, and they give us an incredible amount of money—$2 million—and with that come all sorts of inevitable issues that you have to confront when you work in government. Most of what the Park District does really well doesn't necessarily correspond to what we do. For example, I have been through probably twelve to fifteen different sets of contract negotiations with various musician unions, working with labor attorneys who are labor counsel for the Park District. It's an immense amount of information to understand: how people function in the arts, how their jobs are organized.

"People often wonder why the musicians can't work forty hours a week. Most of our musicians work eighteen to twenty hours a week, and that's very much full time in the music business. Now, if you looked at it as a pure business model, you would say that's crazy. But if you gave the musicians a forty-hour work week—forty hours of people being on stage—they would be dead in two or three weeks. They just can't do that, they also have to go home and practice the music so when they do have rehearsals, they are ready to go.

"Thinking back to my very first concert as artistic and general manager in 1995, I learned something important. The program was with Frederica von Stade, who was one of America's greatest

Artistic and General Director James W. Palermo served from 1995 to 2009, and among other accomplishments, helped guide the Festival's move to Millennium Park.

mezzo-sopranos from the 1970s through the early 1990s. She was the 'it girl' of opera, and she opened our season in 1995. I was a little starstruck. I remember meeting her and just being so awed by her: she was a famous singer and she was so nice.

"I will never forget, we had a reception after the concert at the restaurant La Strada. We were standing in a receiving line, and a woman came up and said, 'Miss von Stade, I remember hearing you sing Mimi in Puccini's *La Bohème* twenty years ago, and I have never forgotten it! Thank you!' Von Stade graciously smiled and thanked her, and the woman walked on. I looked at her and said, 'You didn't sing Mimi in *La Bohème,* did you? It's the wrong voice-type for you—it's a soprano role.' She said, 'No, I've never sung it, but why tell her that and ruin the experience for her?' She was so concerned about being nice to the lady that she wouldn't want to embarrass her by telling her that she had the wrong role. She was so classy and so lovely. That was a great way to start my tenure here."

Daily Life at the Concerts in the 1990s IN THEIR OWN WORDS

The Petrillo Tanning Salon

Mary Stolper, principal flutist, 2002–present, remembers a shining moment at the band shell:

"One funny story I remember: one of the first things that Catherine Cahill did when she took over as general manager was to really spruce up the place, the old Petrillo Bandshell. Flowers were added at the front of the stage. All sorts of things to help dress it up and make it look elegant.

"One day we came to rehearsal, and they had painted all the metal chairs in the audience from a gray to a kind of beige color. They were a little brighter and they looked cleaner. It actually had a nice effect. They sat on black asphalt, these chairs, and when it got really hot, that asphalt generated a lot of heat. Well, during a break in rehearsal, when we went downstairs to the dressing room, we noticed that Gladys Elliot, principal oboe at that time, looked as if she'd been under a sun lamp for hours. She was really pretty severely sunburned. In fact, she was sent to the hospital.

Sure enough, several other people in the orchestra with fair skin were burned as well.

"It turned out that the reflection of all those newly painted, lighter chairs reflected a lot more sunlight into the shell and caused all these musicians to get sunburned. From that day forward we all had to wear sunscreen while we sat in the shell. All because of those chairs! We couldn't believe it. That was the only explanation: the brightness of five thousand beige chairs was throwing light into the band shell and burning the musicians!"

Flexing Musical Muscles

Brian Ferguson, bassist, 1974–present, talks about the preparation it takes to play a piece:

"I teach a lot, and I use the analogy that musicians are actually athletes but using a different set of muscle groups.

When the Petrillo Bandshell was built in 1978, it was designed to be easily disassembled at the end of each summer, although it was never taken apart. Photo circa 1980.

That covers a lot of territory because in football season you look at these athletes who have these humongous moves and things that they do with these large muscle groups, and we're doing it all with the small muscle groups. There's also the feeling of the music and the thought process that goes through that as you are playing. For bass players, usually we aren't supposed to be playing a melody, but the melody is usually being played by somebody else. We're playing an underlying role, and what we have to think about is how do we make that melody sound the best that it can? How can we shape our phrases to make them sound better?"

Bolero in the Rain

Peter Szczepanek, cellist, 1983–present, remembers a charming moment of weather-induced solidarity:

"I remember when we did a performance of Ravel's *Bolero* at the Petrillo, and it started raining—without a strong wind,

straight down, so we could keep playing, since the orchestra wasn't getting wet. The piece starts very quietly with just the snare drum playing the bolero rhythm. Instruments are added on, and the piece gradually crescendos throughout, for about fifteen or eighteen minutes, getting more intense. Because of the rain, people started walking up towards the edge of the stage, umbrellas and all, just trying to escape the rain the best they could. It was a great experience. As the piece crescendoed, so did the number of people who gathered at the edge of the stage. By the end it was just this big, shared event. There was a very unique, communal feeling, having all these people huddled together, up close to the stage.

"We have always been so affected by the weather; we have such a relationship with it. One of the things we love about this job is being out in the elements. If we had to be indoors all the time, this job would lose some of its uniqueness. Instead we get to spend our summers outdoors, and we get to watch the city and the people in the audience."

The Petrillo Bandshell provided a unique blend of casual concertgoing mixed with high level performances and programming. Photos circa 1995.

Secrets of the Music Library

One of the lesser known facets of the Festival is the fact that, tucked away backstage, the Festival has its own music library, with thousands of scores and a small team of librarians who undertake the task of preparing scores. The Grant Park library is overseen by Grant Park Orchestra violinist Michael Shelton who speaks about how the library functions:

"It is cost effective to have a library because a lot of the music we play can be purchased. If we didn't purchase it, then we would have to get new parts every time we played a piece. In the library, we do all the work of putting bowings in and markings. We do purchase a lot of music. We have a lot of music that is out of print now, as well as a lot of music from the Soviet Union that has gone back into copyright. It used to be in the public domain but the GAP Treaty put a lot of Soviet music back into copyright."

Battling the Lawnmowers

Grant Park Music Festival Artistic and General Director James W. Palermo describes one of his battles to obtain silence during rehearsals:

"One of the banes of my existence was that we could never quite work effectively with the people who cut the grass. The orchestra would just get started, and suddenly there'd be this terrible, 'RrrrrRrrrr...RrrrrRrrrr...' out on the lawn. I'm sure the orchestra and chorus probably laughed when they saw me run out there shouting, 'No!! You've got to stop! They are in rehearsal!' The people cutting the grass had no concept that you have a rehearsal and it has to be quiet. I'd make phone calls, give them the rehearsal schedule for the entire summer, and say, 'Would it be possible to schedule the leaf blowers and grass cutters around this?' Then I would think, 'Okay, I did it! Problem solved.' But the next day, during rehearsal, there it would be: 'RrrrrRrrrr...RrrrrRrrrr...' And I'd be running out into the grass all over again, shouting, pulling my hair out."

A dramatic view from behind the percussion section at the Petrillo Bandshell, 1984.

Adventurous Programming in the 1990s

The crowds on the lawn at the Petrillo Bandshell for the Grant Park Music Festival concerts were often a reflection of Chicago's vast and varied population. The lawn had space for more than thirty thousand people. Photo circa 1995.

It's easy to neglect new works by living composers, especially for an outdoor, summertime festival, where audiences supposedly crave frivolity and the familiar.

As music critic Alex Ross notes in his highly acclaimed history of classical composition in the twentieth-century, *The Rest Is Noise,* new work often, "sounds like noise to many. It is a largely untamed art, an unassimilated underground. While the splattered abstractions of Jackson Pollack sell on the art market for a hundred million dollars or more, and while experimental works by Matthew Barney or David Lynch are analyzed in college dorms across the land, the equivalent in music still sends ripples of unease through concert audiences…Classical music is stereotyped as an art of the dead, a repertory that begins with Bach and terminates with Mahler and Puccini. People are sometimes surprised to learn that composers are still writing at all. Yet these sounds are hardly alien. Atonal chords crop up in jazz; avant-garde sounds appear in Hollywood film scores; minimalism has marked rock, pop, and dance music from the Velvet Underground onward…Music is always migrating from its point of origin to its destiny in someone's fleeting moment of experience—last night's concert, tomorrow's solitary jog."[8]

The Grant Park Music Festival has very often found a way to include a healthy helping of contemporary music. In 1992 alone there were nine Grant Park premiers and eight Chicago premiers, including works by such composers as Alfred Schnittke, Stephen Paul, William Schuman, and Roberto Sierra. What follows are some of the more interesting examples of composers whose works were presented at the Festival in the 1990s, each of whom brought remarkably unique sounds to Chicago's lakefront concert series.

Ray Wilding-White

Wilding-White was a student of Aaron Copland and Luigi Dallapiccola. He came to Chicago in 1967 to teach composition and establish an electronic-music studio at DePaul University. He also developed programming for WFMT radio and recorded *Music Chicago Style,* a history of music in the city. His *Concerto for Violin and Small Orchestra* was performed by the Festival in 1991. The *Chicago Tribune* described this exceptional world premiere at the Festival:

"Wilding-White is one of Chicago's true Renaissance men who, despite his many activities, has managed to keep writing music at a steady pace. The violin concerto is the first big score he has given us in years.

"As one who has admired many of Wilding-White's scores, I must confess to finding the concerto an oddly schizophrenic affair. The violinist emerged as a Jekyll-and-Hyde figure who held your attention only when he was being wicked: Witness the wild violin-and-percussion cadenza that, among its other Cagean gimmicks, required the concertmaster to roll a pair of dice across the stage. (On Wednesday a passing ambulance added an unscripted wail that the composer may wish to make a permanent part of his piece.)"[9]

Frank Abbinanti

Abbinanti has long been active in new music in Chicago. Starting in the early 1970s, he helped to form the Modern Music Workshop, which presented contemporary pieces at the Museum of Contemporary Art. His cantata, *Like a Force of Light,* was performed in Grant Park in 1991. The *Chicago Tribune* captured the experience in the following review:

"For centuries, Columbus' voyage of discovery has sparked the imagination of forward-looking writers and artists. So, aptly enough, the Grant Park Festival's Columbian quincentenary commission is from one of the city's vanguard young composers, a piece that celebrates the spirit of enlightenment. Frank Abbinanti's cantata debuted Saturday night…Titled 'Like a Force of Light,' it juxtaposes the words of three radical Italian poets in an impassioned appeal to the illuminating power of the intellect.

"The percussion-heavy music begins ferociously, evoking a primordial world. Immediately, the singers babble, croon, and shout, demanding to be heard above the ruckus. The tenor launches into a speech, a passage from Dante, like an agitator at a political rally….In a way, the meaning of the texts from Dante, Giacomo Leopardi, and Pier Paolo Pasolini is secondary to Abbinanti's purpose. Only towards the end does the music soften as the quartet of soloists, in harmony for the first time, ease into a lulling praise of the nurturing moon….Even though non-lyrical and cantankerous at times, 'Like a Force of Light' is riveting in its rage."[10]

Andre Hajdu

Hajdu studied with Szabo (composition) and Kodaly (ethnomusicology). He was involved in research about gypsy musical culture and won first prize with his *Gypsy Cantata* at the World Festival of Youth competition in Warsaw. The five-hundredth anniversary of the expulsion of the Jews from Spain was celebrated with the world premiere of *Dreams of Spain.* The *Chicago Sun-Times* expressed the mood of the piece:

"Sung in Latin, Hebrew and Spanish, the text is powerful, opening with a passage from Genesis in which God reveals that Abraham's children will wander the earth.

"Working mainly with chorus and orchestra, Hajdu deployed his forces for maximum dramatic effect without resorting to the overly obvious….Much of the drama was in the interplay of orchestra and the intense singing of the Grant Park Chorus."[11]

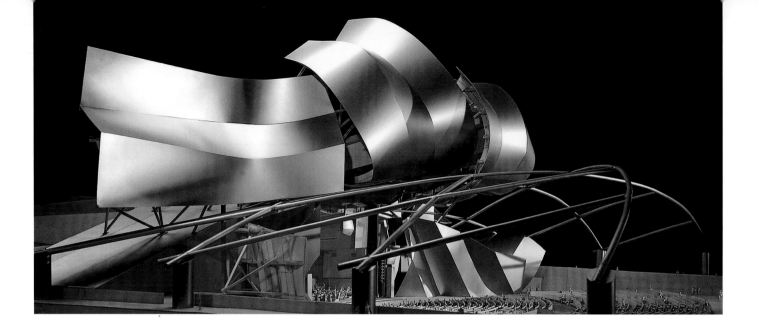

Looking Ahead to the Millennium and a New Home

By the decade's end, a tremendous buzz had begun to build around the rapidly evolving plans for a new concert venue for the Festival in Chicago's Millennium Park. Plans for the park were continually shifting (in large part due to upgrades and more ambitious ideas about the park's scope). By the end of the summer concert season in 1999, there was still expectation that the Festival would be settling into its new home by 2001. While the big move to the Frank Gehry–designed Jay Pritzker Pavilion wouldn't actually happen until three years after that, in the summer of 2004, the anticipation and impatience was palpable in this newspaper account from the decade's end.

FROM THE ARCHIVES

"If all goes according to plan, the orchestra will be playing its 2001 concerts in a new pavilion designed by noted architect Frank Gehry in the new Millennium Park south of Randolph between Michigan Avenue and Lake Shore Drive. 'It seems like the stars are aligning,' said James W. Palermo, the festival's artistic and general manager. 'We've got a new principal conductor looming on the horizon. We're getting a new facility. We're also looking for a new chorus director. All these things will be happening in short succession. It will really signal a new era for the festival.'...

"The city has talked for years about finding a new home for the Grant Park Symphony, but the talk finally has become reality with the Millennium Park project. Palermo is pleased that the designers are taking the festival's musical requirements seriously. 'I've been working with the Millennium Project people closely on the design issues,' he said. 'I've been involved with all of the meetings, working with all the acousticians and architects. They place a very high level of importance on those matters. I'm really confident they're looking at the fact that this is a concert facility, and we have to have an aesthetic and practical environment for audiences and a really superior space acoustically. We all know that sound has always been an issue in years past (at the Petrillo Music Shell). What you're going to experience in the new facility will be light years ahead of where we are now.'"[12]

A model of Frank Gehry's design for the Jay Pritzker Pavilion and BP Bridge for Millennium Park.

Opposite: Millennium Park under construction, 2002. The southeast corner of the construction site is the future home of the Lurie Garden, while the north end is the future home of the Jay Pritzker Pavilion and the Harris Theater for Music and Dance.

CHAPTER NINE

The 2000s

Millennium Park, a Bold New Pavilion, and the Future

The Grant Park Music Festival underwent a change of unimagined proportions in the summer of 2004 when, during the Festival's 70th season, it relocated just a couple of blocks north to Millennium Park's newly opened Jay Pritzker Pavilion. Designed by Frank Gehry, the new pavilion provoked a deluge of awestruck reactions. A visiting journalist from the *New York Times,* for instance, wrote, "I passed beneath Mr. Kapoor's gleaming stainless steel ellipsis [*Cloud Gate*], which forms a grand entrance to the park, and stood agog at the Gehry pavilion. Its maw of curling steel looks like a celestial gateway to another universe."[1]

Crowds for Grant Park concerts at the Jay Pritzker Pavilion are often immense, averaging nearly ten thousand people per night. Photo 2008.

A Breathtaking Venue

The Jay Pritzker Pavilion, this otherworldly outdoor concert hall, was six years in the making and instantly became one of Chicago's icons. With four thousand fixed seats and space for another seven thousand on the lawn, a state-of-the-art digitalized, concert-hall-quality sound system, and extraordinary accessibility to the heart of downtown Chicago, the Jay Pritzker Pavilion instantly became a peerless venue. The Grant Park Music Festival shares the space with several other programs, including a regular world music series (Music Without Borders) and a jazz series (Made in Chicago), as well as a host of special events including annual performances by the Steppenwolf Theatre, Lyric Opera of Chicago, and the Chicago Symphony Orchestra. The Festival is very much at the center, however, with the Grant Park Orchestra and Chorus presenting concerts on the Jay Pritzker Pavilion stage almost every Wednesday, Friday, and Saturday evening for ten weeks throughout the heart of the summer.

Average crowds of nearly ten thousand swarmed to the new pavilion to hear the Grant Park Music Festival present the likes of Beethoven, Brahms, Mahler, and Shostakovich, as well as contemporary world premieres by living composers and inventive hybrid concerts mixing classical music with Portuguese fado, indie-rock, a silent film from India with a new score by a British-Indian composer Latin music of all species, Hungarian-Roma fiddling, Neapolitan song, cutting-edge ballet, a gospel choir, and the chanting of a score of Tibetan monks interwoven with Mozart's *Requiem.* The Festival that had begun seven decades earlier in the midst of the Great Depression has become more relevant and vibrant than ever.

FROM THE ARCHIVES

The Jay Pritzker Pavilion was born out of a unique convergence of forces and people, all of which is chronicled by Timothy Gilfoyle

in his book *Millennium Park: Creating a Chicago Landmark*. A short excerpt from that work conveys a sense of the complexity and excitement involved in creating Millennium Park and the Jay Pritzker Pavilion:

"No other enhancement in Millennium Park attracted more attention than the $60.3 million Jay Pritzker Pavilion...The exterior reflects Gehry's distinctive style: a series of irregular, stainless steel panels wrap the stage, erupting like petals across the top of the proscenium. The sculptured headdress extends ninety to one hundred feet above the stage. The pavilion's dramatic and flowing form made it the identifying structure of Millennium Park upon opening. Gehry described the flamboyant covering as 'a bouquet of flowers in the park.' The architect wanted this gift to Chicago to be, in his words, 'entertaining, something that's festive.'"[2]

VISIONARY LEADERS

Among the many people who were crucial to the Pavilion's creation were Richard M. Daley, mayor of Chicago, who was a vocal advocate of the entire Millennium Park project; John Bryan, former CEO of Sara Lee, who served as campaign chair for the park, raising funds and generating support throughout the Chicago philanthropic community; the Pritzker family, who donated $15 million towards the Pavilion's $60 million total cost; Frank Gehry, the Pavilion's renowned architect; Ed Uhlir, Millennium Park's director of design, who coordinated the remarkable array of architects and artists; and the Talaske Group, the Oak Park–based sound design firm that created the celebrated sound system.

Much of the story of the Grant Park Music Festival in the first decade of the twenty-first century is intertwined with the creation of its astonishing new home and the Festival's adjustment to it. But the decade was rich in other manifestations of change as well. At the decade's opening, the Festival welcomed

dynamic new artistic leaders, with Carlos Kalmar joining as principal conductor in 2000 and Christopher Bell as chorus director in 2002. Simultaneously, both the orchestra and the chorus matured in experience and quality. The Festival also embarked on a tremendous burst of innovative programming under Artistic and General Director James W. Palermo, presenting new works by living composers as well as producing six highly lauded recordings with Chicago's Cedille Records.

Finally, in the summer of 2009, the Festival celebrated an astonishing seventy-fifth season of free classical music on Chicago's lakefront, with a sense of abundant possibilities for the future.

The Grant Park Music Festival paired with WTTW Channel 11 for its fiftieth-anniversary celebration in Millennium Park on August 20, 2005. The concert was hosted by Joe Mantegna and Irma P. Hall and featured special guests such as Billy Corgan, Otis Clay, Liz Callaway, Ann Hampton Callaway, Liz Carroll, Orbert Davis, and Samuel Ramey.

Opposite: A view from the back of the Great Lawn with a dramatically foreshortened view of Frank Gehry's innovative trellis system, 2008.

Creating the Jay Pritzker Pavilion

The Jay Pritzker Pavilion was designed with the Grant Park Orchestra and Chorus in mind. The Pavilion's proposed form went through numerous incarnations as architect Frank Gehry and others dealt with myriad criteria. Below, several of the key collaborators offer new appraisals of the process of bringing the pavilion to life.

Frank Gehry

Renowned architect, creator of the Guggenheim Museum in Bilbao, Spain, the Disney Concert Hall in Los Angeles, and Chicago's Jay Pritzker Pavilion in Millennium Park.

IN HIS OWN WORDS

"I think there is a relationship between music and architecture, obviously. People call architecture *frozen music,* and I have heard musicians call music *liquid architecture.* But musicians create

spaces with their sounds, and they respond to spaces, and they work in spaces. The musicians are keenly aware of that; they can sense it, feel it, talk about it.

"When I started designing the Pritzker Pavilion for Millennium Park, I began by trying to find ways to fit it into the city as a whole and to play with the skyline. That kind of integration into the awareness of the building and to the city is something important to all my projects. During the design process, for instance, I pushed very hard to include the trellis to hang the speakers from so that it could create a sense of enclosure for the people on the lawn. Because that sense of being under the trellis relates them to the stage. Thanks to the trellis, people on the lawn really have a sense of a coherent space. Sitting on the lawn, you are not just in the wilderness, aware that a concert is happening somewhere over there. Instead, the space psychologically relates you to the stage, and it also, at the same time, psychologically relates you to the city because the trellis

World-renowned architect Frank Gehry stands beneath the skeletal frame of his Jay Pritzker Pavilion, in the process of being constructed in 2003.

Opposite: Gehry accepted the commission to design the Pritzker Pavilion in April 1999. The Pavilion is seen here under construction, 2003.

also frames various views of the city. It's doing a lot of things at the same time. Its basic function is to hang those speakers so that the distributed sound can be modulated so people at the back of the house can hear equally as well as the people in the front. If we hadn't built the trellis, the only way to distribute those speakers would have been on columns or posts, and then there would have been a forest of posts, blocking views. But the trellis also does much more than that.

"Cindy Pritzker was so important in getting me involved in the creation of the pavilion. Of course, in Chicago there's long been this restriction that people aren't allowed to build permanent structures in Grant Park. But art work is allowed. So Cindy's idea was that I would make an art work that would also be useful. Ed Uhlir and John Bryan were both beyond belief in helping create the park. John Bryan's ability to organize funding and donations is incredible. He not only organized the funding for the pavilion, he helped get funding for the two sculptures, *Cloud Gate* and the Crown Fountain, as well as the Lurie Garden. It was a miracle, what he was able to do. Most of all, Mayor Daley…God, he is terrific, you guys got it all in Chicago.

"I remember meeting Barack Obama at a party shortly after Millennium Park opened at some fundraising event in L.A. He came up and said that the park was very special to him, and he asked me how we managed to get it all together and get the park built. [Editor's note: Obama provided narration for a performance of Aaron Copland's *Lincoln Portrait* with the Chicago Symphony Orchestra in the Jay Pritzker Pavilion in 2005.]

"The pavilion and the concerts attract all sorts of people. If I think about kids encountering it for the first time, I'd say first of all it should be explained to them that it's a place for listening to *all kinds* of music. It could be the music they already like, or the music that their parents like, or maybe and most importantly, the music that they *someday may like*.

"All the shapes in the pavilion's design have to do with presenting the music. So maybe people look up and see a trumpet with music pouring out, who knows? A while back some books

on our work were created for kids, pop-up books and that sort of thing, that help answer some of these questions about how architecture works. The space hopefully encourages people to be open to new music, things they haven't heard before, and will encourage them to give it a chance. I really hope the Jay Pritzker Pavilion makes people in Chicago happy for generations."

Lois Weisberg

Commissioner of the Chicago Department of Cultural Affairs and a legendary figure in the Chicago cultural community, Lois Weisberg played a key role in guiding the Festival during the years before and after its move to Millennium Park.

IN HER OWN WORDS
"What Frank Gehry did with the Pritzker Pavilion is wonderful, simply wonderful. Of course there was this whole group of

Mayor Richard M. Daley confers with architect Frank Gehry shortly after the completion of the Jay Pritzker Pavilion in 2004.

people who made it happen, people like John Bryan and Mayor Daley. John Bryan was remarkable: he gathered the support of all these people but he didn't *sell* the park. He arranged to put people's names out there in the park, but in a subtle way. He didn't put up a lot of advertising. John Bryan and the mayor both realized that we had a chance to do something really unusual here. It could have turned out to be a rather ordinary park, but instead something remarkable happened, something that could not have happened in any other city. It took people such as John Bryan going around the world, traveling, talking about the arts, raising money. He is undoubtedly one of the greatest fundraisers we've ever had. Then you've got the Pritzker family, who know people such as Frank Gehry and who can pick up the telephone and convince someone such as him to undertake the project. We wouldn't have that pavilion without them.

"Finally, what Frank Gehry did in designing the Pritzker Pavilion was absolutely marvelous. He gave us this gorgeous theater with its great sound. I remember Yo-Yo Ma's comment, and I know he meant it, 'This is the best place in the world that I have ever played.' There are a lot more people saying that now."

Ed Uhlir

Director of design for Millennium Park and currently executive director of Millennium Park Incorporated, Ed Uhlir worked closely with Frank Gehry and other architects and artists who designed elements of the park. Prior to his work on Millennium Park, Uhlir was director of architecture, engineering and planning and then the director of research and planning at the Chicago Park District.

IN HIS OWN WORDS

"Millennium Park was to a large degree the brainchild of Mayor Richard M. Daley, who was appalled by the fact that we had a big, unattractive surface parking lot at that Grant Park location just across the street from Michigan Avenue and south of Randolph that was used for nine hundred cars. He wanted to get rid of it. My involvement with Millennium Park really began when I received a call from the mayor's office recommending that I take over as the site director of the new Millennium Park project. The assumption was that the Park District would be in charge and that Millennium Park would be ready in 2000. However, because of internal politics the project did not begin until the fall of 1998. John Bryan started getting his blue-ribbon committee together, and they were focused on making the project really interesting in ways that were quite different from the original Skidmore, Owings & Merrill plan.

"The Grant Park Music Festival was a key reason to do the Pavilion. Skidmore, Owings & Merrill had asked Frank Gehry to get involved early on, but he didn't immediately get involved. When I was assigned to the project, I was the liaison between the mayor, the donor group, the city departments, and the designers. Cindy Pritzker, who was on the executive committee, asked what had happened to Frank Gehry, whom she thought was going to get involved in the project. They sent me out to see Frank in Santa Monica, California, and Frank said that he had told SOM that he wasn't interested. I asked him what SOM had offered him for a role in the park project, and he said it was redecoration of the proscenium. They wanted Frank to design some sort of sculptural application of the proscenium, but he said that he didn't do that as a usual project. So instead, I offered him the much bigger role of actually designing the entire pavilion. He got a little more interested, and we created some drawings. Frank said that he had never done a successful bridge before, so I told him that if he did the pavilion, then we would throw in the opportunity for him to design the bridge.

"I think that the final Gehry design for the pavilion is great. Frank has had a long experience with the Hollywood Bowl, and he wanted to make Millennium Park work and look a bit like the Hollywood Bowl. Initially, he advocated raising up the back end

of the lawn about thirty-five feet higher than it is now and having a sloping lawn, down toward the stage. There would have been a major difficulty in maintaining a lawn on that slope, plus the fact that then we couldn't use it for other kinds of activities. So we managed to keep it flat, which I think worked well. People out on the back lawn aren't as engaged in what is happening on the stage. They might be out there playing with their children or playing Frisbee. They might be listening, but they aren't engaged the same way people up in the seats might be. So, it is appropriate to have a space where they can hear, but they don't need that sloping view of the stage. So, all in all, it was pretty successful."

The twenty-four-and-a-half-acre Millennium Park has drawn an average of more than three million people each year since its opening in 2004.

The Opening of the Jay Pritzker Pavilion: "Then the Big Glass Doors Parted…"

A thrilling new chapter in the Grant Park Music Festival's history began on July 16, 2004, when Millennium Park and the Jay Pritzker Pavilion officially opened with a lavish celebration vividly described in the *Chicago Tribune*:

FROM THE ARCHIVES

"The Jay Pritzker Pavilion, its majestic billowing steel sails embracing the cityscape that cradles Chicago's newest civic treasure, Millennium Park, opened at long last with an inaugural gala concert Friday night.

"Officials feared showers would rain on what Mayor Richard Daley, leading the parade of civic and corporate dignitaries who christened the $475 million arts showplace, called 'the most ambitious public and private undertaking in Chicago's history.' But the dark clouds vanished as if by divine decree. The sea of humanity—exceeding the 10,000 capacity mark, by my rough estimate—spilling out of the pavilion to the far reaches of the Great Lawn, breathed a collective sigh of relief.

"Everyone seemed to agree with Cindy (Mrs. Jay) Pritzker's verdict: 'Isn't this the spiffiest thing you've ever seen?' As the Grant Park Music Festival settled into its imposing new home, beginning an inaugural weekend of free events, classical music in the great Chicago summertime suddenly took on a whole new meaning and importance. The mayor's boast that Chicago will be 'the envy of every other city in the world' seemed apt as audiences took in the park's magnificence.

"But beyond the Frank Gehry architectural splendors, the gardens, and sculptures, there was one burning question on people's minds: How did the Grant Park Orchestra and Chorus sound through the new state-of-the-art sound system the Talaske Group, the Oak Park acoustics firm, created for the festival?

"The amplification certainly is a vast improvement over anything Grant Park audiences have known since the festival began, 69 years ago and survived two locations, including the Petrillo Music Shell. For the first time, delighted orchestra members can hear each other….

"Nothing quite like the Talaske system has been tried at any outdoor festival in the world, and it will take time for the audio engineers and festival officials to get it to optimally serve the variety of orchestral and choral music Grant Park is offering this summer. In effect, the festival has been handed the keys to a powerful new Maserati, but it will have to learn through constant practice how to handle all that muscle under the pedal." [3]

Near the back of the Great Lawn, the ambiance is decidedly more casual, 2007.

Opposite: The Grant Park Orchestra, under the direction of Carlos Kalmar, 2007. More than eighty members of the orchestra come to Chicago each summer from throughout the United States and the world.

The Jay Pritzker Pavilion's breathtaking, sculptural trellis system, which covers the fixed-seating area and the Great Lawn, serves to support the state-of-the-art sound system designed by the Talaske Group of Oak Park.

Opposite: A close view of the stage with a glimpse of Frank Gehry's asymmetrical stage lighting.

Photos 2008.

CELEBRATING A NEW HOME

The anticipation and joy of opening night at Pritzker Pavilion is described by several musicians, administrators, and journalists over the following pages.

Mary Stolper, principal flutist, 2002–present: "The excitement of the new pavilion was enough to make any musician feel like they were on a magic carpet. Here we were moving only a block, but magically we were moving from a little shack to a beautiful, new home palace. The excitement helped the orchestra band together. I'll never forget opening night. Number one, the ladies got to wear something other than white and black. I thought that was very special. It just changed the whole thing beyond a concert. It was everything: it was like prom night, a wedding, everything rolled into one.

"The opening of the doors on the Pritzker stage while we played the Strauss fanfare was spectacular. I remember the big red ribbon across the stage door. I had never been a part of anything with that much pomp and circumstance; I will never forget that night. When we started the piece and the doors opened, you could hear how the audience had their breath taken away; you could literally hear that sound. The audience was just mesmerized!"

Diane Ragains, chorister: "Singing in the Pritzker Pavilion is just a fantastic experience. It is a space that is built with a chorus in mind. In the old band shells, we used to be squeezed into those choral risers in the back. Here in Millennium Park, we have these wonderful choral balconies from which we have the greatest view. From the balconies, we can look up and see the gorgeous colored lights reflected onto the sculpture that is the Jay Pritzker Pavilion. It's just a magnificent experience. Here, we get to see the lawn and all people in the city, who are so happy with the park. As singers, we can hear ourselves so well in this space. Nothing can compare to the Jay Pritzker Pavilion."

Timothy Mitchell, Chicago Park District General Superintendent and Chief Executive Officer: "Opening night in Frank Gehry's Pritzker Pavilion in 2004 was so majestic. It really showed how inviting that space is, especially the way the trellis system works, the way it really embraces everyone on the lawn. And, of course, the sound at the Pritzker is just fabulous, especially in comparison with the Petrillo down at Butler Field. The audience is really immersed in the sound. Being there is just such a golden experience. I really believe that coming to a concert there is the kind of experience that can really turn someone, a kid from the city, into a classical-music lover for life. I'd like to imagine a kid coming here, hearing a concert for the first time, catching the bug for classical music, and wanting to come back again and again. Since it's all free, that's really possible."

Wynne Delacoma, *Chicago Sun-Times* classical-music critic: "During the Pritzker's first season, in 2004, I would periodically go out in the lawn and talk to people about what they thought of the sound. I remember one evening, some gorgeous evening, I wandered out into the lawn. It was packed, and I went way back where it was only slightly less packed, and I asked some people what they thought about the amplification and the sound. Two sets of people on opposite sides of the lawn said almost exactly the same thing to me: 'Well, the amplification really is fabulous, we can hear everything just fine, but the speaker near us isn't working.' Well the point was the speaker wasn't broken, but the system was working so well that they didn't hear the sound coming from the speaker but instead they heard the sound in waves. I found that very amusing.

"I always used to say that judging the quality of the Grant Park Orchestra when it played at the old Petrillo Bandshell would be like expecting Michael Jordan to play on some splintered, crummy old gym floor. It's not right. When you have musicians functioning at a certain level, good surroundings are no longer a luxury. The Michael Jordans of the world need their big stadiums, they need their state-of-the-art training, and they need their Nikes that are custom made for them. When you are a musician in that kind of ensemble, then you need the good stuff too. That's essentially what the Pritzker Pavilion was for the Grant Park Orchestra."

Julian Oettinger, Festival Board of Directors: "The Pritzker Pavilion really is a jewel in the city which has done so much to increase the level of tourism to Chicago and has stirred up so much interest from the general public. You really cannot deny that it's been a great thing. I remember the experience on opening night, turning to my wife and saying, 'Look what we've got!'

"Looking back, it doesn't matter what transpired to get there. Sure, it took a little too long to build. However, the end result is phenomenal. One of the consequences of the new space that I find fascinating is being able to come and listen to the orchestra during their daytime rehearsals. It's so inviting for people to stroll around the park and then sit down and listen to a real rehearsal of a concert that might be performed that night or the next night. I don't think you can do that anywhere else. I love the fact that people on their lunch hour, for example, can walk over there, sit down, eat, and listen to this incredible music. Even if they have no previous interest in classical music, it provides a way of drawing them into the milieu and seeing what the Festival is all about."

A picnic on the Great Lawn.

Opposite: A view from the middle of the Jay Pritzker Pavilion seating area. For all Festival concerts, sixty percent of the seating area is kept free to the general public, and forty percent is held for the more than four thousand annual season members.

Photos 2008.

A Maestro for the Millennium: Carlos Kalmar

Many factors have contributed to the growth of the reputation of the Grant Park Orchestra since the turn of the millennium. The orchestra's new home, with its vastly improved sound system, has been a key ingredient, as have the rigorous auditions and the critically regarded series of recordings released in recent years. However, nothing has made more of an impact than the musical leadership of Carlos Kalmar, who has served as the Festival's principal conductor since 2000.

Kalmar was born in Montevideo, Uruguay, to Austrian parents and studied at the College for Music in Vienna. Before working with Grant Park, he served in key conducting positions with the Hamburg Symphony Orchestra, the Stuttgart Philharmonic Orchestra, and the Opera House and Philharmonic Orchestra in Dessau, Germany. He also serves as music director of the Oregon Symphony. Kalmar first performed with the Grant Park Music Festival in the summer of 1998. Below are some thoughts on the unique bond that he and the Grant Park Orchestra have developed over the past decade.

Carlos Kalmar first appeared with the Grant Park Music Festival in 1998 and made his inaugural appearance as the Festival's principal conductor on June 16, 2000.

IN HIS OWN WORDS

From a conductor's perspective Carlos Kalmar speaks about many facets of creating the festival:

"What surprises me about our audiences at the Grant Park Music Festival is the willingness of the crowd to go with us wherever we take them. As we make a point of occasionally thinking outside the box, we need audiences that are not only willing but actually excited about the emotional places to which we take them. The point is that we work every single concert with our own musicians instead of the usual repertoire of only having guest artists. If you can imagine that our orchestra, chorus, and conductors can offer a concert of Latin American popular music in the very same week that they play Brahms's Symphony No. 4, along with an emotionally charged piece like *On the Transmigration of Souls* by John Adams, then I believe that you can appreciate it as an outstanding artistic and unique accomplishment.

"I have had the privilege over the past nine years of working with a huge list of high-quality guest artists such as the joy brought by pianists like Stephen Hough and Valentina Lisitsa. In addition, I have had the special privilege of sharing the podium with John Browning, Kathleen Battle, Jennifer Koh, and Jennifer Larmore, who are all tremendous artists. I have loved working with all of them, not to mention James Ehnes, Alban Gerhardt, Jonita Lattimore, Nathan Gunn, and Nancy Gustafson. They have all been tremendous. I also adore the work that I have done with amazing non-classical artists like Mariza, the Portugese fado singer; Billy Corgan from the Smashing Pumpkins, who was very special; and Maria del Mar Bonet, all artists who have left a huge impression on me.

"As for working with living composers, performing new works, and making recordings over the years, I have had the honor of meeting several leading American composers. I worked with John Corigliano, a very determined and energetic man, who knew what he wanted and who came to enjoy the work with us on such a deep level. I had conversations with Michael Torke, whose *Book of Proverbs* I conducted many years ago, and who is writing a piece for the Festival for the 2009 season. Aaron Jay Kernis was our very intense partner as the composer of many pieces for two consecutive years. His standards during the rehearsals and recording patch sessions and his commitment to artistic excellence were exemplary. And John Harbison, when we played and recorded his *Partita,* was a wonderful example of a quiet, high-quality musician who showed deep trust in our work. So, the chance to work with these individuals, as well as many other living composers (Garrop, Theofanides, and Prangcharoen, just to name a few), makes me proud of being the principal conductor of the Festival.

"In fact, as principal conductor, I have been very happy with the evolution of the orchestra from a good group of musicians to an excellent, tough-working, intense musical family that enjoys the fast-paced calendar that we demand. The chorus has been amazing in recent years, displaying qualities as singers and as a homogeneous group that makes them one of the best choruses in America. Christopher Bell has been the unifying asset that has

made their development possible. I greatly respect his artistic vision and enjoy working with him every summer.

"As for the audience, what is so special is to see the variety of people gathered in Millennium Park during the concerts, including families with children, many different ethnic groups, and attendees across a wide variety of age groups. Since I usually stay during the summer in an apartment close to the pavilion, one of my favorite things to see is the people walking to Millennium Park and the Festival with their chairs and coolers in order to sit on the lawn just half an hour before each concert. I know that they will be sitting there, having dinner or just a sandwich along with something to drink, looking at the beautiful pavilion along with Chicago's amazing skyline while enjoying and listening to our world-class ensemble."

Jeremy Black, concertmaster, 2006–present, and first violin, 2000–2003: "The orchestra always plays its best when Carlos is there. Carlos always puts his heart into the music. It could be an extremely hot day, the ambulances might be wailing, the helicopters buzzing by, and yet he is giving one hundred percent, and the orchestra really respects and responds to that. He has been a great leader for the orchestra, and I enjoy working with him every time he is here."

"Being concertmaster with the Grant Park Orchestra is intense. We perform two full classical programs every week, and often the programming is very ambitious, with pieces that the orchestra may not have played before—and that results in a lot of juggling. At the same time it has been a lot of fun because the orchestra cares passionately about playing the music well. The environment has improved every year, and that lends itself to putting out great concerts night after night."

James W. Palermo, Artistic and General Director, 1995–2009: "Musically, Carlos has always been like a sponge. He was willing to soak up information. When he first came to Grant Park, he knew very little about American music, other than what any

European would know, which was *Porgy and Bess,* or Copland's *Rodeo* or *Billy the Kid.* There is a whole world of American music out there, and he seemed very interested to absorb all he could.

"Carlos is such a warm and inviting person. He is an intense musician with uncompromising standards. Sometimes it is provocative, and he challenges the orchestra. He is a true orchestra builder. There are people who can come and conduct an orchestra, and they do a nice concert and they leave. But Carlos can bring an orchestra to a much higher level."

Janet Carl Smith, Deputy Commissioner, Chicago Department of Cultural Affairs: "I served on the search committee for a new principal conductor which led to Carlos Kalmar's being chosen in 2000, and it was a fascinating process that lasted several years. It started with the Festival and Jim Palermo, who invited potential candidates to come and conduct, to get to know the orchestra. It was a rather large and fascinating group on the committee. The musicians' union contract stipulates that there be a certain involvement of the musicians in the process of hiring a principal

conductor, and there were two musicians on the committee, as well as two chorus members.

"It was quite interesting during the search because we would all sit in the basement over at Petrillo Bandshell, where the musicians' dressing rooms are, and have long conversations about what qualities were important in a conductor to lead this particular Festival—beyond, of course, just good musicianship. We agreed that a willingness to engage with the public was definitely a high priority. We also felt that having an interest in the educational aspects was crucial. The goal was not just to hire someone who was a quality conductor, but also someone who understood that the programming needed to reflect the city and its makeup as a whole. The role of the principal conductor was much more than just getting up on the podium.

"Carlos really stood out for a lot of us. Of course, his musicianship was extraordinary, and we relied on the musicians' input for this. But he also had remarkable charisma. His mixed Latin American and European background was also a plus. He brought a lot of qualities that seemed to be more than just what

Left: Each summer, the Festival presents nearly fifty free, daytime open rehearsals, all of which feature talks by Grant Park Music Festival docents. Here, docent Tim Halloran gives some insight to a work in progress.

Right: Principal Conductor Carlos Kalmar has been with the Festival since the year 2000.

Photos 2008.

he did on the podium. Looking back, now almost ten years later, I think that everyone agrees it was a fantastic choice."

Jonathan Boen, principal horn player, 1997–present: "I think any conductor has to learn how to have a relationship with the group, and the group has to learn not only what the gestures look like but how you command the details to get what you want. You have to have good time-management skills to survive here. We have had some conductors who might have a fine career somewhere else, but they do not have the time-management skills to do what they need to do in two rehearsals. That is something that you adapt to, or you cannot function in this environment. Carlos has learned to do that very well. Part of it is the familiarity that we have as a group, just understanding what he wants style-wise. One of the things that cracks me up about Carlos is that when he starts counting, he mixes up his German and Spanish. It is the funniest thing. So he counts in German and Spanish and speaks in English to us."

John von Rhein, *Chicago Tribune* classical-music critic: "Carlos Kalmar demonstrates, through his enthusiasm, his vitality, his commitment to music, the way the orchestra should receive that music themselves and how we should be listening to it. I think that, in a nutshell, is one of Carlos's great gifts. He doesn't do anything halfheartedly, that vigor with his hair flying on the podium is real. It's an expression of his energetic involvement in the scores he conducts, and I think that has added a lot, certainly a visual element, but it's added a lot to the music-making dynamic of this orchestra.

"Carlos's approach can make the difference between a performance that has just managed to be rehearsed and all of us listening have to keep our fingers crossed, and a performance that has real shape and real conviction. Over the years, I've heard more than a few of those lucky sight-reading performances at Grant Park, where the players get through by the skin of their teeth, and by the end you think, 'Well, that was nice, but I would

rather go home and put on my recording of that piece.' But with Carlos, the preparation is very thorough, and this results in a real interpretation.

"His energy and appearance help draw people into the experience. That's important in a big populist venue like that. You have people just drifting in and out of curiosity, tourists or whoever, who may have never heard a Brahms or Beethoven symphony before. I think Carlos is able to sell that on a certain visual level, and then the park does the rest. The quality of the orchestra and then the fun of being in that ambiance, I think, pull people in so incredibly well.

"Carlos has certainly been a tremendous asset to the Festival. He is very well-liked by the orchestra, the chorus, the audience, the critics. When you think of it, his repertoire is amazing. He has many more American pieces in his rep than a number of other American conductors do. He does it very well, with real conviction, and he believes in it. He's been tremendous, and the orchestra has definitely seen artistic growth under him. I hope we can keep him as long as he wants to be here."

Principal Conductor Carlos Kalmar and violinist Isabelle Van Keulen at a post-concert TalkBack, 2006.

Vocal Splendour: The Chorus and Christopher Bell

The Grant Park Chorus has long been the secret weapon of the Festival. Since the chorus's founding in 1962 by Thomas Peck, it has been a treasured part of the Festival and has been recognized far beyond Chicago as a unique, first-rate body of singers (having won the Chorus America's Margaret Hillis Award for Choral Excellence in 2006). Christopher Bell, the Irish-born, Scotland-based choral director, first conducted the Festival shortly before the millennium and became chorus director in 2002.

IN HIS OWN WORDS

Bell, Grant Park Music Festival Chorus Director, 2002–present, describes his experience with the chorus:

"Now, I should say that the Grant Park Chorus was, for me, something rather unique because it was a large group of professional singers. I had worked with professional singers before, but never with quite so many and not within the structure this Festival has. The chorus members recognized that I was in a position to work with them.

"As far as goals are concerned, we had a few conversations about what the chorus was capable of and what we would like to be able to achieve. This chorus has to be all musical things during the course of a single summer: we have a wide variety of repertoire to do, and that includes the standard choral repertoire, opera evenings, maybe light opera, and even Broadway. In addition, because of Taste of Chicago and Lollapalooza, we also have opportunities to work off-site, and what we've done in the past is an a cappella concert. So, that being said, the sort of voice that just sings opera isn't necessarily the voice that sings a cappella and isn't necessarily the voice that sings Broadway. So, with the Grant Park Chorus, we are looking for a rather versatile group of people.

"Before we moved to Millennium Park, there was always the feeling that at the Petrillo Bandshell, there was a jewel that perhaps wasn't presented in its best setting. You will hear

Christopher Bell, who became the Festival's Chorus Director in 2002, was born in Belfast, Ireland and studied at Edinburgh University. Photo 2007.

jewelers talking about diamonds that aren't shown off to their best advantage because the mounting, the setting, isn't right. You then take a diamond, slightly re-cut it, put it in a new setting, and the same diamond looks like a million dollars.

"At the Pritzker, there is a connection between the gallery and the orchestral position on the stage so that singers feel they are connecting with the performance, not suspended above it or hidden behind it. They are part of it. In the past, we were hidden behind the orchestra. Quite frankly, we could have been wearing shorts and Wellington boots, and I don't really think anyone would have noticed. To stand on the stage and look out and witness the sea of faces looking up at us, to be in the choral gallery, which actually gives you an even better view of the crowds, is truly a thrill."

James W. Palermo, Artistic and General Director, 1995–2009:

"When the position of chorus director became vacant in the late 1990s, we took a few years to figure out how to find a new leader. When we started to search, we decided to cast a much wider net as far as the people who were out there and think of the chorus with much more of an international perspective. We started auditioning people from all across the United States to become the new chorus director, but we didn't find the right person. However, our principal guest conductor at the time, James Paul, told me that he had just worked with a fellow in Scotland named Christopher Bell. He said, 'I really enjoyed working with him. He is really top-notch, and we might want to consider him.'

"So we brought Christopher to conduct in 2000 and again in 2001, along with other candidates. Finally, we had to ask ourselves, 'Who is the one for us who really represents the future, somebody who has uncompromising standards, is personally very warm, and is committed?' We decided that was Christopher. It was one of the best things to happen to the Festival."

John von Rhein, *Chicago Tribune* classical-music critic:

"The Grant Park Chorus was always a very fine chorus. Tom Peck was a first-rate chorus maestro, bless his soul, and so when Christopher Bell came in, he already had a very fine group, and he proceeded to augment that. On a night-to-night basis there is no finer chorus in the city, no finer symphony chorus certainly. Look at all the repertoire, they don't hesitate to do all of the big works: the *Missa Solemnis,* the *German Requiem, A Sea Symphony,* the Verdi *Requiem.* The biggest choral pieces have been well within their grasp, and that has been great. A lot of the pleasure of my going to Grant Park concerts is to hear the choral masterpieces like Walton's *Belshazzar's Feast.* The incidental music from Beethoven's *Egmont* was done complete one year with the choral parts. Guest conductors have commented on that, and they come in and find an incredibly prepared chorus who can do anything they want them to do. That has been a huge asset, and I couldn't be more pleased. We are so lucky to have Christopher Bell. He would be a catch for any organization."

The Grant Park Chorus performs a concert of recent American choral works during an off-site concert at Holy Family Church in 2007.

The Thrill of the New:
World Premieres and Living Composers

The Grant Park Music Festival has always had a penchant for presenting new and challenging works. During its history, the Festival has performed contemporary pieces by composers such as John Adams, Leonard Bernstein, Benjamin Britten, Aaron Copland, Tan Dun, Osvaldo Golijov, Nitin Sawhney, and Dmitry Shostakovich.

The following are some reflections on working with the Grant Park Music Festival by five of the most exciting contemporary composers working in the United States today.

John Corigliano

Pulitzer Prize–and Academy Award–winning composer of such pieces as the *Violin Concerto—Red Violin* and the opera *The Ghosts of Versailles,* Corigliano's work was first performed by the Grant Park Music Festival in 1980, when his Piano Concerto was presented featuring pianist Sheldon Shkolnik. More recently, during the 2004 inaugural season of the Jay Pritzker Pavilion in Millennium

Park, the Festival chose to feature this American original's music all summer long. Corigliano discusses the experience of having his works performed by the Grant Park Orchestra.

"It is obviously a great honor and a wonderful experience to have a lot of your works played in one period of time by the same orchestra. It also usually provides for better performances because once the musicians have played one piece, by the time they get to the second, third, fourth piece, they understand what you are getting at.

"Carlos Kalmar and the orchestra were quite extraordinary. I am always afraid that, if I am not at the rehearsals, a piece could go awry. It could be fantastic or not because there are so many pitfalls. I use a lot of new notation, new ways of cuing, and new ways of having the orchestra respond to the conductor. It is very important to be a teacher as well as a conductor.

"I think that the Grant Park Orchestra now is as good as any major orchestra in the country. Having had a summer with them, I think that their performances are on the level of the orchestra across the street. I really do. When I heard these absolutely thrilling performances by Carlos and the Grant Park Orchestra, I said to myself, 'Okay, when I am dead and not around, these pieces can be done well without me, and I can accept the idea of giving a certain freedom of interpretation back to the conductor.'

"Well, I had not visited Chicago much before I became composer-in-residence, but I did visit Sheldon Shkolnik, a dear friend of mine who was a pianist. I came to hear him perform my Concerto for Piano and Orchestra in Grant Park in 1980.

"Shelly had a way of always just barely making a concert. I will never forget when he was doing the Rachmaninoff Third Piano Concerto with the Grant Park Orchestra. We started from his house up on the north side of Chicago, driving down just before the concert. On the way down, all the bridges across the Chicago River were suddenly open. We were racing from one bridge to another, trying to get across to Grant Park! He got there just in time for the downbeat. But despite all that, I remember it as a wonderful, spirited, and totally intimate performance."

Aaron Jay Kernis

A Pulitzer Prize–winning composer whose *Sarabanda in Memoriam, Symphony in Waves, Newly Drawn Sky,* and *Too Hot Toccata* were recorded by the Grant Park Music Festival and released on Cedille Records in 2006 and 2008, Kernis reflects on working with the Festival.

"The first time I heard of the Grant Park Music Festival was 1996, back when Hugh Wolff was music director. Before that I had never been to Chicago, and it was unfamiliar territory for me. My piece *New Era Dance* was performed in the old Petrillo Bandshell. I have a visual memory of it; of the space and a lot of buzz within the audience. The orchestra as a joke nicknamed it *Nude Era Dance.*

"One of the more unusual aspects of the piece is that at a certain point the orchestra chants, 'New era, new era, new, new, new, new era.' Orchestras in general, especially at that time, were

thought of as being a bit staid and tradition-minded. The piece had some sense of my relationship to my neighborhood in Washington Heights, New York. It reflected the music I was hearing in the neighborhood at the time: early rap, jazz, and salsa. I thought, 'What better way to assist in breaking that staid way of thinking about the orchestra than involving them in a more theatrical way and making the piece a mini-theatrical concerto?' It was a deliberate wake-up call to do something different and to get involved in a different way instead of just playing instruments. At the Grant Park Music Festival performance, there was surprisingly good energy about the piece from the orchestra and the audience.

"With the recording sessions in 2006 and 2007, there was really a level of mutual concentration among everyone involved. There was the sense of a team among Jim Ginsberg [president of Cedille Records], Carlos Kalmar, Jim Palermo, and me. With all of the dialogue back and forth, all of the tweaking, there was just a very fine level of detail that I had never seen before or experienced directly. It felt very organic, organically developed. I remember that when I first started at the Grant Park Music Festival, Carlos was an open book, just voracious about learning about music. He didn't know much about American music at all. What is pretty interesting about Carlos is that he is very discerning about what he likes and dislikes, and you usually understand exactly why."

Michael Torke

A celebrated composer whose jazz and minimalist-tinged works have received great acclaim, Torke was commissioned to create a major new work for the Grant Park Music Festival based on Daniel Burnham's 1909 Plan of Chicago. Torke's piece, *Plans,* received its world premiere in Millennium Park's Jay Pritzker Pavilion in June 2009. Torke describes his first encounter with the Festival and the process of being commissioned to compose a world-premiere piece.

"My first encounter with Millennium Park occurred the summer it opened. I was with my youngest sister, who lived up in Evanston. We decided to come down because I wanted to see Millennium Park. We sat on the grass. When the rehearsal was over, I saw the chorus director, Christopher Bell, from a distance. I walked over, and we started talking. I was very enthusiastic, never dreaming that anything could come out of it, but a few years later this Burnham project came together. I was just so delighted.

"I received a call from James Palermo in 2006. He said that they were celebrating the one-hundredth anniversary of the Burnham plan for Chicago, and he asked whether I knew Burnham's work. Did I know the book *Devil in the White City?* All of this was new to me. But my father is an architect. I was to write an oratorio-sized piece, much like the *Book of Proverbs,* for this anniversary. As I got to know the subject, I got more and more interested for a variety of reasons.

"What I think is so interesting about Burnham is that he promoted the idea of classicism through Beaux Arts projects like the Columbian World's Fair. It was hugely influential in his time but later lost to the rise of the international style and modernism. It is only now, in the past ten or fifteen years, that there has been a revival in his importance. His return plays into my own thinking about modernism, a style dominant at the beginning of the twentieth century in concert music, which shed certain

ideas which I am very interested in reviving: really simple ideas like tonality, writing music that has rhythms, melodies, and harmonies. In a sense, I have always thought of myself as more of a classicist than a romanticist."

Stacy Garrop

Chicago-based composer Stacy Garrop's work *Shadow* was performed by the Grant Park Music Festival in the summer of 2008. Garrop has served as composer-in-residence at Music in the Loft and is an associate professor of composition at the Chicago College of the Performing Arts at Roosevelt University. Garrop talks about the unique experience of hearing her work at the Pritzker Pavilion.

"For a young composer in the United States, it can be very difficult to get orchestra performances. So I was really touched when Jim Palermo took a look at my work and said, 'Let's do *Shadow,*' especially because it was the piece's second performance in Chicago since its 2001 premiere. To hear it again in 2008 gave me a chance to revisit it, which is a bit like seeing an old friend after a long pause, and seeing how that person has aged and changed.

Frisbees fly and audiences lounge while waiting for a daytime open rehearsal to begin at the Pritzker Pavilion, 2007.

"The nature of the beast is that it is far easier to get a premiere or a reading session done of an orchestra piece than a repeat performance of an older piece, and it is so important for pieces to have second chances or more. Often I will hear a first performance and say, okay, I want to try re-orchestrating this bit here or changing this bit here, but I will have to wait until the next performance to find out if my new ideas work.

"One of the things I love at the Pritzker Pavilion in Millennium Park is to sit a little further back and be able to look around and see the outline of the city all around and realize that, in the middle of this crazy, chaotic city, there is a little oasis. It is an oasis not just in terms of the trees, the flowers, the Bean, and all the interesting structures, but also a musical oasis. The ambiance really means a lot, although it can also add some interesting sounds to your piece in a John Cage–kind of way."

Elbio Rodriguez Barilari

Clarinetist, author, journalist, and composer, Elbio Rodriguez Barilari debuted a number of works and helped organize programs of Latin American music with the Festival in the 2000s. Barilari shares his thoughts on working with the Festival:

"From a composer's perspective, the Grant Park Music Festival is incredible, because each night there are ten thousand people, and they are there because they want to hear challenging music. They could be watching football or baseball or sitting by the lake. When I compose, I think of them. I need to say something that is relevant for each and every person. I think sometimes when the audience leaves, they are right. I am very respectful of that, and I am very happy that all this music, including my music in Chicago, has been able to reach bigger audiences because of Grant Park. Many times at Grant Park after the concerts, people come to me and say, 'Oh, Maestro'—because they love to call me maestro, I think maestro is easier to say than Barilari—'We appreciate what you do because we can relate to that; it is not strange,' or, 'Thank you for using melodies.'

Carlos Kalmar leads a daytime rehearsal, 2008. All rehearsals in the Jay Pritzker Pavilion are open to the public and frequently attended by hundreds of people, providing a fascinating glimpse into the process through which new music is brought to life.

Of course I use melodies; I also often do something weird and challenging, but I put a melody on top or a rhythm underneath, and that gives the audience a means of staying connected.

"Grant Park has requested and premiered a number of my pieces in recent years such as the *Bandoneón Concerto* and *Canyengue,* and has programmed others, such as *Machu Picchu.* The difficulties with my work are different from those of composers such as John Corigliano or John Adams. With my work there's a real challenge for the musicians to embrace the Latino rhythms and syncopations. However, I have the percussionists on my side because they love this. I know that these musicians will be on my side and make the most of it: the tympani, the marimbas, the bongos, and the congas.

"In terms of the future of the Grant Park Music Festival, I do hope that in twenty or maybe fifty years somebody invents some sort of fantastic, little device that will go in the sound booth, and with some special sound waves the technicians can plug it in and isolate the whole of Millennium Park from the outside noise, with a kind of sonic bubble, and then Carlos Kalmar and the other conductors won't need to pause or make a joke about some sirens wailing past in the middle of a piece."

A Rich Recording Legacy

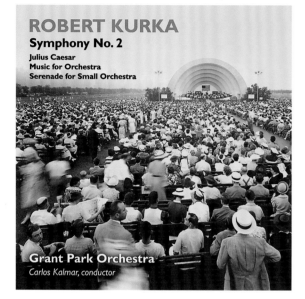

ROBERT KURKA
Symphony No. 2
Julius Caesar
Music for Orchestra
Serenade for Small Orchestra

Grant Park Orchestra
Carlos Kalmar, conductor

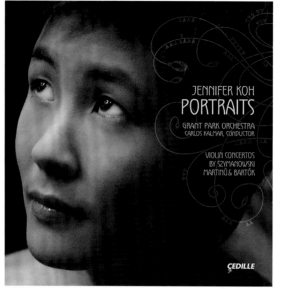

JENNIFER KOH
PORTRAITS
GRANT PARK ORCHESTRA
CARLOS KALMAR, CONDUCTOR

VIOLIN CONCERTOS
BY SZYMANOWSKI
MARTINŮ & BARTÓK

CEDILLE

Symphony in Waves
Music of Aaron Jay Kernis

Symphony in Waves
Newly Drawn Sky
Too Hot Toccata

Grant Park Orchestra
Carlos Kalmar, conductor

CEDILLE

Beginning in 2000, Cedille Records began recording the Grant Park Orchestra. To date it has released six CDs of the orchestra: *American Works for Organ and Orchestra* (with organist David Schrader); *Robert Kurka: Symphonic Works* (which was nominated for a Grammy Award); *American Orchestral Works; Portraits* (with violinist Jennifer Koh); *Symphony in Waves: Music of Aaron Jay Kernis;* and *Royal Mezzo* (with mezzo-soprano Jennifer Larmore). The principal collaborators talk about the process of creating these recordings.

Jim Ginsburg, president and founder, Cedille Records:
"Cedille Records is a label devoted to promoting the finest classical musicians, composers, and ensembles in and from Chicago. Our relationship with the Grant Park Music Festival began with Jim Palermo taking me out to lunch and talking about the fact that this orchestra was entering its seventh decade and had never

made a commercial recording. It had one self-released CD commemorating one of the July 3rd concerts, but other than that, it had no presence in the record catalog, and he wanted to change that. It was Jim's idea to start with a disc featuring Chicago soloist David Schrader (and the newly rebuilt organ in Orchestra Hall) along with the orchestra.

"We made the decision to create the Robert Kurka CD because he was a major and undervalued Chicago composer [born in Cicero, Illinois in 1921, Kurka died just before his thirty-sixth birthday in 1957], and we had recently released a recording of his opera, *The Good Soldier Schweik,* with the Chicago Opera Theater.

"The unfortunate thing was that Kurka died really young. So he never really got to reach his full potential. Many critics have noted that his is the kind of music that appeals equally to the head and the heart. It has emotional strength, but at the same time the logic of it, the structure, is so absolutely perfect. He was

Three of the Grant Park Orchestra recordings produced by Cedille Records.

clearly a very skillful composer. One can only imagine what he would have gone on to if he had lived. But we are glad to have the pieces that we have.

"The Aaron Jay Kernis recording, *Symphony in Waves,* is full of pieces written to really show off an orchestra. To me, it sounds so idiomatic that way I cannot imagine how that piece could have started out as a smaller piece. It has such a gigantic sound, one ideally suited to show off a great orchestra and a great acoustic space. The piece is literally full of these waves of sound that engulf you; it's amazing stuff.

"The advantage of the Grant Park Music Festival's being free is that they can be more adventurous with their programming: nobody is going to complain about the price, and people get to be surprised. It could be a concert that they might not be initially willing to pay for, but they come and make a discovery, whether it's the Kurka Second Symphony or some of the other wonderful works that I have discovered at Grant Park.

"It's been a wonderful experience, and I certainly hope we will be able to continue it. A major part of what our label is all about is promoting musicians, soloists like violinists Jennifer Koh and Rachel Barton Pine; ensembles like the Pacifica Quartet, eighth blackbird, or the Grant Park Orchestra for that matter; and composers such as Stacy Garrop, Lita Grier, and Easley Blackwood. In a larger sense what we are trying to do is really make a document of Chicago's classical music. It dovetails so well with what we are trying to do as a label: what Grant Park has been doing for the public, we're now able to document for posterity."

James W. Palermo, Artistic and General Director, 1995–2009:
"When you add the element of a living composer, things change completely because they're there, the conductor can turn around and say 'What did you mean there?' But also you know it's a living,

breathing work and not a museum piece, but actually a piece that was recently written. For some reason over the last thirty years, some audiences have developed a distrust of anything that is contemporary. In visual art people want to see new pieces. In theater people are interested in going to new theater. But in classical music there is a certain amount of fear. The whole experience of having the composer there allows you an opportunity to communicate with the audience. When you bring in a composer like John Corigliano and he actually talks about the music, you have the opportunity to influence the way people feel about the piece. When we did Corigliano's *Red Violin Concerto,* twenty-five thousand people heard it over two nights. It would take fifteen or twenty performances elsewhere to get that number."

In the Jay Pritzker Pavilion's soundbooth (from left to right): sound engineer Chris Willis, artistic staff member Agnieszka Kozlowska, and Artistic and General Director James W. Palermo oversee the fine tuning of the sound system during a concert, 2008.

Great Artists of the 2000s

In addition to the artists described on the following pages, the Festival saw an abundance of stellar guest artists such as sopranos Kathleen Battle (2000), Dawn Upshaw (2002), Karina Gauvin (2004–2008), and Erin Wall (2004, 2007–2008); tenor Vittorio Grigolo (2008), pianist Stephen Hough (2006 and 2008); violinists Rachel Barton Pine (2002 and 2004), James Ehnes (2008–2009), Roby Lakatos (2007), Christian Tetzlaff (2004 and 2007), and Pinchas Zukerman (2008); vocalists Otis Clay (2005), Mariza (2006), and Maria del Mar Bonet (2008); and rock band the Decemberists (2007).

Valentina Lisitsa

Pianist, 1997, 2000, 2004–2008

Born in Ukraine, Valentina Lisitsa attended a music school for gifted children and later the Kiev Conservatory, where she met her future husband, Alexei Kuznetsoff. Extremely successful as a duo piano team, they both moved to the United States to further their careers.

FROM THE ARCHIVES

The *Chicago Sun-Times* raved over Lisitsa's playing:

"Already memorable, Piano Week at the Grant Park Music Festival was made even more so by Ukrainian pianist Valentina Lisitsa's jaw-dropping performance Saturday of the Rachmaninoff Concerto No. 2. The Rach Second is, like almost every piano work written by the Russian master, a demanding showcase, and one that frightens the less than brilliant. In addition to her formidable technical talents, Lisitsa is a visual delight as she plays. Tall and graceful, her long-limbed frame perches atop the bench, fingers flowing over the keyboard as if attempting to coax magic from it through sheer charm. And from the bell-like opening theme that pealed majestically from the metallic-sounding Baldwin grand, Lisitsa was glorious. Building this music like a romantic cathedral, she was in full control of Rachmaninoff's tempo and mood swings. Lisitsa demonstrated wondrous pace and rhythmic consistency, her swanlike hands linking passages smoothly. Shifting back and forth from martial to romantic themes, Lisitsa impressed with an unerring dynamic sense. Soft passages were so delicate, you were afraid to breathe, while Rachmaninoff's chords thundered effortlessly from Lisitsa's fingers."[4]

Valentina Lisitsa was a warmly received frequent guest artist in the 2000s, performing piano works by Beethoven, Chopin, Grieg, Shostakovich, and others at her six appearances during the decade.

Jonita Lattimore

Soprano, 2000, 2002, 2004, 2006, 2008, and 2009

A Chicago-born, lyric soprano, who has portrayed a variety of roles, ranging from Micaela in *Carmen* to Jackie O, Lattimore has performed with major orchestras across the United States and abroad. She made her Lyric Opera of Chicago debut in Kurt Weill's *The Rise and Fall of the City of Mahagonny*. A frequent recipient of awards, she has been honored by the Birgit Nilsson Competition, the Luciano Pavarotti International Voice Competition, the Sullivan and George London Foundations, and Opera Index, Inc.

In her many appearances with the Festival, Jonita Lattimore has performed such works as Beethoven's Ninth Symphony, Brahm's *German Requiem*, and Szymanowski's *Stabat Mater*. Photo 2008.

IN HER OWN WORDS

"When I was growing up in Chicago, my parents brought me down to the Grant Park concerts. Sometimes we'd make it a family affair. Sometimes we'd make it mother-daughter time. The fact that they were city-sponsored, free concerts was so absolutely important since it created an opportunity for people to be exposed to cultural experiences. It is an invaluable opportunity.

"One thing that I have always wanted to have is a variety of music, a variety of performance opportunities. I never wanted to only do one thing or another. Performing with Grant Park has afforded me the opportunity to be versatile: singing classical music such as Mozart or Beethoven, that type of thing, as well as being able to do the Brahms and Verdi *Requiems,* and also twentieth-century music. To be able to be challenged in all sorts of ways—I mean the languages: the last performance I did, I sang in Polish! That was definitely a challenge. That's a language that I had never been exposed to as far as singing. Now, I have performed in Poland, but all I ever really knew how to say was, 'Dziekuje,' which is 'Thank you.' It wasn't as though I had that kind of exposure as far as languages were concerned. So, it has helped me to grow, to be exposed to a lot of different composers and pieces of music that I wouldn't necessarily have been exposed to. It has allowed me to develop a love for creating new possibilities."

Nathan Gunn

Baritone, 2004, 2005, and 2007

Nathan Gunn has appeared in many well-known opera houses including the Metropolitan Opera, the San Francisco Opera, Lyric Opera of Chicago, the Royal Opera House, and the Paris Opera. He has appeared in the title roles of *Billy Budd* and *Hamlet,* Figaro in *Il Barbiere di Siviglia,* Prince Andrei in *War and Peace,* Buzz Aldrin in *Man on the Moon,* and many more.

FROM THE ARCHIVES

The excitement of Gunn's appearance with the Grant Park Music Festival in 2004 was captured by the *Chicago Sun-Times:*

"Having brought 'hunk' to the opera world of 'hulks,' Gunn is considered one of America's most exciting young baritones. He is boyishly handsome, charismatic, unafraid to tackle almost any role, and seems to be everywhere these days—from the Lyric in Chicago to the Royal Opera House in London to the Paris Opera. His many roles include the title in 'Billy Budd,' Figaro in 'Il Barbiere di Siviglia,' Marcello in 'La Boheme,' and Zurga in 'The Pearl Fishers.'...

"Tonight and Saturday night, Gunn will perform Britten's 'War Requiem' with the Grant Park Orchestra and Chorus in the Jay Pritzker Pavilion in Millennium Park, and he said he can't wait to get back to Chicago, 'where the people don't analyze the music, they experience it.'"[5]

Nathan Gunn performing John Adams's *The Wound Dresser* with the Festival in 2007.

Jennifer Larmore

Mezzo-Soprano, 2003–2007

Beloved mezzo-soprano Jennifer Larmore made her professional opera debut in France in 1986. In the spring of 2008, Cedille Records released the CD *Royal Mezzo*, featuring mezzo-soprano Jennifer Larmore with the Grant Park Orchestra, singing works by Barber, Berlioz, Ravel, and Britten.

IN HER OWN WORDS

"The *Royal Mezzo* CD came about because Jim Palermo suggested doing something that would showcase my acting talent as well as my voice, because I'm a real dramatic creature, and he knows it. I can tell you that Jim is a wonderful person to banter back and forth with about ideas because he knows the voice so well. He knows what fits, especially for my voice, and he's always very respectful of what I want, and so I assume he is very respectful of all the artists that he brings to Grant Park.

"I think the Festival is so important because it reaches a much wider public. It is helping to bring classical music to people who would probably not have a chance to come because the cost would be prohibitive. A lot of people, especially in this economic climate, just don't have the money to spend on extra things. Unfortunately in America, concerts—especially classical concerts—are considered extras. Now, if we were in Europe that would be different, because there you ask somebody, 'What are you doing tonight?' It's a Tuesday, and they are going to the opera. 'What are you going to see?' 'I don't know! It's Tuesday, it's my opera night!' That's just the way it is over there. It is part of their culture. It's not a real big part of our culture. I think keeping Grant Park free and keeping Grant Park moving forward in the best way possible is the best way to bring in more and more people to this fantastic art form."

World-renowned mezzo-soprano Jennifer Larmore made her operatic debut in France, her debut at the Metropolitan Opera in 1995, and has been a favorite of the Festival, making five appearances in the 2000s.

Broadway Programs and Divertimento

Throughout the 2000s, the Festival typically presented spectacular annual programs that blended classical and Broadway styles, often highlighting the work of a specific composer, such as Stephen Sondheim, Leonard Bernstein, or George Gershwin. These Broadway nights were often paired with the Festival's gala benefit party, Divertimento.

Mary Elizabeth Mastrantonio and Brian d'Arcy James light up the stage during a concert devoted to the works of Stephen Sondheim in 2006.

FROM THE ARCHIVES

The *Chicago Tribune's* Chris Jones wrote of the 2006 Millennium Park–wide Sondheim in the Park celebration, for which the Festival presented a centerpiece concert, which Stephen Sondheim himself attended:

"With darkness-loving cabaret artists squinting in the sun and piano keys sticking in the sweaty heat, the song stylings of Stephen Sondheim spouted from all corners of Millennium Park last weekend. Free to all…the mainstage Sondheim show in the Jay Pritzker Pavilion…featured the top-drawer Broadway likes of George Hearn, Brian d'Arcy James, Judy Kaye and Mary Elizabeth Mastrantonio….

"Sondheim introducing Sondheim, followed by Sondheim for dessert. Sun. Warmth. Cheddar. Perchance a semilegal glass of wine. The Gehry. And the company of more than 10,000 fellow aficionados each night. Who'd want to live anywhere else?

"For sure, this was a night for romanticism rather than artistic innovation. But the main stage bill served up Friday and Saturday by musical director Kevin Stites (and stage director Gary Griffin) had some dazzling talent….Sondheim himself showed up Friday night….In Millennium Park this weekend, the grass was green, the atmosphere festive but contemplative, and life felt weirdly good."[6]

Members of the Joffrey Ballet perform an excerpt from *Romeo and Juliet* during their performance with the Festival in 2006.

The Joffrey Ballet

The Grant Park Music Festival's penchant for pairing with other exciting Chicago arts organizations was exemplified by the 2006 program in which the orchestra joined the Joffrey Ballet in a special Millennium Park program celebrating the Joffrey's fiftieth anniversary.

FROM THE ARCHIVES

Hedy Weiss of the *Chicago Sun-Times* chronicled the Joffrey Ballet's performance:

"It was a dazzling example of art imitating art, especially for those familiar with 'The Company'—Robert Altman's film about the Joffrey Ballet, in which there is a scene of a big outdoor benefit performance being nearly washed out by a summer rainstorm.

"On Saturday night, an audience estimated at 8,000 to 10,000 gathered in Millennium Park's Jay Pritzker Pavilion to watch as the Joffrey celebrated its 50th anniversary in a collaborative program with the Grant Park Orchestra. And just as Romeo and Juliet confessed their love—and those warring families of Verona, the Montagues and Capulets, nearly came to blows—a thunder and lightning show from another source came rolling in, causing temporary chaos for everyone but the fiercely focused dancers and musicians.

"Their brilliant Renaissance costumes blowing in the angry wind, the dancers danced on....Decked out in lavish copper and crimson ballgowns and elaborate headdresses, the ladies and gentlemen of the Italian court continued their stately and insinuating formal dances....The storm lasted about 10 minutes, bringing a cooling breeze, and most of the audience stayed where it was, to be rewarded by three more sensationally danced pieces."[7]

Mixing it Up: Movies, Monks, and More

Mixing musical styles and other art forms with orchestral music has long been an important facet of the Grant Park Music Festival. The adventurous spirit and tendency to experiment with innovative programs has been especially prevalent in the years after the millennium. During these years, the Festival brought in such international artists as Chinese erhu player Betti Xiang and pipa player Yang Wei (2005), Portuguese fado singer Mariza (2006), Cuban classical and jazz clarinetist Paquito D'Rivera (2006), Hungarian-Roma fiddler Roby Lakatos (2007), and Mediterranean singer Maria del Mar Bonet (2008). The Festival placed a particular focus on Latin American music during these years.

One of the other exciting means of intertwining diverse art forms has been through projects that involve film. In the summer of 2008, for instance, the Grant Park Orchestra presented the United States premiere of a 1920s silent film from India with a new score by acclaimed composer, Nitin Sawhney, A *Throw of Dice,* for which the Grant Park Orchestra shared the stage with an ensemble of classical Indian musicians and singers.

Below, Neil Kimel reflects on one of the more exciting genre-blending programs in recent years, a screening of the great Russian film *Battleship Potemkin,* with a new score arranged from various works by Dmitry Shostakovich.

Neil Kimel, horn player, 2000–present: "To pair a live orchestra with film really enhances the cinematic experience. We have performed the soundtracks to two amazing silent films in recent years: Eisenstein's *Battleship Potemkin* (2006) and the Indian film, *A Throw of Dice* (2008). We performed *Battleship Potemkin* with a specially arranged score comprised of excerpts from Shostakovich. He really brought the physical conflict to life. This cinematic masterpiece of the early twentieth century was shown on a massive, massive movie screen so even people sitting far back on the lawn experienced the movie in a spectacular way framed by the Pritzker Pavilion, an architectural masterpiece of the twenty-first century. It was such a memorable night for me.

"Some people in the audience told me that they weren't sure if we had planned it beforehand or not, but at the end of the film, when the Battleship Potemkin makes it past the blockade, the sailors are celebrating, and the music is victorious. At this very moment, the fireworks at Navy Pier went off.

"The happenstance of it all was one of those perfect, urban, *Ferris Bueller* moments when everything suddenly connects. There are so many examples of incredible film soundtracks that were written by Prokofiev for symphony orchestras, such as Eisenstein's *Alexander Nevsky* and *Ivan the Terrible,* which would both be marvelous to do in Millennium Park. The Grant Park Orchestra goes places where a lot of ensembles don't dare to go perhaps because, in part, we are not worried about restrictive considerations like ticket sales. We have that luxury."

Tenor Vittorio Grigolo performs as part of a tribute concert to Pavarotti in 2008.

Opposite: The 2008 performance of *A Throw of Dice,* a silent film from India with a new score by composer/ deejay Nitin Sawhney.

MINGLING EAST AND WEST

Another especially memorable cross-cultural program took place in the summer of 2006 when Mozart's *Requiem* was interwoven with excerpts of Buddhist chanting by a group of Tibetan monks.

FROM THE ARCHIVES

Critic Andrew Patner described the experience:

"Multiculturalism is finding itself very much at home in Millennium Park and on Monday evening Yo-Yo Ma will kick off his yearlong Silk Road Chicago Project there with a free concert at the Jay Pritzker Pavilion...

"But the omnivorous Ma himself would surely have been impressed with Friday night's Grant Park program, which was scheduled to be repeated Saturday evening, for the Grant Park Orchestra and Chorus performed a recent edition of Mozart's beloved *Requiem* Mass in D minor, K. 626, punctuated by the multiphonic chanting, gongs, drums and horns of nine Tibetan monks 'on loan' to a Buddhist monastery in Atlanta.

"The idea was more successful than doubters might have suspected, in part because the bass foundation of the monks' chanting resonated with Mozart's bass writing for instruments, chorus, and bass soloist in his final major work. The connections were also well thought out thematically with the five Tibetan interpolations fitting in to the spiritual context of the *Requiem*.... Clad in orange robes with yellow feathered headdresses which looked remarkably like soft versions of Roman centurions' helmets, the visitors were in marked contrast to the white jacketed black-tie players and all-black-clad singers behind them."[8]

Tibetan monks from the Drepung Loseling Monastery perform with the Festival in 2006 as part of a program that interwove Mozart's *Requiem* and Buddhist multiphonic chanting.

Transmigration: A Transcendent 9/11 Memorial

On the Transmigration of Souls, by contemporary composer John Adams, was written to honor the victims of the attack on September 11. At the end of the 2005 season, the Festival presented a particularly memorable performance of that work.

FROM THE ARCHIVES

The haunting performance experience was described by Wynne Delacoma of the *Chicago Sun-Times:*

"In general, few of us consciously crave the work of serious-minded artists to help us make sense of a chaotic world. We can usually keep our larger anxieties at bay with a periodic dip into Hollywood's latest blockbuster or the newest reality TV show. In the wake of 9/11, however, there seemed to be a palpable hunger for something more....

"Doubtless, composer John Adams didn't feel that kind of weighty burden when the New York Philharmonic asked him to write a piece honoring the victims of 9/11.

"Adams' 'On the Transmigration of Souls,' which the Grant Park Orchestra is performing to stunning effect this week under principal conductor Carlos Kalmar may have succeeded.... Composed for orchestra, chorus, children's chorus and prerecorded tape, 'On the Transmigration of Souls' drew its text from everyday speech. Throughout the work, which won the 2003 Pulitzer Prize, a spoken list of the dead progressed with the slow, measured tread of a horse-drawn hearse. It included sung and spoken phrases drawn from newspaper obituaries and the notes left near Ground Zero by those frantically searching for missing mothers, fathers, sisters, brothers, spouses, lovers and friends.

"From such humble materials Adams has created a 30-minute work that captures the bafflement, unreality, despair and struggle for hope instantly recognizable to anyone who lived through 9/11, whether in lower Manhattan or thousands of miles away....

"With its sophisticated acoustical system, the Pritzker Pavilion was an ideal venue for Adams' multilayered 'On the Transmigration of Souls.' While the orchestra and the luminous Grant Park Chorus roamed through its gently contoured melodies and the Chicago Children's Choir sent out bits of fragile, angelic song, we were surrounded by sounds from Adams' recorded tape. The names of the dead came at us from all directions, recited by ordinary children, men and women in the flat, uninflected tones of human beings exhausted by grief. At times, the orchestra coalesced into a monumental force, pressing against long, sustained chords as if fighting to close a massive, glittering metal door.

"There were no gratuitously dissonant outbursts, no noisy clichés of a world gone mad. Far more shattering were the work's subdued tone and the sense of being surrounded by unseen mourners and migrating souls."[9]

One of the most unforgettable events in the past decade was the Festival's 2005 performance of John Adams's *On the Transmigration of Souls,* which paid tribute to the victims of the September 11 attacks.

Cultivating a Sense of Ensemble

After moving to Millennium Park in 2004, the Grant Park Music Festival built many new relationships with people and groups around Chicago. Just as the park subtly weaves together urban and natural spaces and juxtaposes experiences of solitary contemplation and communal celebration, it also brings people together.

For instance, one of the benefits of moving into Millennium Park was the Festival's many daytime open rehearsals, which attract hundreds of people on a daily basis. These include office workers from the Loop on their lunch break, curious tourists, and groups of children on field trips. All of these groups have the chance to ask questions and listen to educational talks by the Festival's dedicated group of music docents, who are the face of the Festival at all rehearsals and a significant part of the Festival's ambition to educate new audiences about classical music.

Millennium Park has also helped bring together organizations with whom the Festival has come to collaborate in recent years. In addition to the Festival's long-standing ties to the Chicago Park District and the Chicago Department of Cultural Affairs, the Festival has built alliances with many other local organizations such as WFMT radio (which broadcasts many Festival concerts), DePaul University and Roosevelt College, both of which provide singers for the Festival's Apprentice Chorale, and the many local music schools that have participated in the annual Community Music School nights. Among the Festival's many other Chicago-area partners in recent years are the Burnham Centennial, the Jewish United Fund, Music without Borders, Luna Negra Dance Theater, Made in Chicago jazz series, the Metro, the Joffrey Ballet, and WTTW Channel 11.

What comes next in terms of new relationships and endeavors is nearly limitless, much as it was when the Festival began in 1935.

The Jay Pritzker Pavilion seen from the bucolic vantage point of the Lurie Gardens, 2008.

Peering into the Crystal Ball:
The Future of the Grant Park Music Festival

As the Grant Park Music Festival celebrates its milestone seventy-fifth season in the summer of 2009, several of the key leaders and commentators in the Festival's recent history reflect on the fascinating and storied legacy of the concert series born in the midst of the Great Depression and ponder the possible role of the Festival in the future.

Lois Weisberg, Commissioner, Chicago Department of Cultural Affairs: "During the past years at the concerts, I have seen so many people bringing their children, children that very well may not otherwise have the opportunity to hear live classical music. They wouldn't have had that without these concerts being out there. It is unbelievable how the majority of the time the kids are so attentive. And of course there's an incredible array of people from different ethnic and economic backgrounds. It's wonderful. These Grant Park concerts are playing a huge role in music education that nobody fully realizes and that nobody might fully appreciate until far into the future."

John von Rhein, *Chicago Tribune* classical-music critic: "The Grant Park Music Festival has thrived in part because of its location. People want to spend their summer downtown, and it is part of the DNA of the city that people have a hunger for quality music in the summer that they wouldn't normally be able to hear. Providing that opportunity downtown was a tremendous boon to tourism and to the cultural life of Chicago at a time when it wasn't always thriving the way it is today. Also, Chicago loves its traditions, and once the tradition got established, it was hard to stop it. Maybe if the Festival had started decades later, say in the 1960s, it might not have taken hold in the same way. The Festival has filled a very real need that nothing else could fill."

Janet Carl Smith, Deputy Commissioner, Chicago Department of Cultural Affairs: "Thinking about the distant future of the Grant Park Music Festival, I hope that it goes on a journey that we cannot even imagine at this point. In another seventy-five years, if it is still an orchestra that comes out onto the stage, sits down in chairs, and plays in this proscenium way on a raised platform to a group of people who sit there and watch and don't clap between the movements—I will be disappointed if that is still the case. While I hope that there is still a group of amazing musicians who play such high quality, well-programmed music for free, beyond that, the look and shape of the Festival could change immensely."

Fred Brandstrader, President, Board of Directors: "I think that there is an even larger audience for the Festival in the city and the suburbs that has yet to be fully tapped into, to be fully reached. Thus, really getting the word out is one of our main missions over the next few years. Hopefully the seventy-fifth season will be a springboard, and the press and others will take a deeper interest, and that will create opportunities for us to tell our remarkable story."

Carlos Kalmar, Principal Conductor, 2000–present: "It is very important for the Festival to continue to be presented for free because that makes it unique. It would be a very different type of Festival if we began to charge for the tickets. I strongly believe that this Park, the pavilion, and the concerts are a part of Chicago and that they belong to the city. The people have made this place their own. It is a place to reflect, enjoy, and be moved, and if it weren't free then it would prevent the public from having a place that over the years has been owned by the people of Chicago. Let's keep it that way!"

Seen from the Aon Building just to the north of Millennium Park, a massive crowd fills the Jay Pritzker Pavilion as the indie-rock band, the Decemberists, performs with the Grant Park Orchestra in 2007.

Endnotes

CHAPTER ONE:
FRONT YARD FOR ALL
THE HISTORY OF GRANT PARK

1   Elizabeth Halsey, *Development of Public Recreation in Metropolitan Chicago,* citing *Chicago Democrat,* November 4, 1835.

2   Daniel Bluestone, *Constructing Chicago,* (New Haven, CT: Yale Univ. Press, 1991), 16.

3   Ibid., 17; "How Grant Park Was Saved for People: Ward's Great Fight Waged 21 Years," *Chicago Daily News,* June 8, 1935.

4   Alfred Lief, *A History of A. Montgomery Ward's Battle to Save Grant Park* (Montgomery Ward and Company, n.d.).

5   "Improvements of 1850," *Chicago Daily Tribune,* December 28, 1850.

6   Ibid.

7   The reader signed his letter, "Forrest." "The Lake Shore Park," *Chicago Press and Tribune,* April 20, 1860.

8   Sandy R. Mazzola, "Bands, Early and Golden Age," in *The Encyclopedia of Chicago,* ed. James R. Grossman, Ann Durkin Keating, and Janice L. Reiff (Chicago: Univ. of Chicago Press, 2004).

9   *Chicago Daily Tribune,* May 15, 1858.

10   "Musical," *Chicago Tribune,* September 2, 1861; Mazzola, "Bands."

11   "Lake Park Concerts," *Chicago Tribune,* June 20, 1869.

12   Ninth Annual Report of the Board of Public Works to the Common Council of the City of Chicago, 1870, 75; Tenth Annual Report of the Board of Public Works to the Common Council of the City of Chicago, 1871, 53.

13   Dennis H. Cremin, "Building Chicago's Front Yard: Grant Park 1836 to 1936," (PhD diss., Loyola University, 1999), 74.

14   Letter from Mr. M. F. Taley, *Chicago Daily Tribune,* February 23, 1874.

15   Horace White letter to Murat Halstead, 1871, quoted in David Lowe, *The Great Chicago Fire* (NY: Dover Publications, 1979), 45–48.

16   Ibid.

17   Joseph Kirkland, *The Story of Chicago* (Chicago: Dibble Publishing, 1892), 354–355.

18   "The South Side," *Chicago Tribune,* November 16, 1871.

19   Cremin, "Building Chicago's Front Yard," 94.

20   "The Exposition," *Chicago Tribune,* September 26, 1873.

21   Cremin, "Building Chicago's Front Yard," 113.

22   Bessie Louise Pierce, *A History of Chicago: The Rise of a Modern City,* 1871–1893 (NY: Knopf, 1957), 3:493.

23   Timothy J. Gilfoyle, *Millennium Park: Creating a Chicago Landmark* (London: Univ. of Chicago Press, 2006), 12.

24   Cremin, "Building Chicago's Front Yard," 118–119.

25   "The Lake-Front," *Chicago Daily Tribune,* June 15, 1884.

26   "For Park Purposes–Judge Ewing Grants an Order Touching the Lake Front," *Chicago Daily Tribune,* May 20, 1893.

27   "Sells' Brothers Show," *Chicago Daily Tribune,* June 29, 1845.

28   "To Be a Fine Park–Plans of Property Owners for Beautifying the Lake-Front," *Chicago Daily Tribune,* January 24, 1893.

29   Gilfoyle, *Millennium Park,* 16.

30   "For Park Purposes–Judge Ewing Grants an Order Touching the Lake Front," *Chicago Daily Tribune,* May 20, 1893.

31   "Lake-Front Plans," *Chicago Daily Tribune,* August 10, 1895.

32   "One Year to Take Park," *Chicago Daily Tribune,* September 15, 1896.

33   Report of the South Park Commissioners to the Board of County Commissioners of Cook County from December 1 to November 30, 1903, 5–9; "Muzzle for Lake Front Watchdog," *Chicago Daily Tribune,* March 18, 1903.

34   Peter B. Wight to John Charles Olmsted, August 8, 1903, Olmsted Associates Papers, Library of Congress.

35   Daniel H. Burnham to Henry G. Foreman, August 20, 1903, Ryerson & Burnham Archives, D.H. Burnham Collection, Series I: Business Correspondence, 14:154, Art Institute of Chicago.

36   "City's Park System and Its Future: Henry G. Foreman Writing in the Century Discusses What Has Been Done and What Is Yet to Be Done to Make It a 'Joy Forever,'" *Chicago Daily Tribune,* January 25, 1905.

37   "Moving to Block Victory of Ward," *Chicago Daily Tribune,* October 27, 1909.

38   "Brookins Soars High Above Loop," *Chicago Daily Tribune,* September 28, 1910.

39   Cremin, "Building Chicago's Front Yard," 306–7.

40   Minutes of the South Park Commission Board of Commissioners, January 14, 1924, 31:147.

41   "Chicago to Have Huge Aquarium," *Chicago Daily Tribune,* March 31, 1913.

42   "Fountain to Be Dedicated Tonight," *Chicago Evening Post,* August 26, 1927.

43   "Clarence Buckingham Memorial Fountain and Garden," Final Landmark Recommendation approved by the Commission on Chicago Landmarks, June 7, 2000.

44   "50,000 Gather to See New Fountain," *Chicago Daily News,* August 27, 1927.

45   "50,000 Attend Dedication of New Fountain—Buckingham Memorial Is Presented to City," *Chicago Daily Tribune,* August 27, 1927.

46   "Speeds Work on Improvements in Grant Park," *Chicago Daily Tribune,* May 5, 1928.

47   "Zeppelin Soars over Chicago for 18 Minutes as Crowds Gather in Parks and Streets," *Chicago Daily Tribune,* August 29, 1929.

48   Lenox Lohr, *Fair Management: The Story of A Century of Progress Exposition* (Chicago: Cuneo Press, 1952), 15.

49   Proceedings of the South Park Commissioners, March 18, 1931, 39:169.

50   Ibid., April 15, 1931, 39:232.

51   "Grant Park Band Shell Now under Construction," *Chicago Daily Tribune,* August 5, 1931.

52   "Ground Broken for Band Shell for the Grant Park Concerts," *Chicago Daily Tribune,* July 11, 1931.

53 Edward Moore, "Chicago Band Opens Season in Grant Park—Thousands Hear First of Outdoor Concerts," *Chicago Daily Tribune,* August 25, 1931.

54 "First Concert in Grant Park at 8 PM Tonight," *Chicago Daily Tribune,* July 8, 1932.

55 Second Annual Report of the Chicago Park District for the Year Ending December 31, 1936, 181.

56 Edward Moore, "Fine Program Launches Park Concert Series," *Chicago Daily Tribune,* July, 2, 1935.

57 John Thompson, "Thousands See 10,000 Youth Join the Navy," *Chicago Daily Tribune,* July 2, 1942.

58 Fifteenth Annual Report of the Chicago Park District for the Year Ending December 31, 1949, 81.

59 "City Bids Queen Good Bye," *Chicago Daily Tribune,* July 7, 1959.

60 "900 March, Picket: Dirksen Won't Budge," *Chicago Daily Tribune,* September 13, 1966.

61 Paul Gapp, "Greening of Grant Park: A Front-yard Priority," *Chicago Tribune,* September 15, 1974.

62 Gilfoyle, *Millennium Park,* 59.

63 Daniel H. Burnham, Edward H. Bennett, and Charles Moore, *Plan of Chicago Prepared under the Direction of the Commercial Club during the Years MCMVI, MCMVII, and MCMVIII* (Chicago: Commercial Club of Chicago, 1909), 30.

CHAPTER TWO: THE 1930s

1 John Beemster, "The Sleep of the Unemployed," *Chicago Daily Tribune,* August 26, 1930.

2 Robert Leiter, *The Musicians and Petrillo* (New York: Bookman Associates, 1953), 46.

3 Thomas Willis, "Petrillo and the Battle of Grant Park," *Chicago Tribune,* June 8, 1975.

4 Ibid.

5 Ibid.

6 Edward Moore, "Free Concerts Add New Star to Civic Crown," *Chicago Daily Tribune,* June 9, 1935.

7 Chicago Federation of Musicians, www.cfm10208.com/display. php?id=100.

8 "Ground Broken for Band Shell for the Grant Park Concerts," *Chicago Daily Tribune,* July 11, 1931.

9 Edward Moore, "Chicago Band Opens Season in Grant Park," *Chicago Daily Tribune,* August 25, 1931.

10 Edward Moore, "Fine Program Launches Park Concert Series," *Chicago Daily Tribune,* July 2, 1935.

11 Edward Moore, "50,000 Hear Symphony in Park Concert," *Chicago Daily Tribune,* July 5, 1935.

12 Edward Barry, "A Gift to the Public," *Chicago Daily Tribune,* August 1, 1937.

13 Cecil Smith, "A Few Thoughts on Grant Park Music for '39," *Chicago Daily Tribune,* September 11, 1938.

14 "Music for the Crowd," *Chicago Daily Tribune,* August 11, 1937.

15 "Free Public Concerts in Grant Park," *Intermezzo,* July 1938.

16 Mrs. Jeanne L. Fay, "Peddlers at the Concerts," *Chicago Daily Tribune,* August 4, 1935.

17 Edward Barry, "Park Concert Given a Taste of Air Raiding," *Chicago Daily Tribune,* August 27, 1937.

18 Ibid.

19 Isabelle Young in "Front Views and Profiles" by June Provins, *Intermezzo,* July 1940.

20 Cecil M. Smith, "Park Concert Pays Tribute to Gershwin," *Chicago Daily Tribune,* July 14, 1937.

21 Ibid.

22 Marcia Winn, "A Single Voice Thrills Record Crowd in Park," *Chicago Daily Tribune,* August 1, 1937.

23 "330,000 at Park to Hear Lily Pons," *Chicago American,* July 25, 1939.

24 Edward Barry, "Heifetz Plays—and Vast Park Throng Cheers," *Chicago Daily Tribune,* August 30, 1937.

25 Edward Barry, "Bobby Sings into Gale—and into Hearers' Hearts," *Chicago Daily Tribune,* August 30, 1937.

26 Edward Barry, "Vallee Croons to 70 Thousand Despite Rain," *Chicago Daily Tribune,* August 18, 1936.

27 Edward Barry, "Helen Morgan Pleases Crowd at Grant Park," *Chicago Daily Tribune,* July 13, 1937.

28 Cecil Smith, "Plan Natural Bowl for Free Park Concerts," *Chicago Daily Tribune,* August 20, 1936.

29 Frank Clemens, "Concerts in the Park," *Chicago Daily Tribune,* April 8, 1940.

CHAPTER THREE: THE 1940s

1 Thalia, "Chicagoans Enjoy Music under Stars," *Chicago Daily Tribune,* July 21, 1946.

2 Claudia Cassidy, "Park Orchestra Shows Promise in 1st Concert," *Chicago Daily Tribune,* July 6, 1944.

3 Thalia, "Chicagoans Enjoy Concerts in Grant Park," *Chicago Daily Tribune,* July 30, 1944.

4 John Thompson, "Thousands See 10,000th Youth Join the Navy: Park Concert Pays Recruit Tribute," *Chicago Daily Tribune,* July 2, 1942.

5 Albert Goldberg, "30,000 Enjoy Army Bands in Park Concert," *Chicago Daily Tribune,* July 5, 1944.

6 Edward Barry, "Tribute Is Paid to Grant Park's Best Customer," *Chicago Daily Tribune,* July 18, 1942.

7 Marcia Winn, "Front Views and Profiles," *Chicago Daily Tribune,* July 22, 1948.

8 Seymour Raven, "Summer Music Takes Quite a Beating Over 4th of July Week-End," *Chicago Daily Tribune,* July 12, 1959.

9 Albert Goldberg, "Malko Directs Park Orchestra in One of Its Best Concerts," *Chicago Daily Tribune,* July 18, 1946.

10 "Solomon's Wives," *Time,* October 30, 1939.

11 Edward Barry, "Classic Music or Swing, They Cheer Benny," *Chicago Daily Tribune,* August 12, 1941.

12 Claudia Cassidy, "Audience Roars Its Approval of Opera in Park," *Chicago Daily Tribune,* July 20, 1947.

13 Edward Barry, "Paul Robeson Wins Ovations from Throng in Grant Park," *Chicago Daily Tribune,* July 29, 1940.

14 Edward Barry, "Leads Symphony at 11; Applause Follows Laughs," *Chicago Daily Tribune,* September 7, 1941.

15 Claudia Cassidy, "Summer Concert Devotee's Dream—a Lakefront Music Court," *Chicago Daily Tribune,* January 20, 1946.

CHAPTER FOUR: THE 1950s

1 Claudia Cassidy, "'Free Music' or Recurrent Nightmare—Anyway, It Begins Again," *Chicago Daily Tribune,* June 25, 1953.

2 "Police Pledge Drive to Clean Up Grant Park," *Chicago Daily Tribune,* August 12, 1952.

3 Claudia Cassidy, "Rosenstock and Tourel Open 23d Season of Free Concerts in Grant Park," *Chicago Daily Tribune,* June 27, 1957.

4 Edward Schreiber, "Sunset Friday to be Hour of Great Conflict," *Chicago Daily Tribune,* August 5, 1958.

5 Seymour Raven, "Park Concert Again Loses to Power Failure," *Chicago Daily News,* August 4, 1955.

6 "Hope for Vote on Band Shell Nov. 3 Waning," *Chicago Daily Tribune,* September 17, 1953.

7 Alex Duff, "Summer Concerts," *Chicago Daily Tribune,* November 18, 1955.

8 Charles Collins, "A New Look at Chicago's Boom!" *Chicago Daily Tribune,* September 25, 1955.

9 Seymour Raven, "60,000 Thrill to Music of Kostelanetz," *Chicago Daily Tribune,* July 11, 1954.

10 Anthony Tommasini, "Beverly Sills, All-American Diva, Is Dead at 78," *New York Times,* July 3, 2007.

11 Claudia Cassidy, "Closing 'Rigoletto' Has Its Points Despite Grant Park Makeshifts," *Chicago Daily Tribune,* August 19, 1957.

12 "The All-American Virtuoso," *Time,* May 19, 1958.

13 Louise Hutchinson, "Shriners Greet Cliburn," *Chicago Daily Tribune,* July 16, 1958.

14 Seymour Raven, "Van Cliburn Is Piano Soloist in Grant Park Wednesday, Friday," *Chicago Daily Tribune,* July 13, 1958.

15 Louise Hutchinson, "55,000 Strong, They Came to Hear Cliburn," *Chicago Daily Tribune,* July 17, 1958.

16 Seymour Raven, "Air in Grant Park Blossoms with Aria Encores of Peerce," *Chicago Daily Tribune,* July 26, 1954.

17 John H. Thompson, "Ask Combined Bomb Shelter and Car Park," *Chicago Daily Tribune,* April 28, 1958.

18 Edward Barry, "It's True: Music Excites Latins!" *Chicago Daily Tribune,* August 22, 1959.

CHAPTER FIVE: THE 1960s

1 "Music in Grant Park," *Chicago Daily Tribune,* July 3, 1961.

2 "Youngsters Attend Concert," *Chicago Tribune,* July 26, 1963.

3 "Four Children Wield Baton for Birthday," *Chicago Tribune,* July 24, 1964.

4 "Miss Anderson Still Soars," *Chicago Tribune,* July 10, 1966.

5 Thomas Willis, "Grant Park Begins 30th Concert Season under the Stars," *Chicago Tribune,* July 2, 1964.

6 Thomas Willis, "Brendel Knits Cloth of Pure Mozart Gold, Arrays Grant Park," *Chicago Tribune,* June 30, 1966.

7 Peter Gorner, "Bernstein Hears 'Candide,'" *Chicago Tribune,* July 14, 1968.

8 John von Rhein, "Grant Park Chorus Tips Scales of Excellence under Director Thomas Peck," *Chicago Tribune,* July 31, 1983.

CHAPTER SIX: THE 1970s

1 Peter Gorner, "Bravo! Grant Park Marks 49 Years of Free-for-All Music," *Chicago Tribune,* June 22, 1983.

2 Rob Cuscaden, "Grant Park's Bandshell Bombshell," *The Chicago Guide,* August 1972.

3 John von Rhein, "Mitch Miller's Oldies Are Best," *Chicago Tribune,* June 29, 1978.

4 Thomas Willis, "Conductor Slatkin Is Find for Grant Park," *Chicago Tribune,* April 5, 1974.

5 John von Rhein, "Slatkin's Magic Brings Together the Best from 40 Years of Music," *Chicago Tribune,* November 4, 1978.

6 Linda Winer, "Uncommon Man at Grant Park," *Chicago Tribune,* July 3, 1972.

7 John von Rhein, "Zinman: Cool Conductor for City Summers," *Chicago Tribune,* July 26, 1981.

8 Linda Winer, "Ballet: Reflections on Bolshoi Week," *Chicago Tribune,* August 13, 1973.

9 Alan G. Artner, "A Warm Crowd Pleaser," *Chicago Tribune,* August 5, 1974.

10 Eileen Ogintz, "A Bang-up Concert Starts the 4th Here," *Chicago Tribune,* July 4, 1978.

11 Marco d'Eramo, *The Pig and the Skyscraper: Chicago: A History of Our Future* (New York: Verso, 2002), 435.

CHAPTER SEVEN: THE 1980s

1 Anne Keegan, "4th of July: Unity out of Dissent," *Chicago Tribune,* July 5, 1983.

2 John Stebbins, "Music Shell Man Has Sweeping Philosophy," *Chicago Sun-Times,* September 5, 1987.

3 Michael Kalk, "Here's to Concerts sans Festival Frills," *Chicago Tribune,* September 9, 1987.

4 Stevenson Swanson, "Bang of a Party Launches 4th Here," *Chicago Tribune,* July 4, 1980.

5 John Gilardi, "Daleys Join Crowd at 1st Grant Pk. Summer Concert–Outdoor Festival Opens 55th Year," *Chicago Sun-Times,* June 25, 1989.

6 John von Rhein, "Bolcom's Ambitious Song Cycle a Grant Park Triumph," *Chicago Tribune,* June 30, 1986.

7 John von Rhein, "Adams' 'Pianola Music' Strikes a Bright Note at Grant Park," *Chicago Tribune,* June 27, 1983.

8 John Von Rhein, "The 'Dale Carnegie' of the Podium Ready to Win Fans at Grant Park," *Chicago Tribune,* July 7, 1985.

9 Robert Marsh, "Shaw's Grant Pk. Concert a Delight," *Chicago Sun Times,* August 13, 1987.

10 Robert Marsh, "Watts, Cleve Offer Food for the Spirit amid Noisy Taste," *Chicago Sun-Times,* July 7, 1988.

CHAPTER EIGHT: THE 1990s

1 Donald Miller, "Colossus of the Prairie," *Washington Post,* August 8, 2004.

2 John von Rhein, "Cliburn's Back on Top: Celebrated Pianist Enchants Nearly 350,000 in Grant Park," *Chicago Tribune,* June 20, 1994.

3 Bill Zwecker, "Clooney's Rich Voice Makes an Unforgettable Evening," *Chicago Sun-Times,* July 28, 1996.

4 Wynne Delacoma, "Grant Park Festival Hustles, Saves Opener," *Chicago Sun-Times,* June 24, 1997.

5 Wynne Delacoma, "Moonlight Serenades—Grant Park Puts Accent on Offbeat," *Chicago Sun-Times,* June 19, 1992.

6 Lewis Lazare, "Grant Park's Loss/Pricey Move/Musical Managers," *Chicago Reader,* May 27, 1994.

7 John von Rhein, "Out of Sight Behind-the-Scenes at Grant Park Suits New Director," *Chicago Tribune,* June 15, 1995.

8 Alex Ross, *The Rest Is Noise* (New York: Farrar, Straus and Giroux, 2007), xii-xiii.

9 John von Rhein, "Wilding-White Violin Concerto Has Its Moments," *Chicago Tribune,* August 8, 1991.

10 Ted Shen, "Abbinanti's Cantata Riveting: Composer's Unconventional Muse Memorable," *Chicago Tribune,* August 17, 1992.

11 Wynne Delacoma, "'Dreams' Takes Powerful Look at Spain Edict," *Chicago Sun-Times,* June 25, 1992.

12 Wynne Delacoma, "Tuning in 2000—Grant Park Looks Ahead to New Home, Conductor," *Chicago Sun-Times,* August 23, 1999.

CHAPTER NINE: THE 2000s

1 Anne Raver, "Softening a City with Grit and Grass," *New York Times,* July 15, 2004.

2 Gilfoyle, *Millennium Park,* 223.

3 Kevin M. Williams, "Valentina Lisitsa at Grant Park," *Chicago Sun-Times,* July 13, 1998.

4 John von Rhein, "Pavilion's Sound a Work in Progress; Quality Changes with the Seat," *Chicago Tribune,* July 18, 2004.

5 Lisa Frydman, "Speaking with Nathan Gunn," *Chicago Sun-Times,* August 20, 2004.

6 Chris Jones, "Sounds of Sondheim Take Over Millennium Park," *Chicago Tribune,* July 17, 2006.

7 Hedy Weiss, "Lightning Rivals Joffrey Show for 50th Birthday," *Chicago Sun-Times,* June 19, 2006.

8 Andrew Patner, "Monks and Mozart Prove an Odd Delight," *Chicago Sun-Times,* June 25, 2006.

9 Wynne Delacoma, "'Transmigration' Lets Us Mourn 9/11 Dead with Art and Dignity," *Chicago Sun-Times,* August 19, 2005.

Photography Credits

FC: GPMF

FF: GPMF

BC: *L:* GPMF
    TR: GPMF
    BR: GPMF

iii   GPMF

iv   CPD

vi   CPD

ix   GPMF

x   GPMF

xii   GPMF

xiii   GPMF

xiv   Courtesy of Van Cliburn

2   Courtesy of *Life* magazine

3   GPMF

4   GPMF

5   GPMF

6   Courtesy of Joe Budtz, Chuckman's Collection

7   CPD

8   CPD

9   Courtesy of Gehry Partners, LLP

10   CST

12   CHM, ICHi-04438

13   CHM, ICHi-37310

14   CHM, ICHi-27382

15   CHM

16   *L:* CHM, DN-0074880
    R: CHM, ICHi-26898

17   CHM, ICHi-02173

18   *L:* CHM, ICHi-61043
    R: Library of Congress Prints and Photographs Division

19   CHM, ICHi-32195

20   CHM, ICHi-02526

21   CHM, ICHi-61047

22   CHM, ICHi-21988

23   CPD

25   CPD

26   CHM, DN-0009314

27   *L:* CHM, DN-0067864
    R: CHM, SDN-009950

28   CPD

29   *TR:* CPD
    BL: CHM, DN-0081336
    BR: CPD

30   CPD

31   *T:* AIC: Grant Park, Buckingham Fountain, Chicago, IL, 1926-1927. Bennett, Parsons and Frost [architects]. Marcel François Loyau, Jacques Lambert [sculptors]. Architecture Lantern Slide Collection, Ryerson and Burnham Archives, The Art Institute of Chicago. Digital File #36644 © The Art Institute of Chicago.
    B: CPD

32   *T:* CHM, DN-0081503
    B: CHM, DN-0089139

33   CHM, ICHi-61042

34   CPD

35   CPD

36   CPD

37   CPD

38   CPD

39   CPD

40   CPD

42   CPD

43   CPD

44   CPD

45   CST

46   CPD, *Brook Collins*

47   GPMF

48   CPD

50   CHM, ICHi-20237.

51   *TR:* CST
    BL: CST
    BR: CPD

52   CHM, ICHi-21109

53   CFM

54   CPD

55   CFM

56   GPMF

57   GPMF

58   CST

59   *T:* CPD
    B: CHM, ICHi-16983

60   CPD

62   GPMF

63   GPMF

64   CPD

66   Wikipedia Public Domain Image Resources

67   CST

68   CPD

70   CST

71   CPD

72   Wikipedia Public Domain Image Resources

73   CST

74   CPD

76   CPD

78   CPD

79   CPD

80   CFM

81   CHM, ICHi-59887

82   CST

83   CPD

84 CPD

86 CST

87 CFM

88 CPD

89 CPD

90 CST

91 CST

92 CST

93 CPD

94 CPD

96 CPD

98 GPMF

99 CST

100 CPD

101 CPD

102 CPD

103 GPMF

104 CPD

105 GPMF

107 CPD

108 CPD

109 CPD

110 CST

111 CST

112 CHM, ICHi-25462

114 CST

115 CPD

116 CPD

118 CPD

119 CPD

120 CPD

121 CPD

122 CPD

123 CPD

124 CPD

125 CST

126 CPD

127 CPD

129 CST

130 CPD

132 CPD

133 CST

134 CPD

135 CPD

136 *L:* GPMF
    R: CST

137 CPD

138 CST

139 CPD

140 CPD

141 CST

142 GPMF

143 *L:* Courtesy of Michael Geller
    R: CPD

145 CPD

146 CST

148 CST

149 GPMF, J. Steere

150 CPD

151 GPMF, Eric Futran

152 CST

153 GPMF

155 GPMF

156 GPMF

157 GPMF

158 GPMF

159 GPMF

160 Indiana University

161 GPMF

162 GPMF

164 GPMF

165 GPMF

166 Wikipedia Public Domain
    Image Resources

167 Courtesy of Sony Music
    Entertainment

168 CPD

169 GPMF

170 GPMF

171 GPMF

172 GPMF

173 GPMF

174 GPMF

176 GPMF

178 Courtesy of Gehry Partners, LLP

179 CPD, *Brook Collins*

180 GPMF

181 GPMF

182 GPMF

183 CST

184 GPMF

185 GPMF

186 GPMF

187 Dmytro Sergiyenko, Wikipedia
    Public Domain Image Resources

188 CPD, *Brook Collins*

189 GPMF

190 GPMF

191 GPMF

192 GPMF

193 GPMF

194 GPMF

196 GPMF

197 GPMF

198 GPMF

199 GPMF

200 GPMF

202 GPMF

203 GPMF

204 Courtesy of Cedille Records

205 GPMF

206 GPMF

207 GPMF

208 GPMF

209 Courtesy of Jennifer Larmore

210 GPMF

211 Joffrey Ballet

212 GPMF

213 GPMF

214 GPMF

215 Courtesy of Alex Dominguez

216 GPMF

218 GPMF

234 CPD

Index